Hitler's
Commanders

Hitler's Commanders

German Bravery in the Field, 1939–1945

James Lucas

CASSELL&CO

Cassell & Co.
Wellington House, 125 Strand, London WC2R 0BB

Distributed in the USA by Sterling Publishing Co. Inc.,
387 Park Avenue South, New York, NY 10016-8810

ISBN 0-304-35315-9

Edited, designed and typeset by Roger Chesneau

Printed and bound in USA
by Creative Print and Design (Wales)

Contents

Preface

Hitler's Enforcers, which I wrote in 1994, described the ways in which it was possible for Germans to become officers in the armed forces, and because this background information is important I am repeating it here.

The precondition which had been essential in earlier centuries, that of noble birth, was relaxed in the latter years of the German Empire and abolished completely during the time of the Weimar Republic, when education and not nobility was the preferred route. In the period of the Third Reich, these two preconditions were replaced by the demand for National Socialist fervour. Bravery in the field had always been a route to a commission, and in the Second World War many men were promoted as a reward for their heroic acts.

The brief biographies that form the text of this book include men who advanced through the military hierarchy via all three of the routes cited above. They include the aristocratic von Arnim, scion of a family which had supplied the German Army with general officers for centuries; the intellectual Westphal, who served as the Ia to several senior officers; and the paratroop hero Schaefer, a sergeant who held the vital position of Cactus Farm in Tunisia. It should not be a source of surprise that men of quite junior rank are recorded here, for their ability, skill and bravery demanded that they be included in these pages, just as it would be incorrect to assume that only senior commanders were capable of bringing a battle to a successful outcome. Walther Koch, the paratroop commander, was a subaltern officer when he led a battalion-size group which captured the vital canal bridges in Belgium and also seized the fortress of Eben Emaël on the opening day of the war in the West in 1940. Scherer, a major-general commanding a hastily assembled battle group, fought a defensive battle at Cholm during the winter of 1941 and defeated the best strategic efforts of an entire Soviet shock army. These men and others like them are among those described in these pages.

As an aid to the reader's full understanding of the text, it is necessary to outline some part of the recent history of Germany. In 1918 the Imperial Army that had gone out to fight in 1914 sought an armistice, out of which the Great War was brought to an end. A defeated and weakened Germany was forbidden, under the terms of the Versailles Treaty, to have heavy weapons, such as tanks, big guns, aeroplanes or submarines. The Army was restricted in size to just 100,000 men. Germany was, therefore, defenceless against two enemies—first, those nations whose armies invaded her territory, and secondly, a political enemy, communism, which sought to overthrow the elected government. In order to defeat the first type of enemy, groups of ex-servicemen banded together into Freikorps, which fought quite literally for hearth and home. In time the enemy incursions were driven out and there was external peace. The second enemy was defeated by the National Socialists (Nazis) when they came to power.

The German Army had always enjoyed the premier position *vis-à-vis* the other services, the Navy and the Air Force. However, discussions at senior level during the years after the Great War had led to the conclusion that all the services were equally important and that a single High Command, embracing all three, needed to be created. This amalgamation took place in the first years of the Nazi Party's government and well before the outbreak of the Second World War, and that body was called *die Wehrmacht* (the Armed Forces). The Wehrmacht then broke down into three component bodies, an Army High Command (Oberkommando des Heeres, OKH), a Naval High Command (Oberkommando der Marine, OKM) and an Air Force High Command (Oberkommando der Luftwaffe, OKL). Although several of the accounts in this text deal with paratroops who were Luftwaffe personnel, it is true to say that they, *die Fallschirmjäger*, fought a ground war as infantry and have, therefore, been included here as if they were part of the OKH forces. Therefore, we need consider the Army as the body responsible for the operations described here.

The Army High Command had its own General Staff system, whose branches included, among many others, the department responsible for the planning of military operations, another department conferred with gathering intelligence on foreign armies and others for the issue of supplies and for the procurement of recruits and reinforcements. That hierarchical structure was repeated, although on a diminishing scale, down to divisional level, a division being the lowest formation capable of undertaking operations on its own initiative. That organisational structure was a very flexible one and was suited to the needs of the commander of the military force undertaking a particular mission. The divisional commander was expected, when faced with a difficult military problem, to use his own initiative, and this he not only was able to do but was encouraged to do

This tri-force structure was then complicated by the growth of a party political army, the SS. The Allgemeine SS was, initially, the only type of SS organisation, but when the Nazi Party came to power, as it did in January 1933, a second branch, the Totenkopf (Death's Head) regiment, was created, to staff the concentration camps. It was so called because the Totenkopf soldiers carried on their caps the badge of a skull and crossbones, a device which then passed into general wear by the whole SS organisation. Quite early in the Party's years of government, the Allgemeine or General Branch began to tighten its control over the nation and started to form regiments which would be used to put down a counter-revolution. These units were armed and drilled as a military force and became, in time, the third type of SS unit, the Verfügungs Truppen or 'units available'. Shortly after the outbreak of the Second World War those groups which had been raised to counter revolutionary activities were combined into a Verfügungs Division. This was the birth of the Waffen SS (the armed SS), an organisation which grew during the course of the war to become a mighty force of thirty-eight divisions.

Reverting to the immediate pre-war years, it has to be stated that there was hostility on the part of the Army generals to the idea of the SS carrying arms, for they saw the rise of an armed Party militia as a threat to their unique position as the weapons-bearers of the nation. The Army generals had also opposed the setting up of the OKW, which they saw as a reduction of their power and influence. For their part, the SS commanders despised the generals as reactionary and lacking National Socialist enthusiasm. That mutual hostility very soon faded on the battlefield, where the SS formations proved their fighting capabilities. In time, the differences in attitude between the Waffen SS and the Army were resolved, and, except for certain differences in uniform, both organisations can be considered as one.

Army, Navy and Air Force personnel wore identical badges of rank, with slight variations. The Waffen SS, however, was different. Not only did it have, to begin with, different rank names from those in the Army, but it also had its own particular insignia. The Waffen SS officers carried on the lapels of their tunics a selection of stars and bars which indicated their rank. However, after the outbreak of war it became clear that having two different sets of names and insignia was confusing. Thereupon the Waffen SS adopted Army insignia for their shoulder boards and added the conventional rank names in the description of their title, although the organisation retained the lapel insignia to the end of the war. Personnel in the Army, paratroop branch and Waffen SS, when dressed in camouflage tunics or white winter jackets, carried on the upper sleeve a pattern of wings, oak leaves and/or bars to indicate rank.

In common with other national armies, the German forces not only wore medals as marks of distinction but had cuff titles and also small metal arm shields to denote that the wearer had been in the action for which the arm badge had been awarded. In the case of the Waffen SS, cuff titles bore either the regimental or the divisional name. The paratroops also wore an identifying cuff title, while in the Army cuff titles were bestowed—usually—for campaigns, as in the case of the Africa cuff title. There were two types of that distinction issued, and it was possible for a soldier to have been awarded both patterns, one being worn on either cuff.

Wound badges were issued in black for up to three wounds, in silver for between three and six wounds and in gold for more than six. The German Cross was an eight-pointed star in black and silver, with a swastika set in a wreath in either gold or silver.

All the men described in this book were awarded the Knight's Cross of the Iron Cross. The Iron Cross was awarded in a series of stages from 2nd class upwards to the Knight's Cross with Oak Leaves, Swords and Diamonds. The German services did not consider a single act of bravery to be sufficient grounds for the premier decoration to be awarded, as is the case in the Victoria Cross. To be awarded the Knight's Cross the serviceman had to gain each stage of the Iron Cross before going on to the next senior stage. It was usual for NCOs or men who had won that decoration to be promoted to commissioned rank. The logic behind awarding or withholding awards for bravery in the German services is confusing. One officer in this book was three times recommended for the Knight's Cross and had his recommendation rejected twice. On one occasion he received instead the German Cross and on the second occasion the Panzer Badge in Silver. This was in line with a recommendation for a Iron Cross 2nd Class, which was turned down, despite the man having carried out a daring mission, on the grounds that, at that time (the early hours of 31 August 1939), no state of war existed between Germany and Poland. The German Army was a mixture of petty officialdom and pragmatic action. It is a fascinating army to study.

Acknowledgements

It gives me considerable pleasure to express thanks for the help which various friends and institutions have given me in the preparation, research and writing of this book. Particularly pleasing is it to render thanks to my friend, the well-known author Mark Yerger, for supplying the photographs which illustrate the text as well as supplying advice on certain of the officers who figure in these pages.

In addition I acknowledge the help given by Vizeleutnant Helmut Eberl and Gill Pratt, both of Vienna, as well as by Professor Rauchensteiner, the Director of the Heeresgeschichtliches Museum in Vienna. I also thank Colonel Busch and the other officers of the archive of the German Fallschirmjäger organization, as well as all the former soldiers of the Para arm of service who helped me, notably Adi Strauch, and the comrades of the German divisions and regiments whose help has contributed enormously to the completion of the text.

I thank my agent, Sheila Watson, for her patience and help when illness stopped me writing for several months, as well as my publisher, Barry Holmes, for his great kindness in extending the deadline because of that illness. To my colleague Gary Shaw I also send thanks, as I do to all those many others who helped me but who are not named here.

However, no expression of thanks would be complete without acknowledging the unfailing encouragement, support and love of my dear wife, Traude. Without her I could never have completed this book.

James Lucas
London, 2000

Generaloberst
Hans-Jürgen von Arnim

The last General Commanding Army Group Africa

Hans-Jürgen von Arnim was born on 4 April 1889 in Ernsdorf, Silesia, the son of a general. The von Arnims were an old military family, and no fewer than thirty of Hans-Jürgen's ancestors had served Prussia, later Germany, and had risen to the rank of General Officer.

As befitted the descendant of such a militarily illustrious family, Hans Jürgen von Arnim was a strong-minded but eminently fair man to his subordinates, with whom he had strong relationships. He did not relish arguments with his superiors, but neither did he avoid them. He was described throughout his service career as ambitious and willing to accept responsibility, and as a calm man who never lost his nerve and who remained unruffled. Early in his years in the Army of the Weimar Republic he was described as having a capacity for hard work and the ability to think and to act decisively.

The young Hans Jürgen was educated in the Görlitz Gymnasium and at Glogau, where he gained his graduation diplomas. He then entered the Army as an Ensign on 1 April 1908, and after completing his officer training course was commissioned, on 19 August 1909, in the 4th Regiment of Foot Guards.

During the Great War he served on the Western Front, first as the regimental adjutant in 1914; then in 1915 he took over as a company commander in the Reserve Infantry Regiment of the 4th Guards Division. During his time with that unit von Arnim was wounded on three occasions. His service won him several decorations for bravery, including both classes of the Iron Cross, the Wound Badge in Black, the Hamburg Hanseatic Order and the Hohenzollern House Order. Later in the war he was posted to the Eastern Front, where he served in the Guards Jäger Division. He was promoted to the rank of Captain on 27 January 1917, and nine months later he was given command of an infantry battalion, with which he continued to serve when it was returned to France and Flanders during 1918.

At the end of the war he was one of the officers selected to serve in the 100,000-man Army of the Weimar Republic and was employed in the standard German Army fashion, with alternating periods of regimental and staff duties. The latter were chiefly with the 'Troops Department', the cover name for the General Staff. The victorious Allies had ordered the German General Staff to be disbanded and, indeed, the name was discarded, but the structure and the function of that body remained intact.

By the autumn of 1928 von Arnim had risen to the rank of Major in a new regimental post and was given command of the 29th Infantry Regiment in Charlottenburg. His next command was that of the Ortelsburg Rifle Battalion. In 1932 came promotion to the rank of Lieutenant-Colonel, and six months later he began a two-year tour of duty commanding the 1st Battalion of the 2nd Infantry Regiment. Three years later he reached the rank of Colonel and an appointment as Ia (Operations Staff Officer) to the 23rd Infantry Division. In October 1935 he took command of the 68th Infantry Regiment, which was garrisoned in Brandenburg, and three years later he received promotion to the rank of Generalmajor (Brigadier-General).

In 1938 von Arnim was appointed—some said it was a demotion—to the post of Chief of the Army's 4th Service Department, another cover name for a staff post and one which saw him as the equivalent of a divisional commander, although he did not lead a division until after the outbreak of war, when his post as General Officer Commanding 52nd Infantry Division was announced on 8 September 1939. The division he was to command was forming in the Saarpfalz region and he led it against the Allies during the war in the West. It was in that campaign that he won the clasps to both of the classes of Iron Cross that he had been awarded during the Great War. He was promoted to Generalleutnant (Major-General) on 1 December 1939, and during 1940 he was given command of the 17th Panzer Division. That formation then moved to Poland to prepare for Operation 'Barbarossa', the German invasion of Russia.

For the opening battles of the war against Russia, in June 1941, von Arnim's division was part of Guderian's 2nd Panzer Group in Army Group Centre. The Panzer group had the task of thrusting through eastern Poland and advancing through western Russia, via Smolensk, and ultimately to attack Moscow. During the advances of those early weeks and months, Guderian and the Panzer formations under his command took part in the vast encirclement battles that marked the German Army's careering progress in that first summer and autumn of the war on the Eastern Front.

But that is to anticipate events. Within days of the opening of the Russian war, von Arnim was wounded on the outskirts of the town of Schklov, and so seriously that he was first evacuated to Lemberg and then to Berlin for treatment. Before that wounding he had already had one lucky escape. On 24 June two Russian T-25 tanks appeared suddenly on the western edge of the town of Slonim, which his 17th Panzer Division had just captured. The enemy machines opened fire upon the group of German officers standing at the side of the road discussing the next stage of the advance. Among that group was Guderian, the Commanding General of the 2nd Panzer Group, Lemelsen, the GOC of the 48th Panzer Corps, and von Arnim. The generals managed to avoid the fire of the Russian tanks, both of which were destroyed by German artillery. On 4 September von Arnim was awarded the Knight's Cross of the Iron Cross, and shortly afterwards was also promoted to the rank of General of Panzer Troops (Lieutenant-General).

The need for convalescence after his wounds had healed meant that it was not until 17 September that von Arnim was able to take up command again of the 17th Panzer Division, which he then led during the encirclement battle of Kiev and, subsequently, in the battles to destroy the Red Army holding out in the pockets of Vyasma and Briansk. One of the great successes of this period was the capture intact of the Desna Bridge as well as the strategically important junction of Briansk. Not long after his return, Operation 'Typhoon' began the German offensive to capture Moscow. In the closing stages of that operation, the German Army Group Centre was trying to encircle two Red Army fronts, Timoshenko's 'West' and Yeremenko's 'Briansk'. These operations were on a massive scale: Timoshenko's force numbered six armies while Yeremenko controlled three. As early as the first week of October, German operations against these two fronts had created two huge pockets, which were in the final stages of disintegration. It was the task of the 17th Panzer to close the ring at Briansk.

On 5 October von Arnim sent out a battle group and ordered it to strike across the Red Army's defences to the north-west of Akulova and to cut the Karachev–Briansk road. Behind that battle group spearhead would follow the main body of the 17th Panzer Division. The battle group made good progress and had halted at Glushy to regroup when the Divisional Ia drove up, bringing with him fresh orders from the corps commander that the battle plan had been changed. It is a measure of the German Army's flexibility and a tribute to the spirit that von Arnim had aroused in his men that this alteration was carried out smoothly and without friction. The new orders were that the division's thrust line was to change so that Briansk was to be attacked from the rear. That operation brought victory, and the town was taken on 7 October. Its main defences had indeed faced westwards, i.e. the direction from which the Red Army had expected the German assault to be made.

As a result of the 17th Panzer's swift assault and capture of Briansk, touch was gained between Guderian's 2nd Panzer Group and the German 3rd Army, and that contact closed fast the ring that had been flung around the Russian mass in the Briansk pocket. Towards the end of October, the 17th Panzer was immobilised because it had run out of fuel for its tanks. Once resupplied, it was posted to Orel but was again held fast at Protova, this time by the thick autumn mud. By the time that the 17th was mobile again, von Arnim had been ordered to lay down command of his division in order to take up a new post. He was given a new command—that of leading the 39th Corps, which was in the line to the east of Leningrad. The 39th Corps was in a parlous state, and the situation in which it found itself was one potentially catastrophic for Army Group North.

To set the background, the German and Finnish governments had planned joint operations by both their armies, and the objective given to Army Group North had been to advance rapidly and to seize Leningrad, Russia's second city. The Finns were, however, reluctant to invade Soviet territory and were prepared to advance only as far as that part of the former Russo-Finnish border which ran along the Swir river. There they intended to halt and wait for the offensive by Army Group North to reach them. The German drive, rising from the south, was to begin at Cudevo, a town in the Volkhov swamp on the Moscow–Leningrad autobahn. The German advance was then to be carried to Tikhvin, a town to the south-east of Lake Ladoga on the main railway line between Leningrad and Vologda. From the railway junction at Tikhvin, Army Group North was then to advance north-westwards and gain touch with the Finnish forces along the Swir river. That, at least, was the OKW plan.

Strategically, the most important town in that area of northern Russia was Tikhvin, and a measure of its importance was the fact that Stavka, the Red Army's Supreme Command, had reinforced the area with élite Siberian divisions, together with masses of tanks and artillery. Stavka was determined to hold Tikhvin at all costs, and the scale of the fighting for that sector was such that casualties to the Red Army were said to be the highest of any single major offensive of the Russo-German war. Despite the most strenuous efforts by the 39th Corps, it had not been able to reach the Swir river and to gain touch with the Finns. As a consequence, the corps' right flank was completely open—a situation which Stavka quickly exploited. It was this heavily embattled corps that von Arnim had been ordered to take over. The journey to reach his corps headquarters was a difficult one, and it was not until 15 November that he completed it, having finished the last part by sledge.

The situation he faced was that the Red Army was attacking using divisions of storm troops marching behind waves of T-34 tanks. Corps, which had been forced on to the defensive even before von Arnim arrived, was unable to withstand the onslaught and as early as 9 December had been driven out of Tikhvin. The Red Army, encouraged by that success, intensified its attacks, and these came in from both flanks, creating the danger that von Arnim's corps might be cut off and destroyed. The only order that the corps commander could give was for his battered formations to fight their way back across the ground they had gained at such cost and to retreat to the Volkhov river.

Three days before Christmas 1941, von Arnim led the last elements of the 39th Corps back across the river in an intense cold, which dropped at times to minus 52 degrees. The corps structure was intact, but its component units had suffered such terrible losses that one, the 18th (Motorised) Division, had been reduced to just 741 men, while the 12th Panzer Division had sunk to 1,144 all ranks.

The corps did not leave the line until the end of March 1942, and it then moved to another sector of that northern front where a new crisis was building up. The land bridge at Cholm, a junction of several roads in an otherwise swampy area, was not only a sizeable town but also a sector of strategic importance. Recent Russian advances in that area had aimed at capturing the town, but although Red Army spearheads had bypassed and isolated Cholm, they had not been able to capture it. The German defenders, a garrison of some 5,000 men, had been ordered to hold the town and, under the command of Major-General Scherer, had every intention of obeying that order.

Von Arnim, aware of the weakness of the Cholm garrison, ordered an attack to be made to push the armour of the 12th Panzer Division through to Scherer's group. But the tracks of the German Panzers could gain no purchase on the icy ground and the attempt had to be called off. It was left to von Arnim's 122nd Infantry Division to carry out another assault, which they did wading through waist-deep snow. For a brief interlude these infantrymen gained touch with the Cholm garrison and co-operated in helping to beat off the Red Army's attacks, but they were too weak in numbers to raise the siege and were forced to withdraw to avoid themselves being surrounded and cut off in the beleaguered town.

The corps commander, determined to do everything in his power to supply the cut-off garrison, then sent in lorry convoys to take forward clothing, food and supplies, but only one column broke through. The Red Army then managed to cut off Cholm completely, but still the garrison held out and fought on. By 1 May the improved weather had not only thawed the snow but had also dried out the ground. Once again von Arnim launched his corps into an assault and, despite the furious resistance of the Red Army, it broke through to reach and relieve the besieged garrison.

Throughout the summer and autumn of 1942 von Arnim's corps was committed to minor actions in and around Rzhev. It was while it was engaged in that fighting that von Arnim received a signal ordering him to report to Hitler's headquarters at Rastenburg. On 3 December 1942 von Arnim reached the Wolfsschanze and was surprised by the news that the situation in Tunisia was such that a new formation, the 5th Panzer Army, was to be set up and that Hitler had chosen him to command it and had promoted him to the rank of Generaloberst (Colonel-General). Upon being told by the Führer of his new appointment, von Arnim posed the question whether supplies to the African/Tunisian theatre of operations could be guaranteed and asked, also, how many divisions would make up the new Panzer army. Hitler assured him that he would command six divisions, so that, once that force— three Panzer and three motorised divisions—was in place and with the lines of supply assured, it would be possible to halt the retreat of Rommel's desert army and to follow that with a counter-offensive. Why Hitler considered that the introduction of another new hierarchical body would simplify the command structure in Africa is unclear.

The situation in Tunisia was at that time certainly menacing. An Anglo-American force had landed at a number of strategic ports in Algeria and Tunisia and was heading eastwards. The aim of the Western Allies was to reach Tunis and then by rapid reinforcement to place a powerful military grouping at the back of Rommel's Axis armies which were carrying out a fighting retreat through Libya. To prevent that military disaster, Hitler had ordered troops to be sent to Tunisia. The first of these, chiefly the battalions of Koch's 5th Parachute Regiment, Witzig's Para Engineer Battalion and the Barenthin Glider Regiment, together with miscellaneous German and Italian groups, were flung into battle and had soon established a flimsy perimeter to the west of Tunis.

There was fighting in northern Tunisia along a line running inland from the Mediterranean Sea as the Axis troops endeavoured to expand their perimeter westwards while the Allied invasion force, driving eastwards out of Algeria, sought to destroy it and to capture both Tunis and the major port of Bizerta. During January and February Rommel's Axis army was finally driven out of Libya and began to enter southern Tunisia, where it proposed to take up positions in the French frontier defences at Mareth. The race to take Tunis had failed, and the Allied host eventually divided along national lines, with Anderson's British 1st Army (an army in name only) in the north of the country and the American 2nd Corps in the centre. The British 8th Army, coming up out of the desert, would eventually join up with the Americans and the Axis troops would then be encircled. In the American sector of the front there were several passes through the mountains, and it was clear to the Germans that the Americans would debouch from these in an endeavour to reach the sea and thus strike Rommel's Panzer Army Africa in the back. In the winter of 1942 the fighting in Tunisia was, therefore, in the north, by the British 1st Army—represented by the 5th Corps—around Medjez el Bab, with the objective of capturing Tunis, and with a second Allied effort, by the US 2nd Corps, which was to drive through the mountains and to reach the sea. The American effort was reinforced by French forces.

Hitler had assured von Arnim of both men and supplies and had, indeed, already given the same guarantees to Lieutenant-General Ziegler when he came to report to the Wolfsschanze in Rastenburg. Ziegler had also been told that a 5th Panzer Army was to be created, and that the extraordinary military situation in Tunisia made it imperative that that army be led by an officer capable of rising to the challenge of such a command. Hitler then told Ziegler that he proposed to make von Arnim the General Officer Commanding that new army and that he, Ziegler, was to be the commander's official deputy. In that way, Hitler went on, the problem that had always existed with Rommel—that he was so frequently absent from his headquarters without giving clear orders to his Ia—would be overcome, because whenever the army commander visited his troops in front-line areas there would always be an official deputy at the army's main HQ empowered to act on the army commander's behalf. Ziegler then put to Hitler the questions of the supply position and of the flow of reinforcements to the new theatre of operations. He was told that within a short time there would be three new Panzer and three new motorised divisions in Africa. Armed with this information, Ziegler asked whether for so great a number of troops a flow of supplies could be guaranteed. Hitler reassured him, and Ziegler felt confident that he could believe the word of his Supreme Commander.

Let us, at this point, consider the terrain in the Tunisian battle area. In the north of the country this consists of a mass of mountain peaks, many of which are over 3,000 feet in height. Those mountains are bisected by the Medjerda river, which flows into the Mediterranean between Tunis and Bizerta. In southern Tunisia the mountains are more regular in shape and they divide into two chains, the Eastern and the Western Dorsals. These stretch like an inverted V, and between them the ground becomes a plain. The Eastern Dorsal ends in a vast salt marsh, which provides an ideal defensive position.

When von Arnim and Zielger met in the Wolfsschanze later that day there was an immediate rapport between them, a mutual trust which was strengthened when they flew to meet Kesselring, the Supreme Commander South, in his headquarters in Frascati, near Rome. From Frascati von Arnim and Ziegler then continued their journey and arrived in Tunisia on 8 December. There they had discussions with General Nehring, commander of the 90th Corps, who had created the perimeter around Tunis with only a handful of soldiers, mostly paratroops and a miscellany of fragments of units that had been stationed in Sicily, Italy and Greece. The arrival of the two senior commanders was a shock to Nehring, who had not been told that he was to be replaced. He had planned an offensive designed to expand the area of the perimeter and showed the battle plan to his two superiors. They agreed it and confirmed the details.

The battle that opened on the following day seized the 900-foot high Longstop Hill, and it was the quick capture of this feature by the 2nd Battalion of the 7th Panzer Regiment and elements from the 754th Infantry Regiment that secured the northern sector of the Tunisian battle zone. As a result of this swift operation the Allies were unable to strike for Tunis until they had recaptured the Longstop peak. The January rainfall then brought an end to the major military operations of both sides, the Italo-German Axis on the one side and the Anglo-American-French forces on the other. By 31 December the 5th Panzer Army, which had been only weeks earlier nothing but an idea in Hitler's mind, had been created and had a strength of over 150 tanks of the III and IV classes as well as eleven of the Tiger or Panzer VI type.

Von Arnim considered the priorities of his new command. The principal one was to expand the Tunisian perimeter so as to shelter Rommel's armies. The second one was dependent on the first—to prevent the Allies from capturing Tunis and destroying the perimeter. Once those two tasks had been completed successfully, he could turn his attention to the third task. That would be in southern Tunisia, where he would stop the Allies—chiefly the Americans—from striking through the passes and reaching the sea.

Quickly von Arnim amalgamated most of the miscellaneous German units into the von Broich Division and placed this on the northern Tunisian sector, i.e. on the seaward flank. The 10th Panzer Division, the paratroops and detachments from the 334th Infantry Division were in the centre of the German battle line facing the British and the Americans, while the Italian 'Superga' Division held the left, or deep Tunisian flank. But von Arnim was unhappy about the reliability of the Italian troops holding that sector and replaced them with German units. He then turned his attention first to northern Tunisia and opened an offensive with limited objectives. Then, on 18 January 1943, he struck the French and British forces in that sector using the heavy Panzer (Tiger) battalion and elements from the 10th Panzer and 334th Infantry Divisions. This local offensive, having taken prisoners as well as equipment, was broken off during the night of 23/24 January, and von Arnim's troops then successfully fought off the Allied counter-attacks, which came in on the 24th.

In the early days of February 1943 von Arnim's attention switched to southern Tunisia, and he attacked the French forces in that area. There had been a reinforcement to the 5th Panzer Army at the end of January when the 21st Panzer Division from the Afrika Korps came on strength. That increase in Panzer numbers emboldened von Arnim to use it in an attack, which was carried out against the Faid Pass. This was to be an operation undertaken by the 21st and 10th Panzer Divisions. The 21st, as we have seen, came from Rommel's desert army and the 10th Panzer had been posted to Tunisia at the end of 1942. A few days later von Arnim attacked the French forces again, and, although these were supported by the US 2nd Corps, he scored another tactical victory, destroying a whole French division as well as the 168th Infantry Regiment of the 34th Division.

At this point we should mention the surprising fact that von Arnim and Rommel had not met, although they were both commanders in the same theatre of operations. It was not until Kesselring insisted upon it that a meeting took place. The three commanders got together on 9 February and agreed a plan. This was for the combined forces of Rommel's Africa Army and von Arnim's 5th Panzer Army to strike and to destroy the Americans in Tunisia. Rommel's armour was to capture Gafsa in the south, while von Arnim's Panzer formations were to strike through the mountains in the north and capture Sbeitla. The combined German Panzer force would then swing northwards to take Bône and thereby would not only pre-empt the anticipated Allied offensive but might even destroy the British in the north of the country.

Von Arnim and Rommel held divergent views on their respective positions. As von Arnim saw it, his task was to hold a bridgehead and to provide a lodgement area as a base for future operations. It was his duty to prevent the destruction of that bridgehead, and in pursuit of this aim he was content to mount offensives that had limited objectives. Rommel was the bolder commander. In the matter of rank von Arnim was the subordinate, but he led his own army, the 5th Panzer, and was ill disposed to lose his authority over it and over the Panzer divisions he now commanded.

Von Arnim's battle to seize the Faid Pass and advance upon Sidi bou Zid began on 14 February 1943 and lasted two scant days and nights. The German attack burst through the pass, bypassed the 168th Regimental Combat Team, a largely infantry body, and forced Combat Command 'A' (CCA) of the 1st US Armored Division out of Sidi bou Zid. Overwhelmed by the German success, the US 2nd Corps pulled out of Gafsa, a strategic town which Rommel's forces promptly occupied. In an effort to restore the situation, the US 1st Armored Division put in an assault aimed at rescuing the beleaguered 168th Regimental Combat Team. The 1st Armored put in Combat Command 'C' and part of Combat Command 'B' but their attacks failed.

They were dispersed by Stuka aircraft, and only four of the attacking US vehicles were able to drive away from the battlefield, the remainder of the American machines being scattered or destroyed. Von Arnim had won another short, sharp victory.

Then Rommel came back on the scene. He had been in Mareth preparing his Africa Army for the anticipated British offensive there. With his return came the question of the new Axis operation. At TAC headquarters a conference was in progress when Rommel arrived and promptly offered to support the attack with his mobile units by taking them out of their positions in the Mareth Line, which was dormant at that time. Von Arnim, who was advised of Rommel's offer as well as the battle plan that the Field Marshal had prepared, turned down both. Rommel wanted to strike deep, to capture the crossroads village of Feriana and advance either upon Tebessa or upon Kasserine, where he would join forces with von Arnim's Panzers marching from Sbeitla. Von Arnim wanted to carry out only limited operations and would not place his 10th Panzer Division under Rommel's command. Kesselring, to whom both commanders appealed, would not give a wholehearted decision. The result of his indecisiveness, coupled with Rommel's energy and contempt for von Arnim's more cautious approach to the situation, produced a crisis in the Battle for Kasserine Pass. The Panzer divisions failed to effect a breakthrough and the Axis forces began to withdraw.

As von Arnim was to write in post-war years,

> It was in the Tebessa sector that a new, dangerous thrust began to grow. The first move, as I saw it, would be [an American thrust] against Gafsa, Sened and the Faid Pass. This would have been a major threat to our rear, in the Mareth Line, which was being defended by General Messe's 1st Italian Army. Everything hung on being able to beat off the Americans . . .

Von Arnim turned down Rommel's battle plan. He considered that his superior's proposal was a dangerous risk which the Axis resources would be too weak to exploit, and it, being weak, could not guarantee success. Von Arnim's own operation, 'Spring Breeze', began at dawn on 14 February, and the opening attack saw the 10th Panzer Division rolling through the Pass while the 21st Panzer drove southwards in an outflanking movement through the desert. The advance by the 10th

Panzer was successful and by fire-and-movement tactics the Panzers broke through the Pass, bypassed Jebel Lessouda and were there confronted by the tanks of the 1st US Armored Division. The Tigers, commanded by Major Seidenstücker, opened fire and every salvo destroyed more and more US vehicles.

While the tank battle of Sidi bou Zid was raging, the 21st Panzer Division, which had fought its way forward, reached the planned junction point with its sister-division. The US tank men were now under fire from three sides, and Combat Command 'A' was very soon destroyed. Combat Command 'C' fought hard and desperately to reach the armoured component of the 168th Combat Team. It was an unequal struggle. The Americans in their light armoured fighting vehicles were facing Tigers armed with 88mm guns, and soon more than 70 US tanks had been shot to pieces and lay as burning wrecks.

During the night the Panzers of the two divisions united to form a single battle group, and early in the morning of 15 February Ziegler, who was the commander on the ground, ordered the advance to continue towards Sbeitla. En route to that objective the two US armoured commands, now brought back up to strength by reinforcements of fresh tank units, contested the Panzer advance. It was a gallant attempt but one that ended in defeat. The Germans moved forward during the 16th when the 10th Panzer Division struck at Pichon, but then the attack upon that place was cancelled. Developments in Rommel's area led to the belief both in Rome and at Führer HQ that his plan, which had seemed to be too ambitious only days earlier, now appeared to be realisable. The OKW took both Panzer divisions from the 5th Panzer Army and placed them under Rommel's command. At a blow Ziegler's Kampfgruppe was dissolved.

Kasserine Pass had become the new objective, and it was attacked without success by each of the Panzer divisions in turn. The task finally fell to Stotten's Panzer battalion, and his thrust, allied to the other Panzer operations of those days, cost the Americans 169 tanks, 95 reconnaissance vehicles, 36 self-propelled guns and 50 pieces of artillery. It was during those days that the 10th Panzer Division reached Thala. Then fighting opened for the last pass before Tebessa. But the offensive had lasted too long and the German Panzer crews were becoming overstrained and overtired. The Panzer weapon had lost its cutting edge and the US Armored Command 'B' easily held the Afrika Korps' next thrust. The 21st Panzer Division had as its new objective the town of Pichon, but its advance was halted at Sbiba by a minefield.

Von Arnim had always had doubts over the feasibility of Rommel's battle plan, and events had shown the Colonel-General to be right. To add to the worry and confusion which abounded, alarming news came in from the south, where the British 8th Army had attacked the Mareth positions earlier than expected. In view of this new development, Rommel was authorised to pull back his forces.

The events of the past few days had demonstrated the positive need for a really simplified command structure in Africa, and as a result 'Army Group Africa' was created and given authority over both Rommel's forces and those of the 5th Panzer Army. Rommel led the new army group for a fourteen-week period before he returned to Germany to undergo hospital treatment. Von Arnim, who was then named as his successor, had been working on a plan for an offensive to improve the positions of the 5th Panzer Army and which would pre-empt a future Allied offensive. The operation, code-named 'Ochsenkopf', opened on 26 February but was closed down only two days later after it became clear that too little ground had been won. After Rommel's departure on 9 March, von Arnim officially took over the post of GOC Africa with Ziegler as his deputy. On the 23rd the new army group commander paid a visit to the Italian 1st Army, where he authorised its commander to pull back his forces to the Wadi Akarit positions.

The first British attack of the new offensive against Wadi Akarit was flung back, but in the following weeks von Arnim was forced to issue orders for his soldiers to retreat so as to avoid their being totally destroyed. One of his many humanitarian gestures at this time was to forbid Axis aircraft to fly combat missions so as to conserve the petrol that they would otherwise have consumed. That fuel von Arnim used to transport the sick and wounded of his army group. The supply position remained as ever precarious, and when he was accused of always looking over his shoulder he agreed, adding the qualification that he did this in the hope of catching sight of a single supply ship.

The military situation became critical, and because of the supply position all the Flak batteries that could be spared were placed to the west of Tunis town, there to be employed in an anti-tank or field gun capacity. There was a shortage of mines and barbed wire, and in the whole area there were no natural anti-tank ditches. The most bitter of all the shortages was that of artillery shells and anti-tank projectiles. The 5th Panzer Army was reduced at times to half a day's consumption. As von Arnim remarked drily after one dispute with OKW, 'It is not possible to fire shells which lie at the bottom of the sea.' To see his problem in true perspective, Arnim's new command, Army Group Africa, had sunk to a strength of 34 battalions of German infantry and 14 battalions of Italian infantry. There were only 49 batteries of artillery, 33 of which were light field guns. The total strength in AFVs was 89 German and 24 Italian machines. The Axis forces in Africa were bleeding to death, and no one back in Europe seemed to care. Indeed, the Chief of the German General Staff replied thus to a question put to him about Africa: 'Africa? I have already written Africa off.'

Whether it was a question of the right hand not knowing what the left was doing or whether it was a deliberate lie on Hitler's part, when the Führer was made aware of the critical supply position in Africa he promptly ordered the tonnage to be raised from 90,000 per month to 150,000, but omitted to specify how this target was to be reached. The only decisive statement to be issued to Army Group Africa was the unrealisable order that the positions in the Mareth Line were to be held to the last; not only that, but any British offensive operations were to be met by Axis counteroffensives. In view of the catastrophic fuel situation in Africa, there could be no chance of Army Group Africa's mounting such operations.

There was then a confrontation between von Arnim and Kesselring, the Supreme Commander South. The latter began by criticising von Arnim's handling of his army group, and when von Arnim had the chance to question his superior officer his first question was to ask for the role of the 5th Panzer Army to be defined. Kesselring's reply was that it was to weaken any Allied advance in the north of Tunisia while Mareth had to be held to the last. When von Arnim returned to the supply position his remarks were ignored and Kesselring repeated his criticism of von Arnim's handling of his Panzer divisions. It seemed incredible to the Colonel-General that his superior seemed to be unable to grasp that in the north of Tunisia there was an Allied army growing daily stronger, while in the south of that country there was an American military force whose strength he estimated to be three divisions, and that against that US group he could commit just one single regiment.

The final battle opened at the end of April 1943, but up to 4 May the line in north and central Tunisia, along the course of the original perimeter, was held. On the day that Tunis fell, 7 May, a crisis developed. A ship loaded with 700 British prisoners of war was attacked by RAF aircraft. The Italian crew abandoned the ship and it was left to the German harbourmaster to contact von Arnim's headquarters and to tell a colonel on von Arnim's staff of the situation. The Commander-in-Chief had a message sent in clear to Sir Harold Alexander, the British GOC, telling him that British aircraft were in danger of killing their own men. Alexander halted the air raids.

On 12 May, at Ste Marie zu Zit, von Arnim decided to end the pointless struggle. He sent an officer emissary to British headquarters, and that officer was then taken to the headquarters of General Anderson, the Commander-in-Chief of the British 1st Army. While awaiting that officer's return, the Germans made preparations to destroy the last of Rommel's caravans and to tip into a wadi the last two of Rommel's command tanks. Von Arnim had refused Hitler's offer to be flown back to Germany. It was his intention that, come what may, he would share the fate of the men he commanded. The Commander-in-Chief was taken to Alexander's TAC headquarters, where he was asked if there was anything he would like. His answer was an immediate 'Yes'. He had saved the lives of 700 British prisoners, and he asked in return that a similar number of badly wounded Germans be returned home in a hospital ship. Alexander agreed to the wish of the last commander of Army Group Africa and then von Arnim left to spend years as a prisoner of war in Britain, the USA and finally Germany. During his time as a prisoner of the Americans he was able to intervene to prevent his companions from being ill-treated by their guards.

At the end of four years' imprisonment von Arnim was released and returned to his family. The estates that the von Arnims had owned in eastern Germany had meanwhile been confiscated by the Russians, and he had to set up a new home in Bad Wildingen. He died there, at the age of 73, on 1 September 1962. At his graveside General Westphal gave a valediction that ended with the words: 'Colonel-General Hans-Jürgen von Arnim was what a senior military officer has to be—a man, a person and a gentleman.'

Generaloberst
Eduard Dietl
The hero of Narvik

E duard Dietl, the hero of Narvik, was born on 21 July 1890 in Aibling, Bavaria, and entered the Army as an ensign. He was gazetted as a Leutnant (2nd Lieutenant) in the 5th Bavarian Infantry regiment in 1911, and served throughout the First World War. When the armistice was signed, Dietl was one of the regimental officers who were retained in the Army of the Weimar Republic.

He rose steadily through the commissioned ranks and on 1 May 1938 was given command of the 3rd Gebirgs Division. The 3rd had been raised out of two former divisions of the Army of the Austrian Republic, the 5th and the 7th. When the amalgamation of those two formations had been completed, the 3rd's order of battle was two infantry regiments: the 138th, made up of three battalions, which had Leoben in the Steiermark as their depot town; and the sister regiment the 139th, also with three battalions, but garrisoned in Klagenfurt in Kärnten. The divisional artillery component, the 112th Gebirgs Artillerie Regiment, also fielding three battalions, was located in Graz, the capital of the Steiermark.

The 2nd and 3rd Gebirgs Divisions were combined to form the 18th Corps, the title of the latter being enlarged during December 1941 to include the identifying word 'Gebirgs' (Mountain). The Sudeten Crisis of 1938 saw both divisions of the 18th Corps deployed in Lower Austria, to be used if required in a war against Czechoslovakia, and the units of the 3rd Gebirgs Division were located along the border with Moravia and were placed on the right flank of the 2nd Gebirgs Division. The Sudeten emergency passed, but in the summer of 1939 a new one arose on the question of Poland and her access to the sea via the Polish Corridor. There was a fresh deployment of forces, although the 18th Corps was not involved in those new dispositions until the middle of August, when a move was made into Slovakia. Dietl's 3rd Division was concentrated around Rosenberg (Slovakia), on the left of the 2nd Gebirgs Division and with the 1st Gebirgs Division on the right flank.

The German campaign plan for the war against Poland was for a double encirclement of the Polish Field Army by two army groups, North and South. The 18th Gebirgskorps formed part of Army Group South and it was foreseen that when 'Case White', the code-name for the war against Poland, opened, as it did on 1 September 1939, the 18th Corps would strike for the Galician capital of Lemberg (Lvov in Polish.) The attack upon and capture of that city would bite deep into the southern flank of the Polish defence and would hinder, if not halt altogether, the road and rail communications network which ran through Lemberg, thereby cutting the line of retreat of the armies in the west of Poland.

The 18th Corps faced two problems at the outset of the campaign. The first of these was the high mountain range that formed the frontier between Slovakia and Poland. The second problem was that, once through the mountains, the divisions of the 18th Corps that were located on the southernmost flank of the 14th Army would have to foot-march from the mountains to reach Lemberg. To begin with, the problem of piercing the mountain barrier, the first of the two tasks facing the 18th Corps, was an academic one for Dietl's division. The opening moves by the sister division would take it and its flank neighbour, the 1st Gebirgs Division, on divergent courses which would lead to a gap opening up and widening as both advanced. To cover that potentially dangerous situation, those units of Dietl's 3rd Division that were already in position around Rosenberg were to hold the line and were to be reinforced as other divisional units reached the Corps concentration area. In essence, that remained the role of Dietl's division throughout the days of the campaign. The division spent most of its time on the left wing of the Corps, guarding the sister formation against Polish attacks mounted by units withdrawing to the line of the River Bug. Dietl's 3rd Division was not even in Poland when the campaign closed. It had been en route to Lemberg when an order was received that it should halt and prepare itself for a move to the Western Front.

Throughout the first winter of the Second World War the 3rd Gebirgs Division lay in positions in the valley of the Ahr river, and there it was joined by the 2nd Gebirgs Division, which had finished the campaign in Poland. It had been anticipated that both divisions would take part in the war that would soon open in the West. This was not to be the case. The next move by the 3rd Division was northwards from the Ahr river to harbours in northern Germany and thence to a new campaign in the Scandinavian countries.

The demands of war are such that prodigious amounts of raw material are needed to produce the guns and weapons with which to equip the fighting forces. Germany lacked the basic iron ore it required but Sweden had enough—and to spare. In fact 11 million tons of ore that were essential to the arms industry or the Reich reached Germany by two principal sea routes. One was from ports in the south of Sweden and thence by ship to Germany and the other was from the Norwegian town of Narvik, down the length of the Norwegian coast and finally to German ports. To the OKW it was clear that Great Britain, which also relied heavily upon Swedish iron ore, was very likely to invade Norway with the aim of cutting off supplies of this vital raw material to Germany. A second advantage that Britain would gain from an occupation of Norway would be strategic: she would outflank Germany to the north.

Because of the threat of a British invasion, OKW took the view that Germany should pre-empt the British attack and occupy Norway. Were she to do this, then it would be the Third Reich that controlled the iron ore supplies, and with the ports along the Norwegian coast under its control the Kriegsmarine would have facilities on Norway's Atlantic seaboard from which U-boats and commerce raiders could sail. Early in 1940 the Royal Navy had begun to lay mines in sea routes off the Norwegian coast and the Western Allies had produced a plan to violate Norwegian neutrality. In view of the aggressive mining operations, OKW produced a plan to attack both Denmark and Norway. Denmark had the harbours and airfields from which the attack upon Norway would have to be launched. Norway, with a two-century long tradition of peace, was expected to offer little or no resistance.

To undertake the operation OKW proposed that only minimal forces would be required, and Hitler set the opening day of Operation

'Weserübung' for 9 April. The objective of the new campaign was Narvik, and that town lies in the far north of the country. In order that the German invasion forces were in place on the morning of 9 April, the ships carrying the soldiers had to be on the high seas well before D-Day for the invasion. But the German Navy was not well equipped with fast-moving vessels such as destroyers, and so the invading forces would have to be small—a regiment in strength—and the soldiers would be packed into the destroyers.

The scene is then set, and it shows three battalions of Gebirgsjäger embarking on to a flotilla of ten destroyers at Wesermünde. It needed ten destroyers to carry the three battalions of Dietl's regiment because the function of a destroyer was to be a fast gun platform. It was not built to carry passengers. Nor was a destroyer a comfortable vessel in which to sail; indeed, the degree of discomfort was such that in the Royal Navy destroyer crews were given a 'hard lying' allowance to compensate them. If a destroyer was not a comfortable berth for sailors, consider the condition of the Jäger who were packed into every available space below decks. Many of the men of the 139th Regiment of Dietl's division had never sailed on the sea before; some had never even seen it.

The companies embarked during the night of 6/7 April, and after the last man had been taken on board the destroyer flotilla set out from the German Bight and took course for the north of Norway. Outside Wesermünde harbour the 'Narvik' flotilla joined forces with a battleship group, and they all headed out into the teeth of a Force 8 gale. The ferocity of the storm increased during the second day at sea to Force 9, and the Jäger lying on the cold, unyielding, water-soaked decks were flung from one side to the other as the vessels crashed their way through mountainous seas. Late in the night the Jäger noticed that the pitching and tossing had eased off and had been replaced by a rolling motion from side to side. What had happened was that the convoy of ten destroyers and other ancillary craft had entered the calmer waters of Ofotfjord and was steaming towards Narvik. Dietl had the companies alerted and mustered on deck. The Jäger stood in a blinding snowstorm ready to enter the boats that would take them to the shore.

Dietl had worked out the debarkation arrangements and had prepared a battle plan. His 1st and 3rd Battalions were to seize Bjervik at the far end of Herjangsfjord while the 2nd Battalion was to go in against Narvik itself. At 0500 hours the Jäger piled into their assault craft and were soon heading for the shore. The Jäger at Bjervik encountered a cavalry patrol and took its men prisoner. There was no other contact with the enemy, and Dietl knew that he and the 139th Regiment had won the race to reach the area. By 0600 hours Dietl was ashore and promptly demanded the surrender of the Narvik area as well as of its garrison, a battalion of the 13th Norwegian Infantry Regiment. With his force ashore, and without having suffered a single casualty, Dietl now had to prepare the area against the attacks upon Narvik that the Anglo-French allies would be certain to make.

Narvik lies at the entrance to Beisfjord. From the little town a railway line led from Beisfjord in the south along Rombaksfjord and thence to the iron ore mines in Sweden. Dietl deployed the 139th Regiment in a semi-circle so as to defend Narvik and the railway line. To the north was the 3rd Battalion and below it the 1st Battalion. Both were positioned to the north of Rombaksfjord, while the 2nd Battalion held the town and secured the ground on the southern shores of that fjord.

With his Jäger battalions in position, Dietl waited anxiously for the arrival of the three supply ships, one of which was carrying a 15cm mountain gun battery. Not one of the ships reached the Narvik area, and it was presumed that they been intercepted and sunk by vessels of the Royal Navy which were heading towards the area. The only artillery assistance upon which Dietl could depend was the guns of the destroyers that had brought in the Jäger, and that defence was likely to be of short duration. The destroyer flotilla was under orders to return to Germany once the warships had been refuelled. That process was certain to take a great deal of time. One fleet tanker had reached the area, and that single ship could service only two destroyers at once.

It was while the tanker was fuelling two of the destroyers that five destroyers of the Royal Navy swept up Ofotfjord and opened fire upon the German vessels. The opening shots sank some of the German ships, but unknown to the British commander was the fact that part of the German flotilla had sailed higher up the fjord and upon hearing gunfire had swept back down again and had gone into action against the British vessels. However, all ten German destroyers were sunk.

Now Dietl's Jäger were isolated and seemingly defenceless, but the general rose to the challenge. He ordered naval diving teams from the survivors of the shelling to locate the sunken destroyers and to cut away the guns from the decks. Other teams were then sent down to bring out the shells and other ammunition from the ships' artillery lockers. When those two major tasks had been completed Dietl could be satisfied that he now had heavy weapons to defend Narvik. But his men also had to eat, and the food they needed was at the bottom of the fjord in the sunken naval vessels and in the hold of a sunken Norwegian whaling ship. The divers were sent down again, this time to find food and warm clothing. One lucky dive brought up a ship's radio, and this was soon repaired and put back into service. Now, at least, Dietl's garrison was in wireless contact with Germany and could ask for supplies to be flown in.

Dietl took stock of his position. A perimeter of defences guarded Narvik. His garrison now included 2,000 sailors, all of whom could be put into the defence of the area, either as gunners or as infantry—once they had been trained. He now had artillery support and anti-aircraft weapons, but, on the negative side, he was totally isolated and with no possibility of reinforcement.

With the garrison in position, Dietl's troops—naval and Gebirgsjäger—held a defensive perimeter that, in the 3rd Battalion's area, ran from Fagevere promontory and around the harbour down to the ferry point at Taraldsvik. The battalion commander concentrated the greatest infantry strength and most of the heavy weapons deployed to repel any Allied attack from the sea. Dietl anticipated that the assault by the Western Allies was most likely to come in against the northern sector where the 1st and 3rd battalions held post. Although he had 2,000 sailors on strength, and although these were being trained in infantry warfare and tactics, he did not have enough men to hold a firm and unbroken line. Instead his men were in positions, large slit trenches holding two or three each. The trenches in which the Jäger lived and in which they were to live for the next two months were holes in the ground blasted out of the solid rock, so widely separated that they were not mutually supporting. When it came to combat, each little group would have to fight its battle in isolation.

The land fighting for Narvik began on 13 April when a Jäger patrol, working its way along the iron ore railway, struck a Norwegian battalion. This was an alarming encounter for Dietl. He knew now that detachments of the Norwegian Regular Army stood between his forces and Sweden, the source of the coveted iron ore. Swiftly he organised a small battle group. In view of his manpower shortage it had to be a small one—a single company in strength but accompanied by an 'armoured train', with, on the open right flank of the Jäger company, a ski platoon. The approach of the Gebirgsjäger towards the northern railway bridge was greeted by small-arms fire from the Norwegians. It was obviously the intention of the commander of the enemy force to destroy that bridge. Were he to succeed, then the link to Sweden would be broken and this would isolate Dietl's force. Coming under fire, the Jäger company commander deployed his men and directed his snipers to keep the Norwegian engineers from placing their charges of explosives while other snipers shot at, hit and destroyed the charges that had already been placed.

It is not surprising that the Jäger snipers had such a high degree of proficiency. Most of them were country people who made their living from hunting animals that were fleet of foot. Their peacetime skills, allied to high-power sniping sights, gave them the ability to hit such small targets as packets of explosive with accuracy. However proficient they were, however, the Jäger were unable to destroy one charge which was blown up and whose explosive force destroyed part of the fabric of the bridge.

The Norwegians, with their long tradition of peace, were no match for Dietl's men, who were skilfully handled by their company commander. The end of the firefight was not long in doubt, and a senior Norwegian officer, together with 45 of his men, came in to surrender. That action was followed a short time later by a group of 150 Norwegian soldiers who crossed over the Bjornfell and through the railway tunnel to enter Sweden, preferring internment in a neutral country to life as prisoners of war.

The defeat of the Norwegian group brought an end to the patrol's operation. It had been in action for three days and, despite being inferior in numbers, had been victorious in battle. Dietl could be well pleased with his men and the success they had gained. They had cleared the Norwegians from positions between the town of Narvik and the Norwegian–Swedish frontier. The immediate danger to the iron ore railway had been removed. This had not been the only military activity in the area of the iron ore port. To the north of Narvik the British Army's 24th Infantry Brigade had landed, had gained touch with the Norwegian 6th Division and had partly encircled the German force. On the positive side for Dietl was the fact that a flight of Ju 52s had touched down upon a frozen lake and had unloaded a battery of mountain guns. The defenders could have confidence that the homeland had not forgotten them, and, indeed, the newspapers in Germany were filled with reports of the conditions in the mountains which the Jäger were enduring. The reassurance that they were not forgotten did not last long, however—the war in the West removed all details of Dietl's force from the headlines.

On 14 April the British brigade went into action and in conjunction with the Norwegian troops exerted such pressure upon Dietl's men that they had to abandon the town of Narvik and pull back along the railway line to the Bjornfell tunnel. The wireless signals sent back to OKW alarmed Hitler, who promptly sent a reply that is quoted in full in the Divisional War Diary. It reads:

> . . . the forces of General Dietl are to hold out in the Narvik area and if compelled to withdraw are to destroy the iron ore railway so as to make this unusable to the enemy for a long period of time. If the area forward of the Swedish frontier can no longer be held then an attempt must be made to form a cadre of soldiers trained in mountain warfare who are to withdraw in the direction of Boetobodoe and who are to be supplied from the air while the remainder [of Dietl's command] may, in emergency, cross into Sweden . . .

This directive led to another decision from the Führer: if Dietl and his force were not able to defend and to hold Narvik, then the general would be given authority to break out and to march southwards until touch had been gained with the main German body in Norway. General Jodl, in the Führer HQ, had to point out that a march by exhausted troops across difficult terrain and in extreme weather conditions was impossible. Undaunted, the Führer suggested that Dietl and his men could be airlifted out. Once again, Jodl had to point out that the lack of suitable airfields meant that only a limited number of Jäger could be brought out. Hitler, accepting that escape was not an option, ordered that the troops in Narvik were to fight to the last man. Even when, late in May 1940, Dietl and his force came again under terrible pressure, Hitler offered them the chance to escape into Sweden. Again Dietl declined the offer: he and his men had no intention of surrendering the town.

The days passed in patrol activity and in attempts by the Jäger to improve their living conditions and to supplement their poor rations. There were indications of a renewed Allied offensive, and moves came in on each of the Allied sectors in turn—British, French, Polish and Norwegian. But the attacks were not properly organised and Dietl was able to move his Jäger from one threatened sector to another to meet the newest problem. Although the attacks were at first unco-ordinated, each of them brought fresh casualties which reduced the numerical strength of the garrison. It was soon clear to Dietl that the Allied thrusts were coming in parallel to the Swedish frontier so as to reach the railway line and thereby cut off his battle group on the landward side. Under the now co-ordinated Allied pressure the Jäger defence line was forced in at one place after another.

Even with this contracting battle line the Jäger losses were such that not all their defensive positions could be manned, and the gaps between the posts grew wider and wider. Dietl knew that his men would hold; they would hold despite their falling numbers; they would hold although they were now desperately exhausted; they would hold despite the poor rations which were cut and then cut again; and they would hold although no hot food was coming forward and despite the fact that fires could not be lit. Dietl, aware of the suffering his men were undergoing, sent off a string of signals asking for reinforcement.

In time the OKW responded to his messages for help. Towards the end of May groups of paratroops were dropped over Bjornfell, and these were followed by two Jäger companies from the 139th Gebirgs Regiment that were parachuted in. Despite this reinforcement, it was not enough when the Allies, facing defeat now in Western Europe, decided that they would make one last effort to take out Dietl and his determined men. The Allied operation was a pincer movement, one pincer to the north and one to the south of the German perimeter. Only shallow penetrations of the Jäger front were achieved in the south, but deeper ones were gained on the northern sector and the attacks in that area forced the Jäger line back to a small perimeter around the railway. Deeply conscious of their precarious situation, the Jäger made ready to meet the assault that would come in and crush them. None came. The Allies, all excepting the Norwegian contingent, had taken ship and had sailed away. Patrols sent out on 8 June met no opposition and saw no sign of the enemy.

There is a postscript to the operation that Dietl was conducting in Narvik. In the south of Norway a relief force had been assembled. Its men were told of Dietl's plight, and although they had already covered 1,000km of hostile terrain a renewed and intensive effort was to be made to break through the Allied ring and to relieve the forces in the high north. A special battle group of three 'Narvik' battalions set out to cross a wilderness 800km in extent for which there were no maps and across which there were no roads nor human settlements. The route to Narvik was up and down precipitous slopes, across a glacier and then through rivers in full flood.

Before that relief force could break through to Narvik, however, Norway had surrendered and the operation was therefore redundant. The OKW communiqué of 13 June broadcast that 'a specially selected group of Gebirgsjäger which had begun a march on 2 June . . . across a trackless wilderness gained touch on 13 June with the forces in the Narvik area . . .' The campaign in Norway was over. Among the honours and awards that were made, there was one distinction bestowed on all ranks of all three services that had fought in the campaign. This was an arm shield worn on the upper left arm and inscribed with the name of the town.

Dietl's success in holding the iron ore port for so long against such heavy Allied pressure brought him promotion and he was given command of Gebirgskorps 'Norway.' Then, when the war opened against the Soviet Union in June 1941, part of the long battle line of the Eastern Front was set in the Arctic Circle and a German force was sent to that area. But before the war began against Russia, Dietl put his men to building roads in Lapland so as to improve communications in that otherwise barren area of northern Norway. The move into Lapland was made by his corps, which took up positions inside the Arctic Circle. The reason for this was that British forces had invaded both Greenland and Iceland and the German force was to act as a deterrent. Dietl's corps moved into hutted accommodation in Lapland, but the commanding general decided not to live in the village of Alla. Instead he set up his headquarters on board a captured British ship, *Black Watch*, which was moored in Altafjord. Slowly but steadily the garrison in the highest areas of Norway was built up and prepared to meet the privations of the long and bitter winter that lay ahead.

In the spring of 1941, before the war opened against Russia, Dietl was ordered to report to Berlin to attend a Führer conference. During that conference Hitler declared that the nickel-ore mines at Petsamo were vital to Germany's war effort but that they were in danger from a Russian assault. In the event of a war with the Soviet Union the OKW anticipated a Red Army offensive that would open with the object of seizing those mines. Dietl was told that it was the task of his corps to prevent the loss of the mines and that he was to advance eastwards and capture Murmansk. Dietl knew the area and Hitler did not. The general remarked that there had never been a war in that region because it was unsuited to military operations. He then pointed out that no roads existed in the region, and that if his Jäger were to be put to the task of road building then there would be no soldiers to do the fighting. He had few enough men as it was, and his corps also lacked prime movers to tow the artillery pieces. Moreover, he had almost no self-propelled guns.

Hitler described the 100km that Dietl's force had to cover to reach Murmansk as 'derisory'. Dietl, having pointed out the terrain and climatic difficulties in that frozen wilderness, rejected the Führer's contention that the distance was derisory and went on to point out that it was not, in any case, necessary to capture Murmansk: all that was needed was to cut the railway line that linked the port with the other parts of the Soviet Union and the town would be strangled. Hitler at first accepted Dietl's proposal and then amended it. Dietl's 'Norway' Corps was still to capture Murmansk, while two other corps were to cut the railway line farther south at Kandalushka and at Louhi. Dietl's corps moved into Finland at 0230 hours on 22 June 1941 but did not immediately open its offensive. Orders from OKW did not come for the corps to attack the Soviet Union until a week later.

The Lapland area was considered by the OKW to be a theatre of war of no importance, and one that could be given little priority in the matter of supplies and men. Lacking these basic necessities, it is no wonder that the German campaign in northern Finland was a war of opportunities lost because of the attitude of the German Supreme Command. To begin with, no winter uniforms were issued to the men living and fighting inside the Arctic Circle. There were no mosquito nets, and this is a region notorious for the numbers of those parasites.

In the Lapland Army Dietl led a corps under the overall command of General von Falkenhorst. From his personal experience Dietl knew about the magnetic influence of the North Pole and he taught his officers and men to use the stars to guide them at night. He also knew about the effect of intense cold upon engine oils and repeatedly asked OKW for special winter-grade oils. The opening German offensive by Dietl's corps was launched with the 2nd Gebirgs Division on the left flank and the 3rd Division on the right. Of the two divisions, the 2nd had the more difficult task: it had to reach the Barents Sea, while the 3rd had the task of protecting the right flank. The first offensive failed to reach the objective of Murmansk, but the corps did reach the Liza river, and military operations above the 60th parallel were reduced, principally, to patrols and to small skirmishes.

The failure of the German summer offensive of 1941 was succeeded by a Soviet counter-offensive during the winter of the same year. In the summer of 1943 the Lapland Army's name was changed to 20th Gebirgs Army and Dietl took over command, handing his corps to General Schörner. Dietl did not hold command of the army for long, however: in June 1944 he was killed in an air crash. His body was cremated with full military honours. His decorations included the Knight's Cross with Oak Leaves and Swords.

General der Panzertruppen
Heinrich Eberbach

The Panzer specialist in the East and the West

On 24 November 1895 Heinrich Eberbach was born in Stuttgart, the son of a salesman. At the age of six his father died prematurely and his widowed mother, who was left to bring up five children, did not have an easy time. The young Heinrich was not a good pupil at school. Lessons had little interest for him and he was only really happy in the open air, spending his time hiking and exploring the countryside around his home town. Although he was not a devoted scholar, he took the matriculation examination at the end of his studies and passed. For a boy whose expressed interest it was to become a soldier, he had, by passing the matriculation examination, taken the most important step to gaining an officer's commission. He did not wait long after gaining his matriculation certificate and on 1 July 1914 was accepted into the 180th Württemberg Regiment, which was garrisoned in Tübingen.

Upon the declaration of war in the autumn of 1914, Eberbach's regiment went on active service in the Vosges mountains of southern France. A month later, in September, the 180th Regiment was taken from that sector of the battle line and posted to northern France and to the Cambrai–Thiepval sector. Here the regiment was involved in heavy and close fighting, with a lot of bayonet work. For his service during this period Eberbach was awarded the Iron Class 2nd Class, and this was followed a few days later by his promotion to the rank of Corporal. In the fighting he was wounded in the upper thigh, but he refused to leave his men and go into hospital. During January 1915 he was promoted to the rank of Ensign and only a month later received his commission.

Throughout the summer of 1915 Eberbach was with the 180th in the great battles that were the milestones of that year, and during the French offensive of September, in the Champagne region, his platoon lay in the front line. French infantry attacked the German positions, but the first wave was flung back by the fire of the 108th. Then touch was lost with the neighbouring unit and the French surged through the gap and began to surround Eberbach's platoon.

In such circumstances it might have been wise to retreat, but Eberbach knew that German Field Service regulations laid down that any ground lost to the enemy had to be regained in an immediate counter-attack. If he and his men could hold out they would soon be brought out of the encirclement. For nearly half a day the platoon fought hard against the attacking enemy. Then ammunition began to run low and it looked as if everything was lost. Eberbach decided to make one great effort, break through the encircling ring and regain touch with the rest of his battalion. Placing himself at the head of his dwindling band of men, he led them at a charge across the torn-up ground. He and his little group had not gone far before the French opened fire upon them. Eberbach was struck so hard on the left side of his face that he was knocked unconscious to the ground. When he came to he found that he and his men were prisoners. The wound he had received had carried away his nose.

Nevertheless, he determined to make his escape, but for his failed attempt he was held in a punishment camp. He did not leave there until December 1916, when he was sent to Switzerland in exchange for a badly wounded French soldier. During his time in Switzerland he learned that he had been awarded the Württemberg Order of Frederick with Swords 2nd Class. Eberbach underwent a series of operations and the surgeons built an artificial nose that partially restored his damaged face. He was returned to Germany in August 1917, and he was decorated with the Iron Cross 1st Class for his action of September 1915.

Eberbach returned to active service in October 1917 and was transferred to the 146th Regiment, which was in Macedonia. With that regiment he was posted to Palestine and many times demonstrated his courage and prowess. One happy coincidence for him was that while in prison in France he had learned Turkish, and because of his fluency in this language he was soon attached to the Turkish 8th Army in Tulkerim.

When the Turkish front collapsed in September 1918 and the units began to give way, Eberbach was given command of the rearguard of the Turkish Army, a demonstration of the trust the authorities had in him. One of his first acts was to withstand a series of attacks by British cavalry. For five days he and his men—a mixed collection of Turks, Austrians and Germans—held the line, but then he went down with malaria and was taken prisoner again. It was Eberbach and men like him who aroused feelings of respect in such former enemies as Lawrence of Arabia, who was astounded that the morale of the Austrians and Germans did not break although they were fighting in a hopeless situation in an alien land far removed from Central Europe.

Eberbach was to receive the same sort of respectful treatment from his former enemies after the Second World War. These former enemies were the officers of the American 35th Tank Battalion. However, that second peacetime greeting lay more than two decades distant. Let us stay with Heinrich Eberbach as he rests in a British military hospital in Cairo, and then follow him through his time as a prisoner of war in Egypt and his return home to Germany. There in 1919 he became engaged to Anna Lempf, who had nursed him in 1917 when he was recovering after the severe wounds to his face. Eberbach was not retained in the Army of the Weimar Republic and, like so many of his contemporaries, enlisted into the Württemberg police force. He rose steadily in rank and by June 1933 had gained his majority. Two years later he re-entered the Army and was posted to Schwerin to the newly raised anti-tank battalion that was stationed in that town. Promotion came quickly in the Army of the Third Reich, and in the autumn of 1937 Eberbach was raised to the rank of Oberstleutnant (Lieutenant-Colonel) and then, a year later, was given command of the 35th Panzer Regiment, a component of the 4th Panzer Division.

It was while with his Panzer regiment that Eberbach again went to war. The first campaign was against Poland, and the 4th Panzer Division formed part of Rundstedt's Army Group South. The opening operations ran smoothly until 4 September, when it was realised at Army Group level that a concentration of Polish divisions was withdrawing in a south-easterly direction under the pressure of Army Group North and posed a threat to the flank of Rundstedt's army group. To confront this danger von Rundstedt changed front by swinging his forces round to face the Polish host. While the mass of Army Group South was preparing itself to contest the advance of the Polish divisions, the 4th Panzer, with Eberbach's regiment in the van, struck for the Polish capital, and at 1715 hours its vehicles entered Warsaw. But armour, however skilfully handled and directed, is not a successful medium in urban warfare, and Eberbach's regiment was quickly taken out of the Polish capital and redeployed to support the Leibstandarte SS 'Adolf Hitler' Infantry Regiment which was fighting in the great bend of the Bzura river against a mass of nine divisions of the Pomorze Army. This was a bitter battle. It was not one of mopping up the defeated enemy, but one fought against soldiers who not only were defending their home-land but were determined to smash their way through the closing ring of German forces in order to support the main army inside Warsaw. The withdrawal of the 4th Panzer Division from the Warsaw sector weakened the German encircling ring and the Poles were quick to ex-ploit this fault. On 12 September the Polish 4th and 16th Infantry Di-visions attacked the German units barring the way to Warsaw, but were driven back with heavy loss.

At first light on 13 September Eberbach's regiment, supported by the Leibstandarte, attacked in order to relieve the pressure that was being exerted on the other formations of the 4th Panzer Division. Slowly the balance began to turn against the Poles, and Army Group South started to close in and to destroy the enemy in the bend of the Bzura. In that advance the Polish 28th and 30th Infantry Divisions were struck and forced back towards Modlin. Along the Bzura there was now a solid mass of German armour, which was used to isolate the Polish units and to fragment them.

Eberbach's 35th Panzer Regiment went in and attacked the high ground at Btonie. For this operation he formed his armour into two columns, each of which was supported by an SS battalion. The assault rolled on, and against diminishing Polish resistance the small town of Kaputy was taken. There was to be no halt now. Eberbach ordered the units to keep moving at top speed. The fighting endured for a further few days and then, on 16 September, the 35th Panzer Regiment, sup-ported by the 12th Rifle Regiment and the Leibstandarte SS, struck across the Bzura. Divisional engineer units had already begun to erect a bridge, but Eberbach was unwilling to wait for it to be completed and ordered his vehicles to wade across the wide but shallow river. As the units began to cross, rain fell and soon was of such an intensity that the armour was not able to negotiate the thick and clinging mud that had been produced, nor climb the bank on the Polish side. This meant that too few machines reached that side to go into the attack and it had to be postponed. By 1100 hours enough armoured fighting vehicles had been grouped and the attack began to roll again. The assault, now reduced to a single column, moved forward until Bijmpol was reached, and at that place Eberbach divided his force and deployed it to carry out a pincer attack. On the Polish side, General Kutzreba had concentrated the divisions of the Pomorze Army and had grouped his artillery in order to smash a way through the German lines and to reach Warsaw. The ensuing battle produced a crisis that was not mastered until Eberbach's regiment, together with two battalions of the Leibstandarte, opened a counter-attack. Within an hour the German assault had broken through the Polish front—a movement that headed a general assault by Army Group South and which broke the Pomorze Army.

The most successful and destructive encirclement operation in military history to that date was concluded and had been fought out in the bend of the Bzura river. As his reward for the part that his Panzer regiment had played in the Polish campaign, Eberbach received the clasp to the Iron Cross 1st Class that he had been awarded during the Great War. Ahead of the 4th Panzer Division there now lay the prospect of a new campaign—the war in France and Flanders.

The war in the West ended in another German victory, and Eberbach's Panzer regiment took a prominent part in the first part of the campaign—in Flanders and then in the fighting in the Dyle positions as well as in the capture of Armentières. That town was taken in a night assault—the first in German tank history. The role of his regiment in the operations during the subsequent Battle of France was no less glittering. The thrust through the Weygand Line at Péronne and then the charge which took the regiment up to and then across the Seine, near Romilly, was carried on to occupy the town before midnight. That success brought with it orders to drive to Locre, and this was accomplished by moving through Dijon and then making a swift advance to Lyon.

An example of Eberbach's determination to win came when one of his Panzer battalion commanders asked for a day's rest in order to service the vehicles, which were showing the strain of continual and daily use. Eberbach's answer was a rejection which ended with the remark that one has to pursue a fleeing enemy and that if he, Eberbach, had under his command just the divisional field kitchens he would still continue to attack until the enemy had been brought to his knees. At the end of the campaign in the West, Eberbach was awarded the Knight's Cross for the action at Romilly.

For Operation 'Barbarossa', the invasion of the Soviet Union, the German Army disposed four Panzer groups. One of each of these served with Army Groups North and South. Under the control of Army Group Centre there were two Panzer groups. In this account we are concerned with the 2nd Panzer Group, commanded by General Guderian, which had on its establishment three Panzer corps and one infantry corps. Each regiment of Guderian's Panzer divisions had a higher than usual establishment of battalions—three instead of two. This higher establishment equipped his Panzer group with a total of 930 armoured fighting vehicles compared to the neighbouring Panzer Group von Kleist, which had only 750 machines on its establishment.

The 24th Panzer Corps, of which the 4th Panzer Division formed part, was placed on the left wing of Guderian's group, and the campaign opened disastrously for Eberbach. In the advances of the first weeks he responded to a request from the 3rd Panzer Division for help and immediately changed his regiment's line of advance to support the sister division. In the ensuing fighting the town of Baranovitch was captured in a *coup de main*. Despite this victory, the commander of the 4th Panzer Division threatened to charge Eberbach with dereliction of duty in disobeying his original orders. The charge was not proceeded with and Eberbach led his regiment in the capture of Stary-Bykor, one of the bastions of the Stalin Line, as well as in the capture intact of the bridges at Propaisk. It was the last-named, brilliantly executed Panzer action which led, perhaps, to Eberbach's being named as commander of the 5th Panzer Brigade within the 4th Panzer Division. The storming career of Guderian's Panzer group seemed to be unstoppable, and one after the other major Russian towns fell to the German thrusts.

A situation then developed in the fighting of mid-August 1941. The advance by the right, or inner, wing of Army Group Centre and the left, or inner, wing of Army Group South had been retarded by the terrain phenomenon of the Pripet Marshes. By contrast, the outer wings of both army groups had been more rapid. As a consequence, a vast salient had been created. The westernmost point of this was at Kiev and the eastern end was more than 120km past that city. The salient contained nearly sixty Red Army divisions, formed into five armies, and the possibility existed that that great mass of Red Army soldiers could be trapped and destroyed. But there was a difference of opinion at senior command level as to what was the correct course of action. Should the salient—this ulcer on the German flank—be left or should it be taken out? Among others, Guderian was of the opinion that the salient should be left unmolested until the thrust to take out Moscow had been made and had succeeded. The opposing voices claimed that this threat should be neutralised before the attack was launched against Moscow. That was the course of action that Hitler chose.

The battle plan was for an encirclement by units of both army groups. The Panzer formations of Army Groups South and Centre, already a long way to the east of Kiev, would swing inwards at Konotop (Army Group Centre) and at Kremechug (Army Group South) and encircle the Red Army formations. Meanwhile, the infantry of both army groups would play their part in compressing and destroying the Soviet forces. The task of Guderian's 2nd Panzer Group was to advance eastwards and to capture the important railway junction at Konotop, for the Kiev–Moscow railway line was the channel that supplied the armies in the salient and it would be their principal line of retreat. The advance by Guderian's Panzers was then to continue eastwards to take Romny. Here it was to turn southwards and to meet the Panzer force of von Kleist, which would be striking upwards from Kremechug. The meeting of the two Panzer groups would thus have encircled the Soviet troops of the South-West Front.

When the 13th Red Army was shattered on 17 August, the 2nd Panzer Group reached the Desna river. Guderian selected the 24th Panzer

Corps to be the cutting edge of the offensive that was to drive southwards to meet von Kleist's armour. Model's 3rd Panzer Division, part
of the 24th Panzer Corps, was to spearhead the corps' assault with the
4th Panzer and 10th Motorised Divisions marching closely behind.
Corps forced a crossing of the Desna river, established a bridgehead
and then broke out of this to drive southwards and to capture firstly
Shostka and then Voronezh.

On 28 August the careering advance halted. The two Panzer divisions had outrun their fuel supplies and were stranded, immobile, on
the Ukrainian steppes. On the following day the corps commander
regrouped his forces and, having refuelled them, sent them off again.

The Soviet High Command, belatedly realising that it faced a crisis,
ordered counter-attacks to be mounted by troops outside the salient
and by units inside it. The Command was determined to break the
German ring and to open a passage through which the forces, encircled and trapped, could escape. But each succeeding day the German
armoured ring was thickened and the Red Army's efforts came to
naught.

For the attack to be made at 0700 hours on 1 September, the corps
commander ordered that his Panzer divisions advance and strike shoulder to shoulder. The motorised infantry led the assault, with the Panzer regiments on either flank and the anti-tank guns in the centre. The
armoured wave met no serious opposition until it approached the tactically important road and rail bridges across the Essmayn river. The
storm of fire from the Russian artillery struck the Germans and smashed
their first assault. The armour withdrew, regrouped and then came on
again.

Made aware from captured documents that one of his Panzer groups
was striking near the junction of two Red armies, Guderian moved the
two Panzer divisions of the 24th Corps and set them the task of smashing the Soviet front. The 3rd and 4th Panzer Divisions stormed through
the gap that had been created and by the middle week of September
had completed the encirclement. Thereafter came the destruction of
the Soviet forces, and this was aided by Stalin's blundering order that
the million Red Army men trapped in the salient were not to withdraw.
No fewer than 665,000 of them were taken prisoner.

The Kiev operation had proved that *Blitzkrieg* worked well, and if there is one criticism of the operation it is that there was a weakness in the supply chain that allowed the Panzers to run dry and thus immobilised them. Against a flexibly minded army such an error would have been disastrous, but the Red Army at that time was rigid in thought and action.

After the capture of Konotop, Eberbach's unit was given a rest period of six days and then, on 30 September, received orders to drive northwards and to capture Orel. The first town en route to that objective was Essmany, and during the drive to take out this place Eberbach's brigade met and destroyed a major Red Army tank detachment. Then the advance continued on to take out the next target, the town of Ssevsk. As his armour drove towards the objective, Eberbach saw that the approach road was lined with anti-tank guns. He directed the fire of his Panzers with such success that they had soon broken down the opposition, had taken Ssevsk and had gained the objective given them—Windmill Hill. The brigade commander issued orders for the advance to be continued towards Dimitrovsk by a small battle group while he regrouped the main body.

The 13th Red Army had been attacked because it posed a serious threat to the flank of Guderian's Panzer group. Its units were concentrated around Briansk, an important road and railway communications centre. Not only was it a road and railway hub, it was also a jump-off point for the German attack on Moscow. The 24th Corps broke through the front of the 13th Red Army in fine and dry autumn weather, and the 4th Panzer now took the lead in the pursuit battle that followed. The fuel situation was critical and the question was mooted whether Corps should continue to harry the Russians or whether it should concentrate, regroup and refuel. The corps commander and the commander of the 4th Panzer Division both advised Guderian to halt and regroup, but when he spoke to Eberbach on Windmill Hill he received a fresh and contradictory viewpoint from the brigade commander.

Guderian opened the discussion with the remark that he had been told that Eberbach's Panzer brigade was having to halt. Eberbach responded that he was in pursuit of a fleeing enemy and that in such a situation one did not halt but continued to pursue the foe. In response to Guderian's question on fuel supplies, Eberbach assured his superior that he had enough. Every vehicle driver had set aside a small reserve for such a contingency, and his brigade would continue to chase the retreating enemy. Assured by Eberbach's confident words, Guderian ordered the pursuit to continue. The tanks of Eberbach's Panzer brigade and the other machines of the 4th Panzer Division covered 130km during the day.

By 3 October Orel, a full 200km behind the Red Army's front line, had been taken by Eberbach's men. So unexpected was the arrival of the Panzers in Orel that the trams were still running and soldiers in the streets did not fire upon the German column. Then the weather changed. During the night of 6/7 October the first snows of winter fell, and by the following morning a thaw had melted the snow and thick mud covered the ground.

The advance then continued, and Mzensk fell to Eberbach's Panzers. On the road that led towards the town the Soviets had placed a blocking force of a brigade of tanks, KV heavy vehicles backing and supporting a mass of T-34s. The battle was a hard one, and it soon became clear that Eberbach's brigade would be outflanked and might be encircled. During the fighting his command vehicle was hit and the crew had to bail out. They walked through the explosions and fury of the battle carrying their wounded with them.

On 22 October Eberbach was given command of the 8th Panzer Regiment, which was reinforced with an armoured battalion taken from the 18th Panzer Regiment. The battle group was given orders to take Tula. Eberbach moved his group by night and it struck into the back of the Russian defenders of Mzensk, smashed a Red tank armada and by employing superior tactics destroyed the superior Russian force. When news of the victory was reported to Guderian he increased Eberbach's battle group with elements from the 75th Artillery Regiment, the 3rd Rifle Regiment and the whole of the 'Grossdeutschland' Infantry Regiment. He issued the order to the reinforced battle group that it was to stop for nothing but must capture Tula at best possible speed.

By now the autumn rains had set in, but despite the adverse weather conditions Eberbach used the road northward to gain the objective. Whole detachments of his command lay immobile, trapped in the thick slime. By 28 October the battle group lay only 4km outside the town, and Eberbach proposed to seize it in a night operation. But his proposal was rejected and the attack did not roll until 0530 hours on the 30th. The delay in mounting the operation had given the Soviets time to strengthen their defences, and the first Panzer attack gained only half a kilometre of ground before a mass of anti-tank fire forced it to halt. Then, through the smoke of the Red artillery bombardment, the first wave of T-34s rolled towards Eberbach's battle group. The fighting between the Russian armour and the German Panzers lasted all day, and even when the Stukas were brought in the losses they suffered halted any further air attacks. The battle group went over to the defensive.

The wastage in these defensive battles was such that by mid-November the units of Eberbach's command had sunk from a nominal strength of 300 machines to less than 50. In addition to Russian defensive fire, the bitter cold—minus 22 degrees was recorded on 13 November—immobilised the German formations. Despite these disadvantages, Eberbach took up the attack again and his group fought its way into Uslovaya and then to Venev. Moscow was now only 60km distant. The temperature sank to minus 40 degrees and, despite the biting cold, the attack was carried on until 3 December, when the Tula–Serpukov road was reached and cut.

It was the final, dying effort. Only two days later the army on the Eastern Front was forced to retreat. A vast number of AFVs for which there was no fuel had to be blown up to prevent their falling into the hands of the Red Army. For the efforts that his units had made, Eberbach's name was recorded in the Wehrmacht's book of honour, and on the last day of 1941 he was awarded the Oak Leaves to the Knight's Cross. Further, on 1 March 1942 he was promoted to the rank of Generalmajor (Brigadier-General) and was given command of the 4th Panzer Division.

Throughout the winter of 1941/42 Eberbach remained with his regiment, fighting the defensive battles that marked that bitter period. The strain of command took its toll, and on 15 April 1943 he had to be rushed into hospital with a kidney haemorrhage. Towards the end of November Eberbach was entrusted with the temporary command of the 48th Panzer Corps, and he led it in the first battles for Stalingrad. Within two days he was wounded again, this time in the chest by a shell splinter, which kept him in hospital until 1 February 1943. During this time he was promoted to the rank of Generalleutnant (Major-General) and upon his return to duty was given the post of Inspector of Armoured Troops in the Home Army. On 8 August came his promotion to General of Panzer Troops, and in October he returned to active service with a Panzer corps in the battles around Zhitomir. A month later he was entrusted with the command of Army Group Nikopol. His spell of duty in that post came to an abrupt end when he was again taken into hospital with another kidney haemorrhage at the beginning of December and was then evacuated to a convalescent centre in Germany.

Upon returning to duty, he took up, once again, the post of Inspector of Panzer Troops, leaving when he was given a new appointment with Model's army group. In the first week of July 1944 he left the Eastern Front for a posting to the Western Front, where he was named Supreme Commander of Panzer Group West facing the British 21st Army Group in Normandy. His first action on reaching France was to discuss with Hans von Kluge, the new Supreme Commander West, the current situation and the plans which had been drawn up to counter and to defeat the Allied invasion. Hitler had already sacrificed two of his top commanders for their failure to throw the Allies back into the sea. On 3 July the Führer had accepted Gerd von Rundstedt's offer to give up his post as Supreme Commander West on health grounds, and on the same day he removed Geyr von Schweppenburg from his post as Commander of Panzer Group West. It was to the command of that Panzer group that Eberbach now succeeded.

Having been briefed on the situation, Eberbach drove to meet Rommel and to discuss with him the defence of the Caen sector. Caen was the prime objective of the Normandy campaign, and it had been expected to be taken in the first week's fighting. Among the divisions defending Caen was the 12th SS Panzer Division 'Hitler Youth', and Eberbach visited that formation on 7 July. He arrived shortly after an air raid had struck at divisional headquarters and in time to evaluate reports of the fighting that was taking place along the divisional front and to issue orders for a tank battalion from the 21st Panzer Division to support the 16th Luftwaffe Infantry Division. Throughout the following days Eberbach was engaged in fighting a defensive battle in Normandy, plugging gaps in his front that the Allies—predominantly the British 21st Army Group at this stage of the fighting—had created. All the intelligence summaries reported that Montgomery was building up his forces to open another major offensive. The British commander issued Directive M 505, setting out his plan for the future development of the campaign. He intended to relieve pressure upon the US front by a new offensive in the area of Caen. One result of this was the operation which has passed into British military history under the code-name 'Goodwood'. In that battle Eberbach demonstrated his skill at handling armour both in defensive as well as in offensive operations.

Eberbach's Panzer Group West had under its command for the 'Goodwood' operation the 86th Corps with the 711th Infantry Division holding the coastal sector from the Seine to the Orne estuary. The 346th Infantry Division defended the ground from Franqueville Plage to north of Touffreville. The 16th Luftwaffe Infantry Division together with the 192nd Panzer Grenadier Regiment of the 21st Panzer Division lay to the north of Touffreville from Colombelles and held the line to the Orne bridges to the south of Caen. The 1st SS Panzer Division with the 272nd Infantry Division was positioned from the Orne bridges to the south of Caen and to the west of Eterville.

German intelligence sources expected that the main British effort would fall in the area held by the 16th Luftwaffe Division, which had already suffered heavy casualties in the fighting of the previous weeks. Eberbach ordered the division to be supported in the rear areas to prevent any British breakthrough and disposed the troops to reinforce the Luftwaffe division. These were two battalions of a Panzergrenadier regiment, together with an SP battalion, a battalion of Panzer IVs and one of Tiger tanks. Farther behind the Luftwaffe division were artillery units echeloned in depth.

Eberbach spoke to von Kluge on 17 July and advised him that a major attack was anticipated for the following day and that it would be made by means of three main thrusts. As he had expected, the Allied assault opened at 0525 hours on the morning of 18 July, with the usual artillery barrage by the British and Canadian batteries made upon known and suspected German artillery positions. During this hurricane of fire

1,600 Allied heavy bombers flew towards the western flank of the German positions and smashed the front of the 16th Luftwaffe Division. The air bombardment extended as far back as the forming-up line of the Panzer divisions. Close behind the aircraft came the tanks of the 11th Armoured Division, their advance covered by a barrage from about 700 guns whose fire was supported by a bombardment from ships lying out to sea. That armoured spearhead rolled over the stricken Luftwaffe division, but then it was met by Panzers that Eberbach had ordered forward.

The fighting which ebbed and flowed all day to the east and to the south of Caen ended when at last light the British armour went into laager with many of the day's objectives still not taken. The next major armoured operation came in at around midday on 19 July, and was repeated on the 20th. Then rain began to fall with an intensity not formerly met in the campaign, and the adverse ground conditions that it caused forced Montgomery to break off the 'Goodwood' offensive. The bridgehead east of the Orne had been extended, but this was all that had been gained. Eberbach had demonstrated his successful tactical and strategic command of the German Panzer force in the West. During 'Goodwood' the British and Canadian armies lost 570 armoured fighting vehicles and did not gain the objectives for which they had striven.

On 9 August 1944 Eberbach's headquarters was moved to Mortain at the Führer's direct wish, according to von Kluge. The Americans had broken through the German lines at the base of the Cherbourg peninsula and the Führer had conceived the idea that an armoured thrust could not only seal off the breakthrough but go on and roll the Americans back to the invasion beaches. It was to be Eberbach's mission to accomplish this military miracle.

Hitler grouped the Panzer divisions in that part of Normandy and formed them into Panzer Group Eberbach. Hitler and the OKW were confident that he, with his great experience of armoured operations, would bring the offensive to a successful conclusion. But even Eberbach's skill could do nothing in the face of US tank superiority. He was able, at least, to bring out the Panzer divisions engaged in the Mortain offensive and to regroup them to form a new assault unit. This he led in a limited thrust to bring out some of the units trapped in the Falaise pocket.

On 14 August Eberbach took over command of the 7th Army. The few troops under his command were the burnt-out remnants of the divisions that had once held Normandy. He resolved to build a new front along the line of the Seine river and it was on 31 August, while he was on a reconnaissance in that operation, that he was taken prisoner by units of the British 2nd Army.

Eberbach's health in the immediate post-war period broke down in December 1945, and he was moved during the autumn of 1947 to a US prisoner-of-war camp in Neustadt. He was released from the camp on 8 January 1948 and spent the following months in hospital. Discharged at last, he took up honorary work with a Protestant religious charity and was then associated with commemoration services for wounded and missing soldiers. He lived out the rest of his life carrying out charitable work and forging links between former enemy servicemen.

SS Gruppenführer
and Generalmajor der Waffen SS
Otto Hermann Fegelein

The commander of the SS Cavalry Division
who became Hitler's brother-in-law

Otto Hermann Fegelein was born on 30 October 1906 in Ansbach, the eldest son of a subaltern officer in the Army. When Hermann was six years old the family moved to Munich and in the Bavarian capital city the young boy's passion for riding found expression when his father was posted to an Army school of equitation in the Albrechtstrasse.

The young Hermann's education was that of a middle-class German boy—Kindergarten, followed by high school, from which he passed into university. During his years as a student in the University of Munich, Fegelein served a six-month period with the heavy machine gun squadron of the 17th Cavalry Regiment. A short return to civilian life was followed by enlistment into the police force on 27 April 1927, and in his post he applied himself to his duties with such diligence that he was marked out for promotion. That diligence, coupled with his intelligence, brought him promotion to NCO rank, and after a probationary period of service he was selected to attend a police academy where future senior officers of the force were trained. Fegelein decided not to graduate from that academy at that particular time but instead spent his days travelling around Europe, taking part in equestrian events.

On 15 May 1935 he joined the Allgemeine SS, where his police training stood him in such good stead that he received a commission as an Untersturmführer (2nd Lieutenant) on 12 June of that year. His first posting was to the mounted squadron of SS Gruppe Süd (SS Southern Group), and he later joined the SS Oberabschnitt Süd, where he was appointed to the post of adjutant to Heinrich Himmler, the

Reichsführer SS. In addition to that appointment he also had the duties of a Sonderführer (special duties officer) to fulfil, and he held both
appointments for nearly a year before gaining a new post. This gave
him command of the 15th Reiterstandarte of the SS in Munich. On 20
April he was promoted to the rank of Obersturmführer (1st Lieutenant) and assumed command of Reiterabschnitt V, holding that post
until the formation was broken up during October 1936. In addition to
those posts Fegelein held responsibility as Head of Equitation in Oberabschnitt Süd. Promotion came rapidly to him. He was raised to the
rank of Hauptsturmführer (Captain) on 9 November 1934 and to that
of Sturmbannführer (Major) on 30 January 1936.

During that year the Olympics were held in Germany and Himmler
decided to build a showpiece institution that would become the SS
Riding Academy. Fegelein was chosen to be Director of the Academy,
and both through his work in this institution and through his equestrian reputation he became better known to a wide circle of influential
people. Further promotion came to him quite easily and quickly, and
after having been awarded the Equestrian Badge in Gold he was el-
evated to the rank of Obersturmbannführer (Lieutenant-Colonel) on
30 January 1937. This was followed by promotion to the rank of
Standartenführer (Colonel) seven months later.

Although he had a home of his own, Fegelein named his apartment
in the riding school as his residence, certainly until September 1939.
General mobilisation had been ordered by that time, and this was followed by the outbreak of war. His riding school address then became
his official one. He had expected to take over command of the SS
Totenkopf Reiterstandarte (the SS Death's Head Mounted Regiment),
because the mounted units had been raised originally as part of the
Allgemeine SS, but they were then absorbed into the Waffen SS. Fegelein
had been promoted to Standartenführer in the Allgemeine SS and was
allowed to wear the insignia of that rank, although in the Waffen SS he
only had the rank of Obersturmbannführer. He was made War Substantive in the Obersturmbannführer rank of in March 1940 and was
promoted to Standartenführer in the Waffen SS on 1 February 1942.
For his service during the early campaigns Fegelein was awarded the
Iron Cross 2nd Class on 15 December 1940, and six months later came

---

the award of the Iron Cross 1st Class. On 2 March 1942 he was awarded the Knight's Cross for conspicuous bravery over a month-long period of close combat in the Rzhev area of Russia. He had been recommended for this award by General Schubert, the General Officer Commanding 23rd Corps. The official document recommending him reads:

> The SS Cavalry Brigade was positioned on the south-eastern flank of Corps' front and specifically in the sector to the north of Nikulino–Polovinino–Saizevo–Dimitrovo–Sokolomo. Its task was to halt the advance of strong enemy forces which had broken through to the west of Rzhev and which were about to strike southwards so as to attack the rear of the 206th Division.
>
> The Brigade thwarted every enemy attempt and accomplished this with great dash despite the heavy casualties which it had suffered. Not only did the SS Cavalry Brigade defeat every enemy attempt, but it was also the spearhead of our main offensive operations. The Brigade led the encirclement moves that only a few days later led to the complete annihilation of the enemy forces.
>
> During these defensive and offensive operations personal calmness, exemplary bravery and offensive spirit were shown by the Brigade Commander. In the offensive operations he was at the head of his men and thereby gained all the objectives assigned him.
>
> On 5 February 1942 the Brigade Commander, on his own initiative, ordered an attack against a strong enemy group located to the north-west of Chertolino. The advance was carried out by the Brigade across difficult terrain and in poor weather conditions against a vastly superior enemy holding entrenched positions.
>
> The capture of a number of tactically important places, including the Chertolino railway station, taken only after heavy fighting, enabled our forces to close the ring around the enemy, who was then destroyed at the end of hours of continuous night fighting. These operations were conducted by the Brigade Commander in person against a numerically superior enemy. He led his men with tremendous élan.
>
> The enemy lost 1,800 dead and tons of material while we suffered only minimal casualties. Because of that victory Corps could shorten its front, allowing other Corps units to be freed. The SS Cavalry Brigade by determined attacks tightened its encirclement of the enemy to the south-west of Rzhev. There was confused fighting for the village of Yersovo, which fell to us on 14 February 1942, a victory which finally destroyed the surrounded enemy group.
>
> SS Standartenführer Fegelein was able to destroy completely the enemy forces using a combination of resolute command decisions and bold leadership. His personal bravery and aggressive spirit enabled us to clean up a situation to the south-west of Rzhev.

Before we go on to detail the developing military career of Hermann Fegelein, it must be understood that the greatest part of his active service life was spent on anti-partisan operations. This was brought about, in part, by the special terrain factors that controlled the course of the war in Russia. One of these terrain factors was the Pripet Marshes, which extended across the central sector of Russia and acted as a barrier to any army advancing from the west, as the Germans were. The Marshes were more than 600km long from north to south and over 200km wide on an east–west line. They were an area of waterways and of thick forests almost primaeval in their density. The vast woods were virtually impenetrable, and German patrols were usually able to enter only a few hundred metres into them.

The Pripet Marshes had a few areas of permanently dry ground and across those so-called land bridges ran the railway lines to Moscow and other major cities. The railway tracks supplemented the poor network of all-weather highways. The extensive marshes were a magnet to Red Army units that had been bypassed in the German advances of summer and autumn 1941 and which did not want to surrender to the invaders.

Within this vast swamp the Red Army re-formed its shattered units, and soon supplies began to come through from the 'big country', as those areas of the Soviet Union that had not been occupied by the Germans were called. When they had gained sufficient strength, guerrilla groups then went over to the offensive. This they did with such success that the partisan problem was one that the Germans were never able to overcome. In time the partisan formations grew so strong that they influenced not only the ground war but also that in the air. This they did by forcing the Luftwaffe to issue maps to its air crews showing the sectors of the Central Front over which planes were advised not to fly because of the danger of Soviet anti-aircraft fire. There can be no doubt that a single willing Red Army man who could cope with the peculiar difficulties of the Pripet Marshes required at least three German soldiers to subdue him and that such numerical superiority on the part of the Germans was never forthcoming.

Although Fegelein's cavalry brigade was used exclusively on anti-guerrilla operations, it should not be thought that this was a lesser or a minor part of military operations. The war against an enemy who was indistinguishable from the civilian population but who could and would fight with desperation or, indeed, savagery was in many respects far harder than that fought against the uniformed and recognisable Red Army. Personnel of rear units of the German forces on anti-partisan operations knew that death awaited them if they were captured, and that death would not come easily: they could expect to be tortured and even mutilated before they died.

The German Army made a clear distinction between the operational area, where the major campaign was being fought, and the area behind the front line. This distinction had applied in former wars, but during the Second World War the gulf was widened. The reason was that on the Eastern Front the Russian-German war was less a military conflict than an economic and ideological one. The Third Reich was determined to exploit the human resources of the Soviet Union and determined to conscript the Slav masses into working for Germany either on farms or in factories. Those Russians who were too weak to work were shot, as were those considered by the Nazis to be racially impure. A vast campaign of suppression by terror was unleashed across all the rear areas of the German-occupied zones of the Soviet Union—a campaign that was criticised by most of the conventional and conservative-minded German military commanders. Mention was made above that in military circles the combat zone was separated from the rear areas, and, by decree, those rear areas were controlled and administered by the Nazi Party, whose executive body was the Allgemeine SS. The rear areas of the front were exclusively the province of the Party, and no Army commander had authority there, except by invitation or else as a commander in charge of a military operation that had been planned. In the rear areas the word of the SS was paramount and unchallengeable. Thus in the vast theatre of operations which was the Central Sector of the Eastern Front there existed a world in which Fegelein's word was law, and in it he and his cavalry units fought a bitter war.

Russian morale suffered under the victories won by Fegelein's brigade, and efforts to strengthen Soviet resolve were made when commissars were flown in from mainland Russia. Those ruthless officers of Stalin's system inspired, infused or dragooned their subordinates into action against the occupying forces. Those German forces, let it be understood, faced a hopeless task. For example, a single German security division had to police an area the size of Austria, and there were other examples of German troops spread too thinly across partisan-infested terrain to be effective everywhere or, indeed, anywhere. The reason was that the German security units that were supposed to carry out anti-partisan sweeps were made up of men either too old or too poorly armed to be effective in such operations. Small wonder then that a formation such as Fegelein's brigade, strongly armed and up to strength, was found to be so indispensable that it usually spearheaded military operations in the Pripet Marshes.

Anti-partisan missions were usually overlooked when the war diaries of major units came to be written up, for such operations were minor in scale when measured against the titanic struggles that were being fought by the three main German army groups. The only information which is accessible to post-war historians is that contained in sub-unit war diaries or in the post-operational reports written by officers who commanded those missions. It was standard practice in the German services for reports to be written by the unit commander and forwarded to the next senior, hierarchical level. These wartime reports assume that a reader has a knowledge of details such as the terrain across which the operations were carried out as well as the peculiarities of that terrain. For a reader to follow a unit's movements towards its objectives, accurate and detailed maps of the area are essential.*

In the late spring of 1942 the SS Cavalry Brigade was enlarged to become a division. Fegelein was not with his brigade when this expansion took place. He had been posted to the SS Führungshauptamt (SS Main Headquarters), where he took up the post of Inspector of Equitation and Horse Transport. That change of command brought further promotion, and on 1 December 1942 he was raised to the rank of SS Oberführer (Brigadier-General) and shortly thereafter was once again given a field command—a standard practice in the German Army.

* Research in the archives in which those post-battle reports and sub-unit war diaries are held is a specialist study, and this author was fortunate enough to be guided to the source of many records by the celebrated military author Mark Yerger, whose advice and profound knowledge is deeply appreciated and acknowledged. He had earlier supplied detailed archive material in his books *Riding East: The SS Cavalry Brigade in Poland and Russia* and *Waffen SS Commanders: A to K*—two of his many indispensable reference works.

He was posted from his position on the staff and took over 'Battle Group Fegelein', a unit composed of the 2nd Battalion of the Police Division's 3rd Regiment, a battery of field artillery armed with foreign weapons and another battery of field artillery equipped with German guns. To supplement its field artillery component the battle group also had a few self-propelled guns, and to complete its establishment it had under command a signals platoon and some anti-tank guns.

While in command of this battle group Fegelein was wounded again, and he did not return to active service until mid-April 1943, when he was given command of the SS Cavalry Division and promoted to the rank of Brigadeführer (Major-General) on 1 May. He led the division throughout the summer of 1943 and for his leadership qualities was recommended for, and received on 9 September 1943, the award of the German Cross in Gold. He was extremely active in command of the SS Cavalry Division and on 23 December 1943 was involved in the fighting for Golaya. Two Red Army regiments and an artillery group attacked and struck the German front, determined to break through. The German forces were few in number and tired from the strain of combat, but Fegelein roused them from their lethargy and fought back the enemy thrusts. Six months later, on 17 May 1943, his division encountered a large body of well-organised and well-armed Russian partisans. Fegelein quickly regrouped his forces and struck the enemy so severely that a total victory was won.

At this time a general up-arming of the guerrilla forces, coupled with an increase in aggressive operations against the German occupying forces, seemed to have happened, for only a week later Fegelein was in action against another heavily armed partisan band in battalion strength. He determined to strike at the heart of that guerrilla group and stormed their strongly garrisoned strongpoint. The élan shown by Fegelein and his men was such that the enemy was destroyed in quick time. For that operation his unit was mentioned in the Wehrmacht communiqué of 12 June 1943. A week later the interrogation of some partisans revealed that the earlier operation had destroyed the partisan force in just twenty minutes, leaving 11 guerrillas dead and 22 wounded.

This success was followed by another on 26 August 1943, when the Russians broke out of an encirclement near Bespalovka, using three fresh divisions of infantry, the remnants of two other divisions and a strong force of armour. The fighting was intense, and Fegelein displayed his customary calmness and leadership attributes during the battle. He demonstrated the same qualities during the fighting on 28 August when Red Army units attacked behind a fierce and prolonged artillery and mortar barrage that struck particularly hard against Fegelein's 1st SS Cavalry Regiment. It was estimated that the Soviets had a three-to-one majority and used that superiority to attack using waves of men. The force of their assault broke through the German lines and the Russian troops flooded through the gaps that they had created. They were only halted when Fegelein put his last reserves into combat. The fighting endured for more than eighteen hours, and post-battle reports state that the divisional commander was always to be found where the fighting was most intense. Then, on 9 September, he led a counter-attack against Russian forces that had captured an important hill. His counter-attack group was a weak one, but Fegelein led his men in and not only re-took the hill but inflicted heavy casualties on the enemy troops.

During the final days of his command of the SS Cavalry Division, Fegelein realised that a Russian attack against another tactically important hill would not only give the enemy observation into the German area but could also be a base for launching further attacks against his division. Then orders came in that the hill had to be held until German SPs and Panzers could enter the fighting. At the head of his men, Fegelein stormed the hill and was again wounded, but he refused to be evacuated until the armoured fighting vehicles arrived and had taken over the ground from his units. That wound gained for him the Wound Badge in Silver.

Upon his return from convalescence, Fegelein was posted to Hitler's headquarters, where he served as the liaison officer between Himmler and Hitler. In recognition of his actions during the fighting of the summer of 1943, he was awarded the Swords to the Knight's Cross on 23 February 1944. Himmler introduced him as his new liaison officer, and by that act Fegelein, who had already risen very high and had reached the rank of Gruppenführer (Major-General), determined to reach the most senior circle—that around Adolf Hitler. He exercised his not inconsiderable charm, and in March 1944 asked Marianne Schönmann, a friend of Eva Braun, Hitler's secret mistress, to arrange an introduction. She introduced him to Eva Braun, who was immediately attracted to the tall, athletic and young war hero. Fegelein was invited to lunch.

There is no doubt that there was a mutual attraction between Eva Braun and Fegelein, and he soon became the most popular man in Hitler's entourage—in the words of a woman who worked in the Berghof, he was 'the life and soul of the party'. Having an easy familiarity that made him well liked by the ladies, he could tell the most risqué stories without showing the least touch of embarrassment. As a highly skilled rider he had a perfect sense of balance and moved gracefully, two attributes that served him well in the afternoon and evening dancing parties that were one of the chief ways in which Eva Braun and her friends passed their time.

It soon became clear to all those who attended those parties and the intimate dinners that Eva Braun arranged that the feeling between her and Fegelein was more than just a mutual attraction. She was fascinated by him because of her temperament, but far more than her deep feeling for him was the awareness, the fear, that he would be returned to active front-line service. Eva was determined to keep him by her side. She arranged the ideal solution: he should marry her sister, Margarete. Surely no one could object to Margarete being with her, and where Margarete was so would Fegelein, her husband, also be. In April 1944 the couple announced their engagement, and on 3 June they were married in a civil ceremony in Salzburg, having their wedding breakfast on the Kehlstein mountain. Eva had calculated well, for she was now Fegelein's sister-in-law and could both flirt and dance with him without fear of gossip. In the middle of January 1945 Margarete became pregnant and her husband, fearing for the safety of his wife and unborn child, persuaded her to leave Berlin and to go to Bavaria, in southern Germany.

It was a sensible precaution. Not only were the Allied air raids on the Reich capital more frequent than formerly, and more destructive, but a Russian offensive was building up which would erupt out of the Oder river bridgehead. When that happened the obvious target of the Red armies would be Berlin, into which Hitler had withdrawn. The Soviet offensive opened, and by the mid-April the city was almost surrounded.

In the Reichs Chancellery bunker Fegelein realised that he now faced a dilemma. As an SS officer he had a military obligation to be loyal to Hitler but, on a personal level, he also had an obligation to his sister-in-law Eva Braun. He knew that she intended to stay with the Führer in the Reich capital and was determined to die there with him. In Fegelein's eyes she was committing suicide, and he determined to give her a shock that would bring her to her senses and change her mind.

On 25 April 1945 he left the Reichs Chancellery bunker, accompanied by his aide-de-camp Obersturmführer Bornhold, and drove to Furstenberg to seek the advice of one of the most senior of the SS leaders, Hans Jüttner. In view of that officer's high position in the SS organisation, Fegelein may have concluded that Jüttner was privy to Himmler's secret approaches to the Swedish Count Bernadotte. Those approaches were aimed at bringing the war to an end. By the time that his meeting with Jüttner ended, news had been received that the road between Furstenberg and Berlin had been cut. Fegelein thereupon flew back to the Reich capital, not to the Reichs Chancellery but to his flat in the Bleibtreustrasse. It was from there that he repeatedly telephoned Eva and begged her to leave Berlin and to save herself. She, for her part, urged him to return to the bunker, where his absence had been noted and commented upon. This he refused to do, even though senior members of Hitler's entourage who also telephoned him at first suggested that he return and finally ordered him to do so. He remained adamant, and it was clear that he had been drinking heavily. A group of SS men under the command of Obersturmführer Frick was sent to his flat to collect him. Fegelein, now totally drunk, refused to accompany them.

SS General Johann Rattenhuber, chief of the SD, the Reichssicherheits Dienst (Reich Security Service), was determined that Fegelein should be made to return to the bunker and sent his deputy, Peter Högl, together with some SD officers to arrest the deserter. When the group arrived at the flat in the Bleibtreustrasse there was a red-haired woman with Fegelein and in the struggle to overpower him she escaped. Högl and his group, taking with them the reluctant and obstinate Fegelein, reached the Führerbunker during the evening of the 27 April. Hitler's first action when the drunken officer was brought into his presence was to strip him of his rank, and he then ordered that Fegelein be put into the line as a simple soldier in the defence of Berlin. For Martin Bormann degradation was not punishment enough and he ordered a search to be carried out in Fegelein's room in the bunker. A small case was found which contained a collection of jewellery together with amounts of foreign currency. Then Fegelein's briefcase was opened and was found to contain documents that implicated him in the surrender negotiations that had taken place between Himmler and Count Bernadotte. The possession of such incriminating material changed the whole complexion of the case against him. Fegelein now faced a charge of high treason, and this carried the death penalty. He was tried, condemned and shot to death, although where the execution took place has never been established. One theory is that it was carried out in a cellar in the Chancellery and the firing squad consisted of just two men from the SD.

History has passed two judgements on the career of Hermann Fegelein. The first and wholly condemnatory one claimed that he was not a brave officer but was one who had gained his medals, promotions and advancement at the expense of the men whom he had ruthlessly sacrificed. The alternative view is contained in unsolicited, contemporary letters, citations and reports written by senior officers in the Army to whose formations Fegelein and his cavalry brigade had been subordinated, and these documents speak for themselves. Awards for bravery are not given to officers who lack either courage or the ability to inspire men in battle. Fegelein was awarded every class of the Iron Cross up to that with Oak Leaves and Swords. His other decorations included the German Cross in Gold for repeated acts of bravery, as well as the Close Combat Clasp in Silver and the Wound Badge, also in Silver. The last award showed that he had been wounded in action on three occasions. He also held Romanian decorations for bravery and leadership.

After Fegelein's execution Eva Braun would have had scant time to mourn him for only a few days later she committed suicide in Berlin with Hitler. Fegelein's wife Margarete, Eva's sister, whom he had sent away to Garmisch-Partenkirchen in Bavaria for safety, stayed there until the war's end. Years later she moved home and lived in northern Germany.

General der Panzertruppen
Werner Kempf
Germany's Panzer fireman of the Eastern Front

erner Kempf, who was to become one of the most successful Panzer commanders of the Second World War, was born
on 9 March 1889 in Königsberg, East Prussia. From his ear-
liest years he was determined to be a soldier, and after passing out from
cadet school he joined the 149th Infantry Regiment (Schneidemuhl) in
the rank of Leutnant (2nd Lieutenant). His time with that regiment was,
however, of short duration. In 1912 he transferred services and became a
subaltern in the 2nd Marine Infantry Battalion. This was commanded by
von Lettow-Vorbeck, who was later to win fame as commander of the
German troops in the East African campaigns of the Great War.

When offered the opportunity to train the naval cadets of the training ship *Veneta*, Kampf accepted immediately and, together with his
naval recruits, sailed on a two-year cruise to the Caribbean and South
America. In the course of that cruise a revolution broke out in Haiti
and landing parties were sent from the *Veneta* to protect foreign consu-
lates and to help restore order. Kempf, by this time raised in rank to
Oberleutnant (1st Lieutenant), was in charge of one of the *Veneta*'s
landing parties and acquitted himself well.

When the *Veneta* returned to Germany at the end of the two-year
cruise a European war was imminent, and shortly after the outbreak of
hostilities the 2nd Battalion, in which Kempf had served in peacetime,
was expanded and became the 2nd Regiment of Naval Infantry. The
young 1st Lieutenant Kempf was appointed to the post of regimental
adjutant and he served both in that position and in the trenches. The
German Navy's land units held post on the extreme right of their battle
line in Flanders with their trenches and dugouts literally on the shore of

the North Sea. The 2nd Regiment was involved some of the heaviest of the fighting in Flanders, and Kempf took a prominent part in many of these actions. One of his comrades in the Naval Division was Bernhard Ramcke, who later achieved fame as a paratroop general.

In 1916, after nearly two years' front-line service, Kempf was promoted to the rank of Hauptmann (Captain) and was seconded to the General Staff to be trained for a senior command post. Two years later he was transferred to the staff of the Naval Corps in Flanders.

With the end of the war revolution broke out in Germany and certain foreign powers sought to annex German territory. Units of German patriots were formed to operate against the nation's internal and external foes, and from the former Naval Division a Freikorps unit in brigade strength known as the Eberbach Naval Brigade was raised. Kempf served as a staff officer in that unit.

There then came a new change of service—back to the Army—and Kempf, who was retained in the 100,000-man Army of the Weimar Republic, was posted back to the infantry and served as a company commander in the 4th Regiment. Within two years he had won promotion and was appointed General Staff Officer of the Infantry Inspectorate in Schwerin/Mecklenburg. In 1926, while serving in the Inspectorate, he was asked whether he would consider a transfer to the motorised branch of the Army. He had no previous experience of internal combustion engines or their capabilities but agreed to be transferred and was sent on a training course with the 1st Motorised Battalion.

By the beginning of October that year he had risen to the post of Ia in the Inspectorate of Motorised Units. In that position he became increasingly aware of the necessity for motorisation within the Army as well as the problems of the tactical employment of armoured fighting vehicles. It was clear to him that modern armies had to have armoured units. Despite the fact that Germany was forbidden to have tanks or, indeed, any heavy weapons, the question of the employment of armoured fighting vehicles was mooted, albeit academically. There were also questions asked among those officers of middle rank whether any practical purpose was served in carrying out field exercises using dummy tanks and whether, by using such mock vehicles, the troops could gain any experience of collaborating with, or fighting against, armoured vehicles. It was Kempf's good fortune that his duties kept him close in contact with the Panzer theorist General Lutz and with his Chief of Staff Guderian, both of whom were wholeheartedly in favour of the application of armour and its peace-time instructional role.

In the rank of Oberstleutnant (Lieutenant-Colonel), Kempf was then given command of a Bavarian unit, the 7th Motorised Battalion, in Munich, and in his two years in that post he gained fresh experience in handling motorised units *en masse*. He took over as Chief of Staff from Guderian on 1 July 1934 and continued with the task that his predecessors had begun in pressing for a motorisation of the German Army. One of the most important events during his time as commander of the Munich motorised battalion came in the manoeuvres of 1932. Kempf's skilful handling of vehicles operating across the difficult country of the Frankfurt-am-Oder training ground demonstrated his ability to control a large body of vehicles in a tricky situation. Although he proved, in the 1932 manoeuvres, that he had the practical skills necessary for armoured command, he continued to study the theory of war in the future and realised that with the development of more powerful internal combustion engines warfare had entered a new dimension. He became aware that motorisation increased mobility, and he reasoned, further, that the speed at which an army could move should not be tied to the speed of a marching infantryman. Rather, armour—and he anticipated that the German Army would one day re-arm and equip itself with armoured fighting vehicles—must be an independent arm of service. It would need to be organised into self-contained, all-arms formations, and it was clear that the divisional structure was the most flexible form.

Kempf did not regret that the day of horsed units in battle had passed. Under most conditions the AFV was faster, better armoured and more mobile than the horse. Not only that, but wireless could pass messages between the commander and his subordinates, faster than was possible for a cavalry patrol. The concept of motorized (i.e. armoured) warfare was driven forward by the protagonists of that type of as yet unproven conflict, namely Guderian, Lutz and Kempf, supported by several members of the High Command who had a hard struggle against another group of officers who thought in the conventional way and who saw tanks as being the handmaids of the infantry: in their eyes, the infantry was the arm which decided the outcome of a battle. Hitler supported the armoured concept and promoted Kempf to command the 4th Panzer Regiment on 1 October 1937.

Although Germany had come late to the idea of armoured warfare on the battlefield, her theorists, such as Kempf, had spread the idea so widely within the Army that the principles of what became known as *Blitzkrieg* were widely understood. It was Germany's fate that the mechanisation of the Army was not swiftly acted upon. Certainly there were, as a result of rearmament and reorganisation, several Panzer divisions on the Army's establishment, and these did form a new arm of service, although this did not win official recognition until the middle years of the Second World War. The vehicles with which the Panzer divisions were equipped were in the main lightweight. They were chiefly the Panzer I, armed only with machine guns and suitable for reconnaissance and little else. The Panzer II was an improvement over the Panzer I, but it was still not a battle tank. With the phasing in of the Panzer III and IV, however, the Army at last had machines that were useful and capable—so capable, indeed, that both types were retained as the workhorses of the Panzer arm until the end of the war. Even when the Panzer V (Panther) and the Panzer VI (Tiger) entered service, there were still large numbers of IIIs and IVs within the Panzer divisions.

The German tank specialists had considered that the III and IV, both of which weighed 20 tons and had ranges of between 100 and 125km across country, were sufficiently heavy, well armed and manoeuvrable weapons capable of all-round service. When it became necessary during the war for there to be an upgunning of the main armament, then the construction of the Panzers permitted heavier guns to be fitted without the need for a redesign of the whole vehicle. Moreover, that upgunning allowed the German machines to keep pace with the vehicles of the Allied armies and in some cases to prove themselves to be superior to the enemy types. For example, for several months in 1941 the Russian T-34 was superior to any German Panzer, but the training, skill and initiative of the Panzermen, at all levels, were superior to those of their Red Army opponents and these compensated for the lack of a suitable weapon until the Panzers were upgunned and the crisis was overcome.

In the first campaign of the Second World War the German armed forces met in combat a Polish Army whose tanks were inferior to their own and which were easily 'killed' by the relatively few Panzer IIIs and IVs that were in service. For that campaign Kempf, newly promoted to the rank of Generalmajor (Brigadier-General), was given command of an *ad hoc* Panzer formation. In the summer of 1939 the SS Regiment 'Deutschland' was incorporated into Panzer Division 'East Prussia', later to become known as Panzer Division Kempf. This formation was raised on 10 August and for the invasion of Poland was one of the divisions of the 1st Corps, in the 3rd Army, on the strength of Fedor von Bock's Army Group North. The battle plan produced by OKH was for that army group to thrust for Warsaw and, in conjunction with Army Group South, to encircle and destroy the Polish Army to the east of the Vistula river. Panzer Division Kempf was an experimental unit set up to establish whether the type of division which fielded only one infantry regiment could be as effective as one which contained the standard two infantry regiments. The division was also unusual in that SS and Army troops served together in it— a revolutionary concept at that time.

Kempf moved his division into the frontier region of East Prussia, near Neidenburg. There, when war broke it, it had as its first task to break through the permanent defences protecting the town of Mlava. The SS infantry regiment of Panzer Division Kempf opened its operations on 1 September 1939 and made good progress until it reached the foot of a steep and open slope on whose crest the Mlava defences were located. The first infantry attack could gain no ground and Corps ordered that the aborted attack be made again, but this time it was to be supported by Panzer units. The 1st Panzer Battalion of Kempf's division began its assault but soon found its way obstructed by anti-tank barriers. As the vehicles milled around the area they were struck by Polish artillery fire that knocked out several of them. The Panzer regiment's commanding officer, unwilling to see his command shot to pieces for no gain, ordered his units to pull back. With the assault halted around Neidenburg, Corps moved Kempf's division eastwards to Chorzele, where a breach in the Polish lines had already been made. On 10 September Panzer Division Kempf crossed the River Bug and struck southwards to cut off the Polish units that were marching to reinforce the Warsaw garrison. That advance by Kempf's division was hotly contested by major Polish units, which flung in a succession of infantry and cavalry attacks against the SS and the Panzers.

Polish opposition to the east of Warsaw broke on 15 September. Although the capital was surrounded it could not fall until the forts at Modlin had been taken. Those forts were located to the north-west of the city, and to reach them Kempf's division had to retrace its steps. Panzer operations against the forts were out of the question: this was an infantry battle, which lasted from 19 to 28 September. The role of Kempf's division was then at an end, and with the departure of the SS regiment the *ad hoc* unit was disbanded.

Following the war in the West in 1940, Kempf, by this time promoted to the rank of Generalleutnant (Major-General), took command of the 48th Corps. On 1 June 1941 he was promoted to the rank of General of Panzertroops and led the 48th Corps—two Panzer divisions and the motorised 25th Infantry Division—as part of Rundstedt's Army Group South in its charge through the Russian steppes and across the Ukraine. The first months of the war against Russia saw the German Army carrying out a series of highly successful encirclement battles. In the battle for Uman, Kempf drove his corps towards the town, striking down from the north to meet the upward thrust of another Panzer corps. The advance was not without risks, and Corps was soon in a precarious situation. During the encircling operation a gap had opened between the 11th and 16th Panzer Divisions and the Soviets, ever quick to exploit a blunder, advanced upon the gap, intending to use it as an escape route from the eastward drive of German 17th Army. Forced by that army's pressure, they concentrated their forces and struck hard, hoping to break through the encircling ring and to widen the breach between Kempf's two divisions and thus to escape eastwards.

By 1 August the Panzer divisions of Kempf's corps had reached Novo Archangelsk, to the north of Uman, and the encirclement of three Soviet armies, the 8th, 12th and 18th, was complete. The Soviets, aware of the importance of the town, flung in a succession of attacks and recaptured it.

The ring around the Red Army formations in the Uman pocket had been burst open temporarily, but Kempf rose to the challenge and changed the direction of the Leibstandarte Infantry Regiment's line of advance. In a swift and overwhelming assault, the SS regiment recaptured the town. In the battle for Uman the Germans took 103,000 prisoners, and in an Order of the Day issued on 8 August 1941 Kempf expressed his thanks for the bravery of the SS in the battle for Novo Archangelsk.

There then followed the mighty encirclement operation around Kiev. For this battle Kempf's Panzer corps formed the spearhead of von Kleist's 1st Panzer Army. Conscious of the risks that were being taken in encircling so great a mass of Russian troops with so few armoured forces, Kempf spent much of his time driving from one of his divisions to the other, to inspire and to encourage his soldiers. Throughout the operation he was constantly in danger from Russian counter-attacks and break-out attempts, but he insisted on leading his formation from the front.

The Kiev encirclement was the greatest battle that had been fought to that time. The background to that operation was that the German advance in southern Russia had been so swift that the right wing of Army Group South had driven farther eastwards than its own left wing or that of the inner wing of its neighbour, Army Group Centre. As a consequence, a vast salient had been created. In the west of that salient was the city of Kiev, defended by the Soviet 5th Army, which offered the most bitter resistance. The mechanised units of both Panzer armies found less opposition to their advance in the open country outside Kiev, and on the vast steppeland they had soon advanced to a point over 100km east of the town. Within the salient that the Germans had created there were some sixty Soviet divisions comprising five or six armies. As the encirclement developed, OKH formulated a plan for a double encirclement, the inner one to be formed by the infantry forces of both army groups and the outer one by their Panzer formations. To begin that operation, at the Kiev or western end of the salient, the German 6th Army, an infantry force, was to hold the Soviet 5th Army fast, while the infantry of the German 2nd Army and the armour of the 2nd Panzer Group, once in position, were to drive down from the north to meet the uprising German 17th Infantry Army and von Kleist's 1st

Panzer Group. Von Kleist's Panzer group was weaker in armoured strength than Guderian's, having a total of only 750 machines against the 930 serving with Guderian's 2nd Panzer Group.

During the Kiev encirclement operation there were changes in the composition of Kempf's 48th Corps. The Leibstandarte SS 'Adolf Hitler', which had been on its strength, was posted away to the 11th Army, but such was the rapport that had grown up between Kempf and the Leibstandarte that he was not content just to issue an Order of the Day bidding it Godspeed. Instead he went in person to say goodbye to this élite unit, and the divisional history of the Leibstandarte says of him that not only was he one of the leading Panzer exponents of the Second World War, but he was also a warm-hearted, knightly superior. In an Order of the Day issued on 3 September, Kempf praised the six-week-long collaboration between his corps and the SS that concluded with the capture of Cheson and ended his order with these words:

> If today—and hopefully only temporarily—the LSSAH leaves our Corps, so is it a debt of honour to send to its brave soldiers and to their commanders my thanks and recognition for their achievements. I remember in this expression of my thanks all those courageous heroes who gave their lives for the Führer and for Germany.

The 17th Army began its part in the Kiev encirclement on 31 August. Under the cover of an aerial and artillery bombardment, the Desna river, almost a kilometre wide, was crossed and within a day German engineers had bridged it. Kremechug fell to Army Group South on 8 September and a bridgehead was created around the town. With its capture the time had come for the Panzer formations of Army Group South to move into action. The order was given, and by the morning of 12 September the leading elements of Kempf's Panzer corps were poised ready to break out of the perimeter that had been created. The infantry of the 11th Corps advanced under an artillery drum fire and behind the infantry three waves of Panzers from the 16th Division moved forward into the assault. The waves of German infantry and armour smashed into and then through successive Russian defence lines. Quickly the Panzers passed through those positions and found themselves among the soft-skinned vehicles of the Russian rear areas.

Kempf's formation had achieved total surprise. Within hours it had burst out of the Kremechug perimeter, had then driven for over 30km, crushing resistance, and had smashed every Red Army convoy it met—horse, cart, lorry and infantry. That night of 12 September the 16th Panzer Division laagered in two groups, the infantry at Yaroshi and the AFVs at Karpicna. Not to be outdone, the 9th Panzer Division had captured Mirgorod and on 15 September its leading elements had seized the unblown bridge across the Sencha river and had set up a bridgehead on the far bank. The swift break-out of the Kremechug perimeter had been a total success and set the course for the next stages of the encirclement.

With the infantry force of the 17th Army now in position on the left and the fast units of the Panzer group positioned on its right, Army Group South moved in to complete the crucial stages of the encirclement. For their part in the operation the Panzers were given the objective of the high ground between Lubny and Lochvitsa. Kempf's corps raced towards the Dnieper river through weather that was truly appalling. There was torrential rain of almost monsoon intensity, which fell all day long. Kempf ordered the construction of an emergency bridge, and by the following day it had been completed and the leading elements of the 16th Panzer Division were crossing the Dnieper with Kempf riding with the point detachment. Now the imperative was for Corps to move with all possible speed in order to effect a link up with Army Group Centre and thereby trap the Russian host.

The next important objective of Kempf's corps was Lubny, to the east of Kiev and well behind the Soviet front. Kempf urged his men on, with such success that within twelve hours the 16th Panzer Division had clawed its way 70km through the clinging mud of the Ukraine. To bring their advance forward the Panzer crews had driven throughout the pitch-black, rain-filled night. Behind the 16th came the 9th Panzer Division, the sister formation of Kempf's corps, and together they struck towards the Ssula river which runs north–south between Kremechug and Romy, where the formations of Guderian's 2nd Panzer Group were making their drive down to meet the 1st Panzer Group. On that northern side of the great pocket, Lochvitsa had been taken by the 3rd Panzer Division of Army Group Centre. The jaws of the German pincers were closing fast, although Soviet resistance to the 16th Panzer Division was still bitter and at times fanatical.

Aerial reconnaissance photographs showed that the Ssula river bridges to the south of Lubny were still intact, and Kempf gave orders to the 16th Panzer Division that it was to race forward and to seize them before they could be blown. It fell to the pioneer battalion of the 16th Panzer to carry out Kempf's order. The lightly armoured vehicles of the pioneer battalion roared forward and, under the cover of smoke shells, the pioneers raced on to the bridge, some of them removing packets of explosive charges while others fired through the curtain of smoke to beat down the hail of Russian defensive fire. Soon the pioneers had fought their way into the suburbs of Lubny. But there the advance began to slow and Kempf ordered an infantry regiment forward in order to 'beef up' the flagging attack.

Throughout 13 September the bitter fighting for Lubny went on, but then, on the 14th, as the Panzer units moved out to open a new attack with Kempf, as usual, heading the advance, Russian resistance suddenly broke and the last groups of Red Army men gave up the struggle. With the closure of the pincer jaws now only a matter of time, Kempf formed a battle group out of units of the 16th Panzer and sent this out to contact the point unit of Model's 3rd Panzer Division and thus to complete the encirclement. The sealing of the giant pocket was effected on 15 September when the vehicles of the 16th Panzer Division met detachments of the 6th Panzer Regiment of the 3rd Panzer Division. Once the armoured units were in position, half of the vehicles turned outwards i.e. eastwards, to face the attacks that the Red Army was launching to break open the jaws of the pocket and release the trapped Soviet forces. The machines of the other half of the Panzer ring faced westwards, the direction from which Russian attempts to break out from inside the pocket were being made. When the pocket was finally destroyed and the count was made, 665,000 Red Army men had been taken prisoner and 1,000 tanks had been destroyed or captured, together with 3,718 pieces of artillery. Of that vast total of prisoners, Kempf's corps had captured 109,000.

From Kiev Kempf then led his corps northwards to fight for and capture Kursk, and at that place the major operations by his formation for the year 1941 came to an end. However, throughout the late autumn and the winter of 1941, Kempf and his corps fought in the defensive battles that marked the cold-weather period and throughout the offensives that were fought during those terrible months. In time campaigning weather returned.

For the German offensive of summer 1942, known as Operation 'Blue', Kempf's corps fought as the spearhead unit of Hoth's 4th Panzer Army and was given as its principal objective the town of Voronezh. On 24 June 1942 his corps moved out to open the attack with the 24th Panzer Division in the centre and with the 16th Motorised Infantry Division and the Grossdeutschland Division on either flank. Kempf decided not to launch a methodical assault but to capture the town in a *coup de main*. To ensure that the 24th had maximum flexibility, he gave orders that it was to act independently and as the situation dictated. Within ten days of Operation 'Blue' being launched, Voronezh had been captured. Kempf and his corps stood east of the Don river heading the advance of the 4th Panzer Army as it drove the retreating Soviets towards Stalingrad. That town was reached towards the end of August.

On 1 September 1942 Kempf led the 14th Panzer and the 29th Motorised Infantry Divisions towards Pitomnik, just outside Stalingrad, while his 24th Panzer Division smashed a 20km gap in the railway line between Stalingrad and Karpovka. It was Kempf's plan to surround the 62nd and 64th Red Armies, and in order to complete the encirclement it needed only Paulus's 6th Army to form the northern pincer of that operation. However, the tardy 6th Army units did not arrive in time, allowing the Soviets to escape the trap that Kempf had laid for them.

It was on the Volga river that Kempf handed over his corps and flew to Berlin, where he was decorated by Hitler with the Oak Leaves to the Knight's Cross. After a period of leave he was given command, in February/March 1943, of an army-sized detachment that became known as 'Army Detachment Kempf'. As commanding general of that formation, he was ordered to clear up the situation at Kharkov.

The battle for that city saw the German senior officers in some confusion. There was uncertainty on the part of the army group command on how the operation should be conducted—whether it should be dealt with as a tactical or as a strategic battle. On the one side Kempf and his supporters of the tactical option considered it essential to hold the city as Hitler had ordered. The army group commander, Field Marshal von Manstein, who saw the strategic picture, intended to let the Russians take the city and then, to the west of Kharkov, to strike them a paralysing blow. Kempf and his party pointed to the low numbers in unit vehicle strengths and the poor quality of the roads which made the mass movement of motorised machines almost an impossibility. Von Manstein refused to accept those arguments. The enemy had to be beaten. After that it did not matter if the vehicles were stuck in the mud or not. Despite Kempf's pessimism, the attack went in and smashed the Soviet 3rd Tank Army. At the end of March operations were halted as both sides were held fast in the Rasputitsa, the deep and clinging mud of the Russian steppes.

Kempf had always been known as a commander who protected his soldiers in battle. That he knew how to protect them in other situations also is shown by the following episode. In a telex von Manstein had seemed to criticise the Leibstandarte SS for not conducting operations in an aggressive manner. Kempf reacted immediately and vigorously on behalf of 'the men who are struggling bravely and who are commanded skilfully' and went on: 'The LSSAH has an 80km wide area to cover and has carried out its duties in that area in an effective and aggressive fashion . . .' Accepting the rebuke of his subordinate, Field Marshal von Manstein withdrew his comments and apologised.

It is necessary at this point to set the background to the next major operation. One does not have to be a trained staff officer to see where the German summer offensive of 1943 would come in. The location was obvious. By the time that the Soviet winter offensive of 1941/42 faltered and died, it had created a vast, blunt-headed salient in the middle of which lay the communications centre of Kursk. The task facing OKH was to launch a fast, encircling operation from the north and south of the Kursk salient, so that, when the jaws of the pincers met, a great mass of Soviet divisions would be trapped and could be destroyed or taken prisoner.

The operation, code-named 'Citadel', envisaged that Model's 9th Army of Army Group Centre, fielding three Panzer corps, would descend from the Orel sector. Shortly after the 9th Army had begun its southward drive, Army Group South would launch the 4th Panzer Army. That formation was to drive northwards to meet Model. It is with Hoth's 4th Panzer Army that we are concerned. It had on its establishment the SS Panzer Corps, with three SS armoured divisions, Leibstandarte, Totenkopf and Das Reich. As the SS Panzer Corps struck northwards, its right, or eastern, flank would be protected from Soviet attack by Kempf's Panzer detachment.

This task was one of vital importance, and it is no surprise that the Panzer specialist Kempf was entrusted with that task. The battle plan produced by Army Group included the detail that

> . . . on the opening day of this operation the Panzer army will effect a break-through of the enemy's first-line position on the high ground Belgorod–Korovina. Enemy resistance in the second line is then to be smashed. The enemy armoured forces south of Oboyan are then to be attacked. It must be anticipated that enemy assaults will come in against the eastern flank of our attack and that these will be made by several armoured corps . . .

On the basis of that appreciation the 4th Panzer Army issued its orders at the end of June and directed the east wing formation (Kempf's Panzer detachment) to use its 6th Panzer Division to attack in the direction of Prokhorovka. From an intelligence survey it was clear that the staff at Panzer Group anticipated that the principal effort would be made by SS Panzer Corps at Prokhorovka and, further, that from the success of that attack a salient—later to become one arm of the German pincer—would be created. The advance by the main body of Kempf's armoured group would create a second pincer and between them the Red Army in the south of the Kursk salient would be trapped.

With that phase of 'Citadel' completed, the SS Corps and Kempf's detachment were to unite to create a single powerful fist that would then strike irresistibly northwards towards Kursk. Kempf's detachment had yet another task to fulfil as it struck upwards, holding and defeating the attacks that the Red Army would make against it: it was also to advance eastwards, defeating the Soviet forces it encountered. Once the junction had been effected between the 4th Panzer Army and Model's 9th Army, the Kursk salient would have been pinched out and 'Citadel' would have been brought to a successful conclusion.

The Soviet forces that would oppose Army Group South were three fronts, the South-Western, the Steppe and the Voronezh. Of those three, the Voronezh was the most important for it had on its establishment the greatest number of tank and Guards Tank armies. According to

Soviet military historians, 'the enemy concentrated a powerful assault grouping, about 50 élite divisions including armoured and motorised divisions'. The Soviets did, however, accept that they had a superiority in infantry of 4:1 and a two-fold superiority in guns, as well as a 2:1 superiority in armour, and it was obvious that it was those masses which would be put in most strongly against the German units on the flank of the advance. In the case of the 4th Panzer Army, the heaviest burden would be made against Kempf and his divisions. To bring to bear the full force of these attacks against the right wing of the German advance, Stavka, the Soviet High Command, was prepared, if it became necessary, to take one of its major formations, the 5th Guards Tank Army, out of its strategic reserve. Once committed, it was to be deployed and by aggressive action it would wear down and blunt the two pincers of the Panzer army.

At the end of the fighting of the first few days, the fury and might of the attack by the SS Panzer Corps was such that a breakthrough threatened, and to prevent this Stavka took more and yet more formations from other sectors and rushed them to the critical area, i.e. that in which Kempf's detachment was embattled. Operation 'Citadel' neared its climax, and this soon became apparent to the staff officers at 4th Panzer Army headquarters. One crisis that arose on 7 July was an attack led by 60 Russian tanks followed by several battalions of infantry. That assault had the aim of cutting a main road that was a principal supply route. Kempf called for air support and soon Ju 87 Stuka dive-bombers, all armed with tank-busting cannon, appeared over the battlefield and by their fire destroyed fifty of the attacking Soviet machines.

The climax for Operation 'Citadel' came in the days between 9 and 12 July 1943 when the tank battle of Prokhorovka was fought. In this clash more than 1,200 tanks were deployed and the losses on both sides were enormous. More frightening than the losses, however, was the fact that in order to delay the Germans until the Red Army was prepared to assemble and dispose its armour—particularly the 5th Guards Tank Army—Stavka continued to take units of half-trained soldiers from every sector of the front and put them into action, sacrificing them in order to gain time. The armoured formations that the Soviets put in during those days of crisis were composed of light vehicles, suitable only for reconnaissance. These were shot to pieces and destroyed, but the intention—to gain time—was achieved.

When the 5th Guards Tank Army eventually reached the battlefield and joined the 5th Guards Army it was committed immediately to battle. Stavka knew that the Germans held the tactical advantage. The Panzers' main armament could 'kill' at ranges up to 2km; Russian tanks could not. To nullify that advantage, Stavka ordered that its armoured units were to attack *en masse* and were to close with the enemy. The Germans could not kill them all, and while Kempf's detachment and the rest of Hoth's 4th Panzer Army were concentrating on destroying the Russian light vehicles, the battle tanks of the 5th Guards Tank Army would charge in and clash with the Panzers at point blank range. In the battle which was fought out over those few days the armour of both sides became so intermingled that none could say with certainty who was attacking whom or how the fight was going.

On 12 July the Battle of Kursk reached its turning point. Operation 'Citadel' had failed to gain the objectives that it had been set and Hitler ordered the offensive to end, despite von Manstein's confident prediction that, given a few more days, he could win a decisive victory.

From its successful defence of the Kursk sector, the Red Army went over to the offensive. During August 1943 Kempf's Army Detachment was retitled the 8th Army and was put in to stop the offensive which the Soviet Voronezh Front had launched and which was aimed at recapturing Kharkov. The forces fielded by Kempf and his superior, von Manstein, were too weak to carry out the Führer's order to hold Kharkov, and both commanders decided to evacuate the town and thereby avoid the losses in manpower and *matériel* that a defence of the city would bring about. Hitler considered this decision to be weakness and disloyalty. He removed Kempf from his post and ordered him to be placed in the Führer reserve of officers.

Kempf never held another military post for the remainder of the war. At its end he was arrested by the Allies and sentenced to a term of imprisonment on war crimes charges. Upon his release he accepted that he had lost his home in East Prussia and settled in Bad Harzburg, West Germany. In his retirement he remained actively interested in matters connected with the subject of armour and was instrumental in helping to recreate the Panzer arm in the Bundeswehr. He died on 6 January 1964 and was buried with military honours as befitted one of the most successful Panzer commanders of the Second World War.

Oberstleutnant
Walter Koch

Commander of the Para Assault Battalion
in the Low Countries and in Crete

The man who led the daring airborne operation that opened the campaign in the West on 10 May 1940 had only a short active-service life for he was killed in a road accident during July 1943. But it was upon the shoulders of that subaltern officer, as he then was, that a heavy responsibility had been laid. If his mission had failed, then the whole German Army plan for the war in the West, Operation 'Yellow', would have been jeopardised.

That young officer was Walter Koch, born in the Rhineland city of Bonn on 10 September 1910, the son of a surveyor. Walter had a conventional education and seems not to have been an outstanding pupil, but he left the senior Central School on 1 March 1929 with a matriculation certificate That qualification led to his achieving an officer's commission in his chosen career, which had been, originally, with the police force. He entered the police academy in Bonn as an officer cadet and by 1 January 1935 was commissioned in the rank of Leutnant (2nd Lieutenant) In August 1935 he exchanged services and left the police force to enter the Luftwaffe, and specifically, the élite 'General Göring' Regiment. On 1 September of that year Koch was promoted to the rank of Oberleutnant (1st Lieutenant) and then, on 1 April 1938 to the rank of Hauptmann (Captain).

At about this time the first steps had already been taken to create a formation of paratroops in the Luftwaffe, similar to that which Göring had set up in the Prussian police force. It was to the paratroop barracks at Berlin-Reinickendorf that the young Captain Koch reported. Jump training was given in the Stendal para school, and once he had made his quota of jumps and had passed out as a qualified paratrooper Koch was returned to the 'General Göring' Regiment where, on 1 April 1938, he took over command of No 1 Company in the regiment's 1st Battalion.

In the political world, it was clear that unless the crises of that year could be peaceably resolved then Europe would be plunged into a new war. The most immediate crisis, that in the Sudetenland of Czechoslovakia, was averted by political concessions made by the Western Powers, but then a fresh matter of contention arose about Polish claims for access to the Baltic Sea.

By mid-June 1939 war had become unavoidable, and the German armed forces underwent reorganisation to prepare them for the coming conflict. Among the units striving hard to prepare themselves were the paratroops (*die Fallschirmjäger*) of the 7th Airborne Division. They were to be disappointed. During the war against Poland there were neither para drops nor glider landings, and the airborne regiments played no role in the campaign. With the end of the war in Poland, however, preparations began for the attack in the West, in which the paras were to carry out a number of audacious operations, initially against targets in Belgium and then in Holland. Koch's battalion was used only in the Belgian missions.

The battle plan first proposed by the High Command was, in many respects, a re-run of the Schlieffen Plan, which had been tried in the opening weeks of the First World War. The plan had foreseen an enveloping, scything sweep through the Low Countries followed by a north–south advance through Flanders and into France. A variant of this plan proposed by the High Command in the Second World War was that Army Groups A and B, holding the north and centre of the German battle line, would push the Allied armies back on to the guns of Army Group C in the south. The Chief of Staff of Army Group A, von Manstein, proposed a new plan. The principal attack in his plan would be made out of the Ardennes and would strike towards the Channel coast. He anticipated that the Western Powers would react to the German assault by driving northwards into Flanders, there to confront the German armies. When the Franco-British force did move northwards, a thrust coming out of the Ardennes would strike behind the Allied northern group and separate it from the bulk of the Allied armies—the southern group, which would be waiting to advance from positions to the south of the Aisne river.

The most important innovation in Operation 'Yellow' was the use of airborne troops, para-dropped and glider-landed, and to explain their roles it is necessary to go back to November 1939, when the 'Friedrichshafen Research Unit' was raised by the Luftwaffe's 7th Airborne Division. That name camouflaged a group of specialists under the command of Captain Koch, whose men came from his No 1 Company, the pioneer platoon of the 2nd Battalion under the command of Lieutenant Witzig, and a glider group led by Lieutenant Kiess. The strength of the unit was eleven officers and 482 men, who would have to carry out specialised airborne operations at the opening of Operation 'Yellow' which included taking out Fort Eben Emaël by direct assault and seizing certain bridges across the Albert Canal. The whole operation was to be carried out swiftly so as to facilitate the advance of German 6th Army in its strike into Belgium.

Koch divided his battalion into four groups. Witzig's 'Granite' detachment was to land on the roof of the fort and neutralise its guns, whose fire otherwise would dominate the bridges over the canal. Lieutenant Altmann and his 'Steel' group were to take out the bridge at Veldwezelt, while Lieutenant Schacht's 'Concrete' unit was to attack and capture the bridge at Vroenthoeven and Lieutenant Schachter's 'Iron' group had the bridge at Canne as its objective.

The officers and men of Koch's battalion did not know exactly what their objectives were, but it was clear from the training that was being given, particularly to Witzig's 'Granite' group, that they were to attack a specific and vital target. In the early spring of 1940 joint exercises involving the parachute detachments and the glider units were undertaken. Koch, realising that Allied intelligence might get wind of the new operation, moved his units very frequently and also changed their names. Unit distinctions and insignia were removed and all leave was cancelled. The whole battalion was, in effect, confined to barracks in order to preserve its anonymity. One of the new and highly secret weapons that the men of Koch's battalion would be using for the first time was the hollow-charge grenade. The effectiveness of this device was tested against modern former Czech fortifications.

During the evening of 9 May the groups of Koch's battalion prepared for the forthcoming operation and at 0430 hours an armada of 42 gliders lifted off from airfields around Cologne. The towing machines cast off the gliders at an altitude of 7,000ft and the pilots trimmed their machines to a 1 in 12 dive, an angle which, it was calculated, would carry them nearly as far as their objectives, after which a second and steeper angle would be taken to bring the machines directly on to the targets.

The groups whose task it was to take out the Albert Canal bridges landed by glider and went into action. Both the Schacht and Altmann groups landed and seized the bridges at Veldwezelt and Vroenthoeven respectively, but Schachter's 'Iron' unit, which landed near the Canne bridge, suffered the frustration of seeing the objective blown up before it had seized it. Not only had the group failed to capture it intact, but the Belgian defenders fought hard to prevent the Germans crossing the canal. At the other two bridges resistance was beaten down and the paras managed to set up bridgeheads on the canal's western bank. To support Koch's men, detachments of troops armed with heavy machine guns were parachuted in some forty minutes after H-Hour and their fire completely dominated the enemy. At Eben Emaël the assault launched by Witzig's group was fast and eventually captured the fort.

During the day the advance-guard units of the 6th German Army closed up to the canal and relieved the airborne men. Koch and his men had gained a strategic victory for the loss of 43 killed and 100 wounded. As a result of the successes gained during the airborne operations in Belgium and Holland during May 1940, the OKW issued an order in July 1941 for an expansion of the units in the 7th Airborne Division. Included in this expansion was the enlargement of the assault battalion, which became a regiment, and Koch, now promoted to the rank of Major, was given command of its 1st Battalion. With the creation of the 11th Airborne Corps in January 1941, the assault battalion ceased to be a divisional unit and was taken on to Corps' strength.

At the end of April 1941 Koch's regiment and the other Corps troops were transported to the Romanian/Bulgarian border and from there to Athens. The campaign to capture Crete by airborne assault was imminent, and the 1st Battalion, stationed on Megara airfield, began active preparations for that mission. The orders for the campaign to capture

Crete from the air allowed only a matter of days for it to be begun and completed. There were to be three main zones of battle, the eastern, the central and the western. It was the western group that Koch's battalion joined. The assault regiment was to form part of the first wave of airborne men and it was to land at dawn in a simultaneous glider-borne and paratroop operation. The principal task of the assault regiment was to take out the anti-aircraft guns that were located on both banks of the Tavronitis river, for these guns threatened the follow-up aircraft. While the guns were being attacked a second assault group of men from nine of the gliders were to capture the bridge across the river and cut the road between Maleme and Sphakia. The most important feature lying within the combat area of 'West Group' was a low hill, Point 107, which dominated the airfield of Maleme. Koch allotted to the capture of that tactically important feature only a single company, No 4. The Maleme airfield itself was the objective of the 3rd Battalion of the assault regiment.

In order for the first wave to reach the island before first light, the Ju 52s took off late in the night, and after circling to gain height took a southerly course. Just before dawn the gliders containing the bulk of Koch's battalion—less two companies that had been seconded to 'Centre Group'—landed by glider, as planned, in the dry bed of the Tavronitis river. It had, perhaps, not been foreseen that the river bed would be filled with large boulders. The gliders crashed into these obstacles, killing or injuring the paras inside them. Worse was to come. The anti-aircraft guns mounted to defend the bridge went into immediate action and their fire riddled the stationery machines. Losses were high, and among those severely wounded was General Meindl, the commander of the para assault regiment. Elsewhere on Crete the paras had gone into action but had failed to seize Point 107. In the fighting for that feature Koch was hit in the head and badly wounded. He was among those evacuated to mainland Greece, and he took no further part in the fighting. Thus he was not on the island leading his battalion when the airborne men and the Gebirgsjäger (mountain troops) won the battle and forced the British and Dominion troops to withdraw. The 7th Airborne Division had entered the battle with a strength of about 22,000 all ranks. Of that number 3,250 had been killed. The assault regiment suffered 700 killed and 3,400 wounded or missing.

The year 1942 saw the high point of German military successes in
the Second World War, but there were, as always in military operations, some setbacks. These, it was confidently anticipated in
Führerhauptquartier, would be overcome as the war machine of the
Third Reich drove on to final victory. One of the minor problems,
which affected the war in North Africa, was that the Axis armies fighting in the Libyan desert did not have a major port sufficiently close to
the combat zone through which the German-Italian forces could be
supplied. Tobruk would have been ideal, but it had been captured by
the British in 1940 and they had held it against Rommel's attacks in
1941. Now, in the spring of 1942, with Rommel and the Axis desert
armies fighting a long way east of Tobruk, the need for such a port,
with major facilities, became vital. A proposal had been made to the
OKW that if the British-held island of Malta could be captured, then
this would be an acceptable alternative to Tobruk. Hitler grasped the concept immediately and ordered the necessary preparations to be made.

Thus it was against the Führer's imperative need for a deep-water
port that planning began for an airborne assault that would seize Malta.
Hitler knew that its capture would require a strong force of expert soldiers, and he knew also that it would be an operation which would be
attended with a number of serious risks. Not only would the island
have been prepared to defend itself against attack from the air, but
there would be the most violent British reaction to the Axis operation.
The Royal Navy had a very strong presence in the Mediterranean, but
to counterbalance that domination the Axis battle plan proposed that
its seaborne invasion force would be escorted by heavy units of the
Italian Navy.

During the May 1942 preparations for the Malta operation, Walter
Koch, whose battalion had captured the Maas bridges and the fort of
Eben Emaël in 1940, was ordered to train a 5th Para Regiment which
would spearhead that mission. It had been the OKW's original inten-
tion to employ Koch's unit, which was to form part of the 3rd Para
Division, and which would be used to reinforce General Ramcke's Para
Brigade already in Africa, but military events altered that intention.
The order from Führer headquarters was acted upon and soon, at the
paratroop training ground of Grossborn in Magdeburg, men began to

come in. These first arrivals in Koch's new regiment were mostly experienced paratroop soldiers who had been with him in his original Sturm battalion or else were men who had served with the air landing regiment. Around that cadre of seasoned men a 3rd Battalion was created, its companies fleshed out with recruits from the three main para training schools. Concurrent with the raising of 3rd Battalion, a 1st Battalion was also being created. A 2nd Battalion already existed but had been posted to the Libyan desert, where it formed part of Ramcke's brigade and was known as Battle Group Hubner.

In July the 1st and 3rd Battalions of Koch's regiment were posted to Normandy to undergo intensive training on the French Army's exercise area at Mourmelon to the south-west of Reims. In the event, preparations for the mission to take Malta by airborne assault were cancelled. In Africa Rommel's new spring offensive had finally taken Tobruk and thereby obviated the need to attack the island. Hitler is reported to have qualified his cancelling of the Malta operation with these words: 'Once the Italian admirals learn that the British fleet is under way they will turn their ships around and race back to port, leaving the troop transports defenceless.' Whether that reason was a valid one cannot be confirmed, but the Malta mission was cancelled. Koch's two battalions were then posted to Italy, ready to be transported overseas to serve in the Libyan desert. The Allied landings in French North Africa required as a matter of urgency that all available units in France and Italy be despatched to Tunisia to guard the back of Rommel's desert army.

In the early hours of the evening of 10 November 1942 Captain Knoche's 3rd Battalion was detrained on to the platforms of the Caserta railway station. When news of the Allied invasion of French North Africa was received, both of Koch's battalions had been placed on 'alarm' status. As a result of the hasty troop movements, the arrival of part of Koch's formation solved a problem that confronted Kesselring, the German Supreme Commander South-East. When Hitler learned of the Anglo-American landings he had telephoned Kesselring asking what forces were immediately available to be put in against the invaders. The Field Marshal's reply was that, apart from his own defence unit, there were only the two battalions of the 5th Para Regiment ready for action. Hitler ordered that these be flown to Tunisia with minimum delay.

Both battalions had concentrated in Caserta during the evening of the 10th and as an 'O' group an advance guard was formed consisting of an officer and men from No 10 Company. From Caserta that group was taken to the airfield outside Naples, taking off on 11 November. A refuelling stop was made in Sicily, and when the Ju 52s left on the following day they were forced to fly low over the water to avoid attacks by RAF fighter aircraft. The advance party landed on El Aouina airfield outside Tunis, where an air raid was in progress, and found that they were not the first German troops to arrive in Tunisia. The para group was ordered to drive through the city and to block the westward-leading roads, i.e. the direction from which the Anglo-Americans would come.

The first flight of aircraft carrying men from the 3rd Battalion began to come in during the early hours of the 12th and the soldiers were disembarked in short order. The air crews had been given instructions to unload with all speed, and they flung the equipment on to the runway in their haste to depart. Within hours the Junkers had returned carrying No 10 Company and part of No 12. Already a stream of units was coming in, to build up a defensive perimeter of troops around the capital.

On 15 November the leading elements of Jungwirth's 1st Battalion began to fly in and found that the regimental headquarters had already sent out reconnaissance patrols. One of these had reported that the French were using delaying tactics to prevent the important area of Medjez el Bab, and its town of the same name, from being occupied by the Germans. Captain Koch had persuaded the French to withdraw and to allow his men to occupy the high ground around the town. It was a vital area and at an 'O' group on the 16th Koch proposed that an immediate all-out assault be launched to extend the Axis perimeter westwards. General Nehring, the corps commander, concerned that such a move might result in his resources being overstretched, countered with the proposal that battle groups be formed to capture the town and the bridge across the Medjerda river.

Captain Knoche, commanding the 3rd Battalion, led out his battle group but found upon his arrival in Medjez el Bab that Battle Group Schirmer was already there. That group had arrived in Medjez el Bab announcing, untruthfully, that they were the advance guard of a newly landed parachute regiment. The French may or may not have believed the story, but they began to reinforce their troops in the Medjez area. In the face of a growing French build-up Schirmer decided to pull back his battle group, causing Koch to complain that if his plan of action had been followed Medjez would by that time have been in German hands. Koch had arranged for a Stuka raid for first light on 19 November and gave orders that Knoche was to attack after the aerial bombardment if he detected signs that French resistance was crumbling. If it was not, then he was to remain in position outside the town. Finally, Koch told his subordinate that in any event he was to prevent the Anglo-American forces from driving on to Tunis.

Koch then discussed with Knoche the disposition of the 3rd Battalion and particularly the platoons of anti-tank and anti-aircraft gunners. The regimental commander mentioned that he had pulled the Schirmer group out and that Knoche was to take command of all troops in the Medjez sector. Knoche formed the troops he had been given, some 300 men, into three battle groups. The first objective, he told them, was to be the bridge over the river, and the operation depended upon the result of the Stuka air raid. There was no air raid at the appointed time, but one did come in shortly before 1130 hours. As the dive-bombers swooped down, the paras of Nos 10 and 12 Companies opened fire and then charged the French positions.

The attack succeeded in capturing most of the town east of the river, but the important bridge lay in no man's land between the German and the Allied positions. A contingent of Italian infantry that had been promised for the dawn attack did not arrive until the early afternoon. Even the reinforcement of these fresh troops was not enough to bring the attack forward, and it was cancelled. Late in the afternoon Koch arrived and almost his first action was to criticise the disposition of Knoche's battle group. At an 'O' group Knoche laid before his superior a plan to attack during the night and to seize the town. Koch doubted whether the battle group would be strong enough to gain the objective, and he then left the battle front to return to Tunis. Within hours he was back again, bringing with him a lorry loaded with explosive charges.

The regimental commander and the battle group commander then discussed, once again, the latter's plan of attack. It was agreed that when the main assault went in small groups of paras who would have waded across the Medjerda river were to move in towards Medjez and blow up any enemy positions they came across. Ten such groups were formed, and each was led by a veteran who had fought in Crete. Each group was kitted out with machine pistols, hand grenades and other explosive devices and each was given a sector in which to operate.

Allied artillery fire died down after last light, and at 2300 hours the individual groups reached their jump-off positions. At midnight they set out at intervals to wade across the river. They penetrated the western part of the town and began to work their way towards the centre. Once assembled, they waited in the darkness until it was time to act. At 0100 hours the explosive charges they had placed began to detonate, blowing up lorries and smashing Allied armoured fighting vehicles. The sudden attacks were a complete surprise and in the streets of Medjez there were vicious firefights as the Allies sought to mount counter-attacks against the German groups. The paras formed a hedgehog position and kept up a controlled fire in order to conserve ammunition. The Allied soldiers were held off and then, just before dawn, the sound of tank engines and tank tracks was heard. The noise came from a group of Allied tanks, which were promptly attacked by the paras. Two of the vehicles were destroyed by hollow-charge grenades placed on their exteriors. The Allied troops then pulled out of the town in the direction of Oued Zarga and in their flight left behind not only damaged and undamaged machines but also a store of rations and other things which the paras were able to use.

The first battle by Koch's regiment to take Medjez el Bab had succeeded, but as yet the first Allied troops were only an advance guard. The mass of the Allied armies was moving out of Algeria and into Tunisia. Back in the capital, which was now securely in German hands, the time had come for the Axis troops to change from a defensive to an offensive strategy if they were to extend the area of their perimeter. In Medjez the initiative passed from Knoche's battle group and was taken up by Schirmer's group, which was ordered to pursue the enemy up the road to Oued Zarga. He decided to attack this small town but Koch ordered the operation to be aborted. Schirmer led the infantry guns of No 12 Company through the hills near Beja with his little artillery group and opened fire, causing the Allies a great many casualties.

Meanwhile in the town of Medjez the paras consolidated their positions and pushed patrols out to strengthen the regiment's right flank. One of those patrol groups was attacked during the following night by Spahi cavalry. The detachment's mortar and machine-gun fire crushed the French cavalry attack. The first battle to hold the German perimeter was opened and was to develop into a bitter struggle as the Allies conHtinued to bring in fresh troops in their attempts to destroy the Axis forces in Tunisia.

At this point, as the fighting died down temporarily, let us recapitulate on what both sides had been trying to achieve and how successful, or not, they had been. The Axis armies in the desert had already begun a slow retreat at the beginning of November 1942, when the Anglo-American forces landed in French North Africa. As a result of these landings in Algeria and Tunisia, the Allies had placed a military force at Rommel's back. If the Anglo-French-American armies could establish a dominant military presence in Tunisia, then Rommel's armies would be crushed between the British 8th Army and the Allied host in Tunisia. It was to prevent this catastrophe from coming about that Hitler had sent troops to Tunisia with orders to make sure that Rommel's force retreating through Libya would have sufficient space to concentrate and to regroup.

The Führer's orders had been, first, to form a bridgehead and then to expand this westward. This is what the para groups and the follow-up divisions had been fighting to achieve. Quite early in the campaign Koch's unit had been reinforced by Witzig's engineer para battalion and then another para unit led by Major Barenthin. Then followed German and Italian divisions to strengthen the perimeter. The development of the Tunis campaign was to see the German attempts to extend the perimeter and the Allies to smash this. If the latter could gain the important road junctions, they could bottle up the Axis armies before going on to destroy them completely. In view of the Allies' superiority in manpower and material resources the campaign could only have one end, and although the German-Italian forces were aware of

Above: General von Arnim, here seen as commander of the corps that had responsibility for the defence of Cholm. He is being shown the positions in the town that Major-General Scherer's force held from January until the first week of May 1942.
Right: General von Arnim (left) with General von Värst, Tunisia, 1943.

Above left: A formal portrait of
General Dietl showing him wearing
the Knight's Cross of the Iron Cross
and the Iron Cross 1st Class of the
Great War, together with the Clasp
for the Second World War.

Above right: Dietl in conversation with
an NCO of his division.
Below: Gebirgsjäger of Dietl's 3rd
Division wait to embark for the
invasion of Norway, 1940.

Above: General Dietl and some of his men. Norway, 1940.
Below: Gebirgsjäger officers fighting in Norway observe the enemy from the protection of a stone sangar, 1940

Above left: A formal portrait of
General Eberbach wearing the black
Panzer uniform. He is shown wearing
the Knight's Cross and Oak Leaves.
Above right: Eberbach with General
Guderian. Russia, 1940.

Below: Hermann Fegelein on the
Eastern Front, dressed in the white
summer uniform and wearing the
Knight's Cross of the Iron Cross with
Oak Leaves. He is seen talking to SS
Obergruppenführer Werner Lorenz.

Above: Fegelein poses between two officers of the SS Cavalry Brigade. Below left: Fegelein on the rank of Brigadeführer, wearing the Knight's Cross of the Iron Cross with Oak Leaves.

Below right: Fegelein wearing the collar patches of an SS Standartenführer. At his throat he is wearing the Knight's Cross of the Iron Cross and below this the ribbon of the Iron Cross 2nd Class.

Left: Werner Kempf in a formal portrait, in the rank of General and wearing the Oak Leaves to the Knight's Cross.
Below: Kempf as commander of the 8th Army, arriving at his TAC headquarters shortly before the opening of Operation 'Citadel', the German summer offensive of 1943.
Right, upper: As commander of the 48th Panzer Corps, Kempf spent a lot of time visiting the units he led. One of these was the Grossdeutschland Division, and in this photograph Kempf (wearing spectacles) is seen with General Hörnlein watching an attack develop for the Manytch river, Russia, 1942.
Right, lower: Adolf Hitler poses with the men of Walter Koch's parachute detachment which dropped over Belgium at the opening of the war in the West and captured Eben Emaël and the bridges around the fortress.

Above left: A posed formal portrait of Koch wearing the decorations he won. At the throat is the Knight's Cross of the Iron Cross; below that, tucked into the top button of the tunic, is the Eastern Front Ribbon; to the left he wears the Iron Cross 1st Class; below the row of three badges includes the Parachute Qualification Badge and the Wound Badge; and on the right breast is the German Cross in Gold.

Above right: Koch wearing the Knight's Cross that he was awarded for the actions of his unit in the fighting for the Maas bridges and Eben Emaël, May 1940.

Below: German paratroops of Koch's regiment pause during their advance

Left: A formal portrait of Otto Kumm, seen in the rank of Standartenführer and commanding the 5th Gebirgs Corps in Jugoslavia. He is wearing the Knight's Cross of the Iron Cross with Oak Leaves; on his left breast he has the Iron Cross 1st Class and the Wound Badge; on his right breast he wears the German Cross in Gold; and he is wearing the cuff title that he had been awarded when in the 'Der Führer' Regiment.

Below: Kumm commanding the 7th Gebirgs Division 'Prinz Eugen', seen on a visit to Flak Abteilung 7, in conversation with Sturmbannführer Noneth. Bosnia, 1943.

Above: A formal portrait of 'Panzer-meyer' wearing a camouflage jacket, Normandy, 1944.
Below: Meyer making a speech at the graveside of one of his men

Left: One of the defenders of Cholm. This man is a young lieutenant clad in white—camouflage clothing—and carrying a machine pistol as he sets out to lead a fighting patrol into Russian lines.

Right: Generalmajor Theodor Scherer, who commanded the troops cut off in Cholm. He is wearing the Knight's Cross of the Iron Cross. The decorations on his right breast are the Clasp for the Iron Cross 1st Class and, below that, the Iron Cross 1st Class itself.

Below: Generalmajor Scherer being decorated by officers of his battle group.

Above left: A sentry from Scherer's battle group in Cholm observing the enemy's movements, 1941.

Above right: In the spring of 1942 the melting snow caused more problems for the men of Scherer's command. The freezing water filled the slit trenches.

Left: A posed portrait of Feldwebel Erich Schuster after his award of the Knight's Cross of the Iron Cross.

Left: A more informal photograph of Erich Schuster. He is seen here wearing the Knight's Cross, the Iron Cross 1st Class and the Parachute Jump Award badge.

Below: A paratroop machine-gun post in Tunisia, late 1942. The weapon is the MG 34 in its light machine gun mode.

Above: General Schörner (right), wearing the Pour le Mérite which he won in the First World War and also the Knight's Cross of the Iron Cross. On his left breast, the upper badge is that of the Nazi Party.

Left: After the victorious battle at Vilkovischen, Colonel-General Schörner, commanding Army Group North, paid a visit to the Grossdeutschland Division. In this photograph he is seen inspecting men of the engineer battalion of the division.

Left: SS Gruppenführer Steiner in a posed portrait. He wears the Knight's Cross of the Iron cross, with Oak Leaves.
Below: Steiner seated in his staff car in Russia.

General of Cavalry Siegfried Westphal: a formal portrait taken after the award of the Knight's Cross of the Iron Cross on 30 November 1942 and before he took over command of the 146th Infantry Division.

their impending fate they fought staunchly, launching a series of offensive operations to delay the inevitable.

To return to events at the end of November 1942, Koch had recalled Schirmer's group and had given orders to Knoche to drive to Tebourba and to hold that area with a line of defensive positions intended to protect the Tebourba airfield against possible Allied attack. The consequence of this order was that the German paras were spread out in penny packets from the airfield via Medjez el Bab and on to El Aroussa—a battle line 60km long. Because Koch's units were so divided the paras were nowhere in strength.

Reports came in that Allied armour was on the move and had reached El Aroussa. To check this Allied thrust Knoche moved his anti-tank and anti-aircraft detachments by night. In daylight the paras saw a number of American armoured vehicles moving, seemingly aimlessly, around in the El Aroussa sector. Koch's subordinate had chosen his positions well. He opened a destructive fire upon the US vehicles and after a two-hour hour firefight the Americans pulled back. Then Koch arrived and, after being briefed on the situation, ordered the action to be broken off and told the units that he had brought with him to withdraw into positions between El Aroussa and Bou Arada.

Knoche's battle group was ordered back to Medjez el Bab, where a new crisis was developing. In the Medjez sector there was a build-up of Allied armoured forces whose strength was too great for Schirmer's battalion to withstand. He and his men were forced out of the town and took up positions in the high ground to the east of Medjez. The right wing of Knoche's battalion remained wide open to a possible Allied thrust until a detachment of the 10th Panzer Division came forward and gained touch. From that point onwards the fighting in the Medjez area was in the nature of an aggressive defence by Koch's regiment, fighting, together with the other formations which had come across from the European mainland, with the aim of preventing the Allies from advancing upon Tunis and thereby ending the campaign.

The fighting reduced in intensity during the winter and wet spring of 1943. Lieutenant-Colonel Koch was forced to pull back his regiment to the area west of Massicault and he positioned the battalions on either side of the main road. Just before the end of the year General

Nehring ordered an attack to be made in the Tebourba area. For this he proposed to take Koch's regiment from its positions in the Medjez area and to use them to spearhead the advance into the back of the Allied forces. If that battle plan succeeded, the Allies would be encircled before they realised that Medjez had been denuded of troops. As a measure of just how short of troops the Germans were, for the forthcoming offensive so many had to be taken from rear-area units that Tunis city was defended by just 30 men and two 88mm guns.

It was the task of Koch's regiment to attack from the south and thereby close the southern and south-western parts of the ring. Koch led his men into action on 30 November in an advance up the Medjez road to camouflage the fact that the town had been evacuated. The paras were then to swing westwards so as to fall upon the backs of the US armoured units. The advance of Koch's regiment was led by his 3rd Battalion, and while this moved towards Medjez the main body of the regiment swung towards El Bathan. The 3rd Battalion soon joined the other battalions, and they not only cut off the little town but gained touch with the advance guard of the 10th Panzer Division. The paras then fought from house to house in the town, battling their way forward until they had driven the US forces into panic flight towards Longstop Hill.

The battle had been both a tactical and a strategic success. Strategically, the Germans had prevented the Allies from 'winning the race to Tunis'. Koch's paras moved back to positions east of Medjez el Bab and concentrated in the hills which dot the area. The fighting was then in the nature of patrol activity and small offensives.

In March 1943 the 5th Para Regiment was renamed the Jäger Regiment 'Hermann Göring' and a month later Koch himself was flown to a hospital in Germany for specialist treatment. He was not to return to Africa, where his old unit passed into captivity in the May of that year, but on 28 August 1943, after convalescence, he was placed in the officers' pool for future employment. Two months later, while driving in thick fog on the autobahn near Berlin, Koch was in collision with another vehicle and was killed.

Brigadeführer
and Generalmajor der Waffen SS
Otto Kumm

Enforcer in the Balkans as
commander of the 7th SS Gebirgs Division 'Prinz Eugen'

O tto Kumm was born on 1 October 1909 in the north German city of Hamburg, the son of a staunchly working class family. When Otto left school in 1925 he applied for and gained an apprenticeship in the printing industry as a typesetter. Five years later he joined the Sturm Abteilung (SA), the Brown Shirt organisation of the Nazi Party, initially in a part-time capacity, and served as a member of a unit that was stationed in his native city. A year later, in 1931, he transferred to the Allgemeine or General Branch of the SS, joining that service in December as a member of the 1st Sturm of the 1st Sturmbann of the 28th Standarte. He completed his basic training by the end of March 1932, and was transferred to No 5 Sturm.

During his period of service with that unit, Kumm was given the appointment of Obergruppenführer, a probationary grade, and then, in February 1934, was commissioned in the rank of SS Untersturmführer (2nd Lieutenant). In the following month he was promoted to command the 3rd Sturmbann, and he remained with that unit for the duration of his service with the Allgemeine SS.

At this point mention should be made that there had been originally two types of SS. The first was the Allgemeine, or General Duties Branch; the second was the Totenkopf formation, which staffed the concentration camps. A third type of SS, the Waffen or Armed SS, developed out of the Allgemeine branch. Quite early in the 1930s, certain SS leaders began to work towards the creation of major, armed SS formations because those radically minded senior commanders saw the Army as conservative and reactionary. They intended to replace it with a force based on revolutionary, National Socialist principles. Although discussions within the Party leadership about the creation of an armed SS were confidential, word of them leaked out and alarmed the generals, who saw the Army's role as weapons-bearer of the state coming under threat from an ill-trained Party militia. Hitler, to whom the Army commanders appealed for a decision, was forced to choose between the officers of the conservative-minded Army and those of the radical Party leadership. Hitler chose to support the Army, and that decision reduced the importance of the SA within the Nazi party.

Not that this was a victory for the Army generals. As the SA declined in importance, so did the SS rise in stature until in time it became what the generals had feared—a military body whose allegiance was to the Nazi Party and which was thus outside the control of the regular Army. That the Waffen SS was to go on to ally itself closely with the Army against the Party and that it would earn for itself a formidable fighting reputation on the battlefields of Europe demonstrated that the original fears of the military had not been without foundation. But all that lay in the future. Meanwhile, in the early 1930s, the first moves in creating the Waffen SS began, and within that embryo force preferment was given to those men who had fought in the Great War or else had served with the armed forces in the post-war Army.

Otto Kumm was in neither category. Eventually a second and, in time, larger group of SS officers was created, and this was made up of those whose only military experience had been gained while serving with the SS. These men had risen through the ranks of the SS and had then gone on to receive officer training in one of the SS military academies. As a generalisation, it can be accepted that the most senior command posts in what became the Waffen SS were held by those who had fought in the Great War, while the most outstanding men of the second category—those with specialist SS training—rose to become senior field officers.

In the early 1930s the putative Waffen SS units were disguised under the bland title Politische Bereitschaften (political readiness detachments), with the duty of acting as a paramilitary force against the Nazi Party's internal enemies—whoever these might be. The Party leadership clearly considered that Army detachments might lack the moral

courage or the loyalty to fight against German civilians who were fo-
menting a revolution against the Nazi Party. In the early days of the
Party's history it had been the SA, the Brown Shirts, that had fielded
the detachments that fought the Party's political enemies. With the rise
of the SS, the SA had diminished in influence. Now, within the SS, a
new and élite group, the Politische Bereitschäfte, had been created.
Bereitschaft number two in the hierarchy was raised in Hamburg as a
horsed unit and was financially maintained by the Hamburg civil authorities until 1935, when the German Ministry of the Interior took
over the running costs and then disbanded it.

The unit was promptly re-raised in 1935 and given the name SS
Regiment 'Germania'. Kumm transferred into the new regiment as a
platoon commander in the 1st Sturmbann and was also promoted to
the rank of Obersturmführer (1st Lieutenant). During May 1935 he
was given command of the 4th Machine Gun Detachment and held
that post for more than a year until he was posted away from 'Germania'
in December 1936. To improve his military skills Kumm volunteered
for a number of courses and in July 1935 he attended a commanding
officers' course in Doberitz. On 13 September 1936, having completed
all his courses, including that for a machine-gun platoon commander,
Kumm was promoted to the rank of Hauptsturmführer (Captain).

By this time there had been a reorganisation of the SS regiments
that would one day become the founding bodies of the Waffen SS.
'Deutschland' was one of these, and it was to this regiment that Kumm
was posted. His first appointment was on the regimental staff, with
which he served for more than thirteen months before taking over command of No 2 Company. He left 'Deutschland' in April 1938. After
the annexation of Austria Hitler had ordered the raising of a third Waffen
SS regiment which would comprise Austrian personnel around a cadre
of trained, German SS men. One of those men was Kumm, and he
took over command of No 10 Company of the 3rd Battalion. This was
stationed in Klagenfurt in Carinthia, and Kumm was to serve with the
3rd Battalion of the new regiment for five years, during which time it
received the title of 'Der Führer'. Colours were bestowed upon the
new regiment and cuff bands bearing the unit name were issued during
the Nazi Party's rally on 1 November 1938.

'Der Führer' Regiment was converted from standard infantry to motorised status and during May 1939 took part in the Army manoeuvres in Pomerania. At the conclusion of these field exercises the regiment was posted to Prague, where it was given responsibility for the security of von Neurath, the Protector of Bohemia, and became the resident guard formation. On the outbreak of war in 1939 'Der Führer' was not ready for active service and as a consequence did not fight in the Polish campaign but was held in reserve. At the end of the German-Polish war the formation was returned to Czechoslovakia, not to Prague but to the city of Pilsen.

It was in that area of Czechoslovakia, near the Brody Forest training ground, that the infantry regiments of the future 'VT' Division concentrated under the command of SS General Paul Hausser. The division, not yet fully raised, was, in effect, a milch cow, for some of its units were detached and posted to other VT—later Waffen SS—formations that were in the process of being created. As existing units were posted away from the regiment new ones were created and were posted to the 'Verfügungs' Division, which was being trained for its future role in Operation 'Yellow', the war in the West against Holland, Belgium, France and Great Britain. The 'VT' was the first of the Waffen SS formations to be raised, and so keen were the officers and men on their task that the division was not only up to strength but was declared fit for active service as early as the spring of 1940.

A scant month before Operation 'Yellow' opened in May 1940, Kumm was sent to Königsberg on an Army commanders' course in tactics—instruction that was to prove of great benefit to him during the now imminent campaign. Kumm returned to his company only days before the warning order was issued. That order reached 'DF' Regiment on 9 May; D-Day was 10 May. Because of its fully motorised status, the regiment was given the task of forming the spearhead of the 207th Infantry Division and was to thrust through the first two lines of the Dutch defence. The 'DF' Regiment was to open the way for the remainder of the 207th Division to follow. On D-Day for Operation 'Yellow', it crossed the German/Dutch frontier and struck westwards across the Ijssel river to reach Arnhem and then across the Neder river to reach the Grebbe Line, the principal Dutch defensive system.

On 12 May, during an attack by parts of the 3rd Battalion 'DF' and the 322nd Infantry Regiment, the commander of the SS battalion was wounded. Kumm took over command and under his energetic leadership the unit advanced against stiffening Dutch resistance. By the end of the short campaign the regiment's given task of breaking the enemy's defensive positions had been achieved. It was then taken out of the line and posted back to the 'VT' Division, which was regrouping in Marienburg. For his successful leadership of the 3rd Battalion Kumm was awarded the Iron Cross 2nd Class on 29 May.

By the time this award had been promulgated the 'VT' Division was back in action again fighting in the Merville area against infantry of the British Expeditionary Force as well as Allied tank units. Fighting in the Low Countries ended, and at the conclusion of Operation 'Yellow' the German army wheeled southwards towards the Somme with the aim of defeating the French Army, which was defending the so-called Weygand Line. On 7 June, during the bitter fighting that marked the regiment's actions on that sector of the Somme, Kumm was wounded but refused to leave his men. By mid-June the regiment was embattled on the Langres plateau, fighting its way forward around Coulmier le Sec, driving the enemy westwards. France asked for an armistice in the last week of June, but before it came into force the 'VT' Division had struck southwards and had reached the Franco-Spanish frontier.

At the end of this successful campaign Kumm was not only awarded the Iron Cross 1st Class but was also confirmed in his appointment as commander of the 3rd Battalion of 'Der Führer' Regiment. The Waffen SS Division ('VT' Division) then returned to Holland and took up coastal defence duties in the Army of Occupation. The time in Holland was one of intense training to improve the fighting skills of the regimental units and was marked by the posting away from the division of entire units that went to form the cadres of future SS formations. On 1 October 1940 Kumm received his promotion to the rank of Sturmbannführer (Major) and on 10 December was also awarded the Infantry Assault Badge.

The last months of 1940 and the first of 1941 marked a further period of intense activity in the 'VT' Division. There was, to begin with, a move from Holland to Vesoul, where reorganisation was begun and security duties undertaken. Then in January 1941 the 'VT' Division was retitled Division 'Reich' and during May 1942 Division 'Das Reich'.

The tense political situation in south-east Europe required a military solution, and operations were opened against Jugoslavia. At the start of this new but short campaign 'Reich' Division, which had concentrated in Romania, struck out from that country and by capturing Belgrade brought operations to a speedy conclusion. Preparations for the attack upon the Soviet Union were now in their final stages, and the division was posted to an area in Poland that had been nominated as its forming-up area. From that place 'Reich', as part of Army Group Centre, was to advance and to invade Soviet Russia. The formation to which the division was attached was the 46th Panzer Corps, comprising 'Reich' and the 10th Panzer Divisions together with the 'Grossdeutschland' Regiment.

Although the war with Russia—'Operation Barbarossa'—began on 22 June 1941, it was not until 6 July that 'Reich', acting in the role of a motorised assault formation, crossed the River Beresina and five days later forced a crossing of the Dnieper. During the Dnieper operation the commander of SS Regiment 'Totenkopf' was wounded and had to be replaced by Keppler, who was at that time commanding 'Der Führer' Regiment. Otto Kumm was recommended to be Keppler's successor and took up his new post in early July.

Kumm was to spend the following years on the Eastern Front and during that time rose from commanding a battalion of 'Der Führer' Regiment to become the regimental commander. With that increase in authority came also promotion, honours and titles. It is not possible, because of limitations of space, to detail the actions on the Eastern Front in which Kumm participated as commander of 'Der Führer' Regiment and, accordingly, only major operations will be discussed; less important battles will only be mentioned.

Following the crossing of the Dnieper, Kumm and the 'DF ' were engaged in fighting against seven Red Army infantry divisions supported by two armoured brigades outfitted with the new T-34 machines. The regiment was victorious in those battles around Yelnya and was then moved to Avdeyevka, where it was involved in more heavy fighting. Kumm's leadership brought his regiment up to the railway bridge at Rudnya, then across the river and finally to a range of hills to the south-east of that small town. Thrusting down from the hills, 'DF' regiment pursued the enemy as far as Chernotitschy and not only smashed a Red Army unit but also captured a great deal of military equipment and a number of weapons.

There then followed attempts to capture Priluki, but the first two assaults failed and the third succeeded only in part. Patrols sent out during the night of 16/17 September reported that the enemy was pulling back. An immediate pursuit was ordered and in the northern sector of Priluki concentrations of enemy troops were surprised and scattered. Kumm's regiment took more than 1,400 prisoners as well as a mass of weapons and vehicles.

An example of how well Kumm handled his unit in action came during 22 September 1941 when attempts were made by Red Army units to break into an encircling ring of German forces east of Romny. Kumm swung his regiment from its easterly thrust line to a southerly one, all without a loss of momentum. In this action the 5th Red Cavalry Division was broken with the loss of over 1,000 men.

During the first week of October 1941 Kumm was recommended for the award of the German Cross in Gold and was also promoted to Obersturmbannführer (Lieutenant-Colonel). A recommendation for the award of the German Cross in Gold was not approved at that time but was gazetted at the end of December 1941.

It was now late in the year and there were only few weeks of campaigning weather left. Nonetheless, Hitler ordered an offensive, code-named 'Typhoon', which was to take out the Russian capital before the onset of winter. Compared with the fast advances of summer and autumn 1941, the 'Typhoon' offensive could only measure its advances in single miles, but by 28 November 'Der Führer' Regiment had taken Istra, to the west of Moscow, and only four days later had captured Lenino. At this point the offensive began to fail and the regiments of 'Reich' Division were ordered to dig in. The mass of the division then moved into reserve, leaving Kumm and his regiment to man the line.

During February 1942 the division came under the command of von Vietinghoff's 46th Corps but 'Der Führer' Regiment, which had been returned to its parent formation, was once again detached and posted away. By this time its numbers had sunk to less than 650 men: the regiment had, in effect, been reduced to the strength of two weak battalions. Throughout January and for much of February Kumm's understrength regiment had come under continuous attack as the Red Army sought to split Army Group Centre from Army Group North. The fury of the Russian assaults led to Kumm's TAC headquarters being moved into the front line. Such was the scale of the losses to Kumm's formation that many sub-units were reduced to just one or two men. One company of the 1st Battalion lost two-thirds of its estab-lishment and his 3rd Battalion was almost totally destroyed. By 12 Feb-ruary Kumm had only 126 men still fit for duty.

Describing the fighting of those days, he recalled the infantry at-tacks that had been launched against his lines. The Red Army infantry had marched shoulder to shoulder towards the German lines and the enemy dead had formed 'walls of corpses in front of our positions'. He estimated that the Russians lost 15,000 dead along the front of his regi-ment alone as well as seventy armoured fighting vehicles. When the division was relieved from the line following the fighting of 17 Febru-ary, Kumm marched the remnants of his regiment to divisional head-quarters and went in to report. There he found Model, the commander of the 9th Army, also in the building, and when Model asked questions on the strength of his regiment Kumm was able to reply with truth that his entire regiment was paraded outside the building. There, in the snow, stood 35 men, the survivors of a regiment that had gone into battle 2,000 strong.

During the period out of the line, 'DF' was reorganised as a Panzer-grenadier regiment and following a fresh period in the front line was withdrawn and sent to France on occupation duties. For his leadership of 'Der Führer' Regiment Kumm was recommended for the award of the Knight's Cross, a recommendation that was personally endorsed by Himmler, who praised Kumm's personal leadership during the fight-ing around Kantschalovo. It was there that he had prevented a link-up between the encircled Russian units and other Red Army formations trying to break the German ring. The Knight's Cross was finally be-stowed upon Kumm by Model, the Army commander, on 16 Febru-ary 1942.

Kumm showed bravery of a different sort when the proposal was made to disband his regiment. He spoke out with passion against such a move and took his opinions to the highest levels of authority. His viewpoint prevailed and 'DF' was retained in the newly named 'Das Reich' Division, which formed part of an SS corps fielding the 'Leibstandarte SS', 'Das Reich' and 'Totenkopf' Divisions.

In February and March 1943 the SS corps took part in the battles for Kharkov and at its conclusion Kumm was awarded the Oak Leaves to the Knight's Cross—a 'first' for the division. This came in recognition of his regiment's actions when it was under orders to attack and to drive back a seven-battalion strong force of Russians. A Panzer unit that had been ordered to support the infantry operation could not carry out its part of the task and was forced to withdraw. The regimental commander realised that the task of driving the enemy back depended upon him and his men and he led his regiment into battle with outstanding success and captured the railway line, thereby cutting the enemy's supply and reinforcement route. He later demonstrated his personal bravery and skilled tactical ability when his regiment took part in an operation against Red Army troops withdrawing towards Yefremovka and contributed towards the division's victories.

Following that successful operation in mid-February, Kumm was ordered to report to Berlin to be assigned a new post. Following a brief period of leave he reported on 20 May, and was decorated by Hitler with the Oak Leaves for which he had been recommended. He was also promoted to the rank of Standartenführer and was told that his new appointment was to be the Ia to the commander of the newly created V Gebirgs Corps, Artur Phleps. The promotion of Phleps from General Commanding the 'Prinz Eugen' Mountain Division to Corps Commander left a gap in the leadership that should have been filled by Brigadeführer Carl von Oberkamp. That officer's health had broken under the strain of battlefield command, however, and Oberführer Kumm was promoted from his post as Ia to become the new divisional commander. The 7th SS Gebirgs Division, which was in action in Jugoslavia, was taken out of the line and the new commander regrouped it by disbanding the fourth battalion of both Gebirgsjäger regiments and distributing the personnel among the other divisional formations.

Throughout the spring of 1944 the 'Prinz Eugen' conducted anti-partisan operations in the Mostar area of Bosnia-Herzegovina. Already, within a year of its raising, the 7th had gained for itself a reputation for élan in attack and staunchness in defence as well as improving upon the skills of its Jäger in mountain warfare. It was as well that it was so skilled and steadfast in battle for ahead of it, in 1944, lay a special mission, and then in 1945 would come operations in which the division, acting as a rearguard, sacrificed itself to gain time for the rest of the German army group in the Balkans to pull back towards the Reich's frontier.

To understand the situation that prevailed in Jugoslavia at that time it must be realised that the country had become a major theatre of operations. The Royal Jugoslav Army, which had been defeated in the short campaign of 1941, had dissolved and had been recreated as a communist force by Tito under the name 'Jugoslav Army of National Liberation'. Well supplied and equipped by the British, Tito's partisans had become a new and revitalised military force that was capable of tying down a great number of German divisions that might otherwise have been deployed on the Russian Front. The JANL had to be capable of changing its command headquarters at the shortest possible notice, for the Luftwaffe still dominated the skies over Jugoslavia. As that Jugoslav command system grew ever more sophisticated, so did the time expand that it took to move its headquarters personnel to new locations. This was very soon realised by the German High Command, and it was to disrupt partisan operations that a new offensive, 'Knight's Move' was planned. The German 2nd Army, whose area of responsibility included Bosnia and Croatia, was ordered by High Command South-East to plan the operation and passed the orders it had received to the 14th Gebirgs Corps. From Corps those orders were transmitted down to Kumm and his 7th Gebirgs Division 'Prinz Eugen'.

The directive from the 14th Gebirgs Corps detailed the enemy forces in the area of Drvar in western Bosnia and went on to describe how these were to be destroyed in an operation employing ground and airborne forces. Going on to explain the task of Kumm's 7th Gebirgs Division, Corps' orders continued:

With a regimental group and an assault battalion of Panzergrenadiers, [the 7th SS Division] will smash through the enemy resistance east of the Sana river and will then advance on a broad front between the Sana and Unae [rivers] in and immediately north of the wooded hills . . . They will hunt down the enemy bands . . . take out the supply bases and will prevent the flight eastwards of the beaten enemy groups and headquarters near Drvar . . . The regimental group of the 7th SS will drive from Jajee and will have as their first bound the area south of the Sana wells and the railway station at Mlinista . . .

From the Corps order it was clear that a cordon of ground troops was to move in towards Marshal Tito's headquarters at Drvar but that the actual buildings would be attacked by parachute and glider-borne units.

Paragraphs of Kumm's divisional order laid out how the divisional group of the 13th Regiment was to carry out a forced march to Turbe and there form the divisional left wing. That village would be the start line for the operation and the regiment was to advance behind a screen of armoured fighting vehicles. The main effort would be made on the left wing by the 2nd and 3rd Battalions of the 13th Regiment. The 3rd Battalion, in vehicles, would fight its way across the Rgolje–Mraca road to gain touch with the other battalions. The whole regiment would then go on to play its part in the encirclement by driving westwards towards Drvar, where Tito's headquarters were located. Other units would also be moving towards the objective. In the air, the 500th SS Parachute Battalion would fly in and make an assault using paratroops and glider-borne troops. Those lightly armed paras were, according to orders, to be relieved on D-Day itself, 25 May, by the 373rd Division.

At Turbe the 13th Regiment formed up and moved off. Almost immediately it was met with fierce opposition from Jugoslav troops who had been aware for some time that the Germans were about to undertake a major offensive. Such was the strength and confidence of the JANL that its units did not merely stand on the defensive but counterattacked Kumm's division. Rising out of the elaborate trench systems that they had constructed, the partisans went into one attack after another. These were supported, according to Kumm's own post-battle report, by waves of Allied fighter-bombers. One serious consequence of these aerial attacks was that the 373rd Division could not fight its way forward and relieve the SS paratroops on the first day.

Throughout the night of 25/26 May patrols from the 7th SS went out and everywhere found that enemy resistance had hardened. It was a bad augury, and when Kumm renewed his division's assault in the early morning of 26 May the opposition was stronger and the enemy's counter-attacks not only more frequent but also heavier in nature. Slowly Kumm's men forced their way forward, not allowing the onset of darkness to halt operations. The divisional reconnaissance battalion captured Ribnik during the night of the 26th/27th and that success broke Jugoslav resistance. The JANL began a slow-paced but controlled withdrawal that, its early stages, led to energetic thrusts by the Jäger and the reconnaissance battalion encircling a number of partisan units.

Although it was clear to Kumm and to the senior commanders that Tito had escaped, they were determined to smash the partisan menace in the Drvar area. From reports and radio intercepts it was clear that the Jugoslav divisions in the area had been ordered to disengage and to filter through the German encirclement. The partisans, however, were supremely confident of victory in the Drvar area, refused to retreat and concentrated their counter-attacks against the 'Prinz Eugen' Division— to such good effect that they halted its advance.

The German 15th Corps then decided to extend the duration of 'Knight's Move', and when the new phase of the offensive opened Kumm's 13th Regiment scored advances and not only destroyed several supply depots but also cut a light railway track which had been used by the partisans to transport supplies. So far did the 13th penetrate that it reached an airfield, where hangars were destroyed and mines laid over the area of the runways. Each battalion of the 13th was able to record victories, with significant amounts of stores and weapons destroyed or captured. Those partisan units encountered were engaged and smashed. In the area of the 14th Jäger Regiment, that unit, together with the assault battalion, captured two armoured fighting vehicles.

Kumm's handling of his mountain division had been masterly, and he led his units and formations across the difficult terrain of high, steep mountain slopes and densely wooded valleys to total, if local, victories. At the conclusion of 'Knight's Move' Kumm's 7th Division was singled out for mention in an OKW communiqué, and a Corps discussion group concluded in its report that

> As the only mountain troops employed in the operation, the SS carried the heaviest burden of the battle and was responsible for its main successes. The combat efficiency and élan shown by company and battalion commanders alike, as well as the evidence of good clear orders and first class reporting, are particularly noteworthy . . .

Although local successes were scored on the ground and often scattered and dispersed the partisan units, the JANL units were regrouping with the intention of mounting a new, general and major offensive. The first signs of this imminent and strong enemy reaction came when the 13th SS Gebirgsjäger Regiment came under attack. The regiment had reached a mountain height in the Uvala region and had had no time to consolidate the ground it had won before waves of Jugoslav soldiers stormed into the attack. That first assault was in regimental strength and struck not only the Jäger regiment but also the recce battalion and units from the Brandenburg Division. The fury of the partisan thrusts broke through the German lines and reached as far as divisional headquarters at Ribnik.

But the Jugoslav attack had penetrated too far and in too little strength. A scratch force of the 7th's divisional headquarters rallied and counterattacked and the partisans were driven back. The situation seemed to have been resolved, but it was a false lull and lasted only until 6 June, when it flared up again and trickled on in minor actions or patrol activity until August. During that time Kumm drafted and wrote the post-battle report on his division's part in 'Knight's Move'. While stating that the partisan forces had not introduced new tactics or shown any improvement in their command procedures, he did admit that the enemy had shown unusual mobility because of his familiarity with the terrain and because he was not tied down by a massive train organisation. Supplies which the JANL needed were either man-portered, usually by locally impressed civilians, or were airdropped by the Allies. In the matter of air power Kumm was scathing in his condemnation of the Luftwaffe, which flew no missions at all after the second day of the offensive and often gave excuses for not collaborating in air-to-ground strikes—and this in direct contrast to the Croatian Air Force, which always responded to an alarm call.

Kumm then commented upon the ability of the partisans to march unusually long distances and also mentioned their determination to fight a set-piece battle—which was unusual because it went against all the precepts of guerrilla warfare and also showed evidence of the confidence of the JANL to meet and to fight a German army on the field of battle. Kumm also commented upon the partisans' tactic of screening their front with small patrols. The slightest slackening of the German drive was quickly exploited by the partisans, who would concentrate their forces so as to hold the German front fast while other guerrilla units worked round the flanks and rear to mount a general attack. Reference was made to the marked increase in the use of artillery and other heavy weapons by the JANL as well as to the vast quantities of ammunition that were seized during the offensive, contradicting the claim that the JANL was short of such supplies. Kumm laid great stress on the morale factor in battle and remarked on the absence of training, weapons and leadership in the German forces. Those deficiencies had allowed partisan units to escape from a battle or else to evade capture, and in that context he criticised the waste of ammunition shown by the German forces. Units were opening fire at distances greater than 400m. The partisans, he contended, had to be allowed to approach more closely than that in order for every shot to hit its mark.

It was a hard-hitting document and one that seemed to have been absorbed, for only weeks later Tito's élite 1st Proletarian Division was so badly mauled that it retreated eastwards into Serbia to prevent its being totally destroyed. The final operations connected with 'Knight's Move' came to an end when intercepts of JANL wireless traffic showed that the guerrilla forces in Croatia had been ordered to move into Serbia.

But adverse military events were developing, and in the autumn of 1944 both Romania and Bulgaria broke away from the Third Reich and went over to fight alongside the Russians. This created the danger of a link-up between the partisans and their new allies, Bulgaria, Romania and the Red Army. A combination of these armies would threaten the destruction of the German Army's southern flank. To counter that likely disaster the German Commander South-East determined to prevent the JANL from linking up with its allies by launching a new offensive in which the 14th Regiment of Kumm's division took part. Then came a series of conflicting orders, the last of which indicated that 'Prinz Eugen' was to take up positions from which it could hold open the Bulgarian-Jugoslav border until the German 2nd Army had retreated out of the Balkans and had reached the territory of the Third Reich.

In the confused fighting that then arose, the 7th SS Division was several times isolated and cut off, but it always fought its way back to the main German body. Kumm gave the uncompromising order to the men under his command who were scattered across the countryside in an effort to dominate the areas. That order was to hold out because there would be no retreat.

Soon the 7th was in battle confronting a Russian and a Bulgarian army. Such an unequal situation with a single German division confronting two Slav armies could not long be held and soon the enemy had worked round the division's flanks, forcing the 7th to withdraw. Like most of the German formations of Army Group E, the 'Prinz Eugen' Division had been forced off the main roads—these had all been cut by the JANL—and had been obliged to move into and through the mountains. There then followed a period of almost continual battle as Army Group E sought to escape along the minor roads, but these too were dominated by guerrilla bands. The task of the 7th Division was to form the rearguard of the 34th Corps, and to hold off the pursuing enemy. Kumm wrote a report on his division's role and in that document stated how badly 'Prinz Eugen' had been hit. Most of the vehicles, horses and heavy weapons had been lost, and particularly serious was the lack of anti-tank guns. Kumm reported that, despite these adversities, the morale and fighting spirit of his division were still high due to the 'successes it had gained in the past offensive and defensive operations'.

The retreat continued through the mountains and across the swollen Drina river with the division now down to only 3,460 all ranks—a fifth of its nominal strength; but it was still given tasks that could only have been achieved if its regiments had been at full strength. The withdrawal began on 22 October and continued past Christmas. Then a new crisis arose. The left flank of Army Group E was turned and the enemy broke through, forcing a gap between that crumbling left wing and the right wing of Army Group South. To seal that breach an offensive was planned, code-named 'Spring Storm', and it opened on 17 January. In the ensuing battles the 7th, under Kumm's inspired leadership, fought not just well but heroically, fully earning the praise that the corps commander heaped upon it. During that offensive Kumm was posted away from the 7th and ordered to take up command of the 1st SS Panzer Division, Leibstandarte SS 'Adolf Hitler'.

His new command was but a shadow of its former self. Once it had been the premier unit of the Waffen SS, but by 1945 it was weak in numbers and armoured fighting vehicles and was fighting a retreating battle through Austria. With the war coming to an end there was little that Kumm could do to restore the Leibstandarte to its former high position. Its ranks were no longer filled with volunteers, but at least the unit commanders were all experienced soldiers who still gained victories at local level.

It was in command of a fragmented 1st SS Panzer Division that Kumm's part in the Second World War came to an end. The élite Leibstandarte had been reduced in numbers to only 1,600 men and 16 vehicles. The orders for surrender were that the German formations should capitulate to that Allied army against which it had been fighting. Rather than surrender to the Red Army, however, Kumm ordered his men to face westwards and to engage the Americans who had advanced as far eastwards as Steyr. Most of his division passed into US captivity.

The immediate post-war years were difficult ones for Kumm and his family, but eventually they moved to Offenburg, where Otto took up his former trade in the printing industry. In subsequent years Kumm published his history of the 'Prinz Eugen' and co-operated in the writing of the histories of other SS divisions. He later added painting to his talent as an author, and although now advanced in years and in poor health he is active in the German ex-service organizations, where he is a well-known and respected figure.

SS Brigadeführer
and Generalmajor der Waffen SS
Kurt Meyer

*'Panzermeyer', who as General Commanding the Hitler
Youth Division was one of Germany's youngest general officers*

The officer who has passed into military history as 'Panzermeyer'
was born Kurt Meyer on 23 November 1910 into a working-class
family. When his father died during the Great War it fell to the
young Kurt to become the family's breadwinner, and this cut short his
education. In 1928, at the age of 18, he found employment as a miner
and worked in the pits until the beginning of October 1929. He then
enlisted in the Mecklenburg State Police Force, and although he had gained
promotion within two years decided to leave the force in May 1935.

Kurt Meyer had been a supporter of the Nazis for many years and
had joined the Hitler Jugend (HJ, or Hitler Youth) in May 1925, going
on from the HJ to enlist in the Sturm Abteilung (SA, or Storm Troops)
on 1 October 1929. In the following January he joined the Nazi Party
and in October 1929 he volunteered for the SS. His first posting was to
a newly raised SS formation, the 22nd Standarte, which was stationed
in Schwerin. Meyer was accepted as a full member of the SS within
four months and was commissioned as a Sturmführer (2nd Lieutenant) on 10 July 1932. Two years later, on 15 May 1934, he transferred
into the élite Leibstandarte SS 'Adolf Hitler' (LSSAH) in the post of
platoon commander. He served in the motorised platoon of the Leibstandarte until September 1936, during which time he was promoted
to the rank of Obersturmführer (1st Lieutenant), and in July 1936 was
appointed to command No 14 Anti-Tank Company. He held that post
for three years, during which time he received further promotion, this
time to the rank of Hauptsturmführer (Captain). On 12 September
1937, as was common in the German services for officers of subaltern

rank, he was sent on a series of courses, including one for engineers and another for which he was posted to a staff officers' college in Muhlhausen.

Meyer served in the Polish campaign and on 7 September, during the fighting of the first week of the war, was struck in the shoulder by a bullet, resulting in an injury that earned for him the award of the Wound Badge in Black. Returning to his unit and to active service with minimum delay, Meyer was given command of No 15 (Kradschutzen) Motor Cycle Company. To reward him for his services during the fighting in Poland he was also decorated with the Iron Cross 2nd Class. He served with No 15 Company during the war in the West and led the unit in Holland. An example of his aggressive attitude on active service was seen during the advance upon Zwolle when, obstructed by determined Dutch resistance, he and another officer commandeered a civilian car and drove through enemy fire to the office of the Mayor. Meyer demanded that the town be surrendered, and such was the force of his argument and the threats he made that Zwolle capitulated. The advance continued

The swift drive by Meyer's company to the Ijssel was not fast enough to prevent the destruction of the bridges over the river. Overcoming them throughout the following days, his unit pushed on towards Rotterdam. En route another heavily defended bridge stopped the advance, but once the SS fire had beaten down the Dutch opposition the problem remained of how to lower the footbridge which the Dutch had raised to obstruct the Germans. Meyer solved this by driving the reconnaissance vehicle's two front wheels on to the roadway. Their weight brought down the footbridge, allowing the motorcycle company to continue the drive into the heart of Rotterdam.

For his actions in the fighting in the Low Countries Meyer was awarded the Iron Cross 1st Class. The unit he commanded was then renamed and reorganised in the early summer of 1940, and Meyer was promoted to the rank of Sturmbannführer (Major).

It was during the Balkan campaigns, during the spring of 1941, that Meyer's star began to rise. In Jugoslavia he led a night drive across country southwards via Skopje and Prileb, with his unit fighting its way across rivers where no bridges existed and forcing back the Serbs across the Zrna river to take Bitolj. From there Meyer and part of his company advanced and captured Vovi. The Leibstandarte then struck into northern Greece and drove back the Allied forces that were defending it. The northernmost provinces of that country are very mountainous, and these mountain barriers are pierced by only a few passes. The mountains represented a terrain factor that favoured the defence, and as a consequence the German advance southwards was slow.

Ahead of the Leibstandarte in those April days was a range of mountains that had only a single pass—the Klidi. For this operation the LSSAH headed the advance by the 40th Corps, to which it was attached, and having successfully penetrated the Monastir gap went on to strike for the Klidi Pass. This was defended by a mixed Australian brigade group and the SS men waited for the dawn, when the German artillery was to open a barrage. Under that bombardment the SS attacked, and despite hand-to-hand engagements the pass, the key to the Allied positions in northern Greece, was taken. The Leibstandarte poured down out of the mountains and drove across a narrow plain towards the next mountainous feature, the Klissura Pass.

Towards the middle of April the Leibstandarte regiment was approaching Lake Kastoria, intending to carry out the advance to Korca by passing on either side of the lake. The orders from Division for 17 April were that the Leibstandarte regiment was to send out a battle group, and those orders went on: 'It is the task of that battle group to destroy the headquarters of the 3rd Greek Corps [at Koritsa] and to bring about the collapse of the northern wing of the Greek Albanian Army . . .' A reconnaissance carried out by the SS showed that the southern road around the lake was impassable because of deep mud, and this meant that the northern road would have to be used by the whole regiment. That press of traffic would slow down the advance of the regiment's vehicle columns considerably. The route was blocked by the Klissura Mountains, and the only pass through that barrier was 1,400m high. Meyer was ordered to take it.

He and his men moved out at 1330 hours to break through the pass, which was defended by the 21st Greek Division who had carried out extensive and skilful demolitions. To bypass the Greek defenders there remained only one route that led up to the pass—a single narrow track—and the opposition offered to the SS soldiers continued to be both determined and bitter. The ground was too steep for armoured fighting vehicles to be used, and there was no level ground on which the artillery pieces could be mounted. An advance by a motorised reconnaissance battalion across mountain tracks seemed to be impossible without the support of heavy weapons, but Meyer was determined to succeed. At 1530 hours the head of his column came across a bridge that had been destroyed by an explosion that had torn a huge hole in the surface of the road. Meyer sent out a point group with orders to cross the gap and to set up a defensive perimeter on its far side in order to protect the motorcycle combinations that would have to be manhandled across the broken ground. As the point unit moved off enemy fire swept the gap and so dominated the area that the men of that point unit could neither move forward nor back. Meyer decided to launch an attack using both motorcycle companies in the role of infantrymen and called them forward.

The SS troopers worked their way along the narrow pathway, under fire, to reach their commander. Once the companies had assembled, Meyer regrouped them and ordered a small body of men to draw the enemy fire. He divided the remainder of his company into three small battle groups, one of which he led himself. The advance to the position from which the final assault would go in was strenuous. The men who followed Meyer along the narrow goat-track to the summit could only scramble up the steep slope and were able to carry just their personal weapons; those groups which found easier going portered mortars, bombs and other close-support weapons. Both companies moved silently and soon realised that they had found the flank of the Allied positions. They began to pass round it but then found that in the darkness of the moonless night the men in the columns began to lose touch with each other, forcing Meyer to halt the advance until his groups had closed up again and had concentrated.

Shortly before first light the SS men began to prepare for the bayonet charge that would clear the enemy from the commanding heights. By this time a battery of 88mm guns had been dragged forward, and although the crews risked being knocked over the edge of the precipice each time the guns were fired they opened a barrage, under cover of which the men of Meyer's unit stormed forward. The fighting opened at 0500 hours, and despite heroic resistance on the part of the Greeks the pass was in German hands by 1700. A very important position had been taken.

Meyer and his men moved swiftly on. Stuka dive-bombing was needed to break the Greek resistance, but when it came it was total and 12,000 prisoners of war were taken for the loss to Meyer's unit of one officer killed and one wounded together with eight men killed and seventeen wounded. From the mountain summit the men of the reconnaissance unit dominated the roads along which the Greeks would have to retreat, and soon the Allied forces had begun to pull back to the south of Greece with Meyer's battalion close in pursuit. The SS reached the Straits of Corinth, only to find that the British forces had been shipped across the water, but Meyer, determined to bring the British to battle, commandeered a pair of fishing boats and brought the whole of his battalion across the straits. His men then went on to clear the southern coast of the Gulf of Corinth and there linked up with men of the 2nd Fallschirmjäger Regiment who had dropped over the Corinth Canal. The war in the Balkans then came to an end, and for all his decisive actions, but chiefly for opening the Klissura Pass, Meyer was awarded the Knight's Cross of the Iron Cross.

The war against Russia, Operation 'Barbarossa', opened on 22 June 1941 but the Leibstandarte SS 'Adolf Hitler' did not cross the frontier into the Soviet Union until 2/3 July. The regiment was on the strength of the 29th Corps of the 1st Panzer Group. Paragraph 5 of the LSSAH's regimental orders laid out the march formation. The column was to be led by a detachment of Meyer's reconnaissance battalion, supported by some 5cm Pak and 2cm Flak guns.

Throughout the weeks and months of the German drive in the summer and autumn of 1941, Meyer's unit spearheaded the advance of the Leibstandarte, smashing its way through one line of defences after another as well as carrying out the pursuit battles that marked that storming advance. The first recorded encounter of a unit of the reconnaissance battalion with the enemy came at 0500 hours on 2 July when a group of Red Army men digging in at a crossroads was fired on. A second and more serious encounter came in during the evening of that same day when a group of Russian tanks was observed near Zwierov.

Fire was opened, and in the ensuing battle two of the Soviet machines were destroyed. The other vehicles moved off. The Stalin Line was attacked on the 4th and in a battle that lasted for three days was penetrated and overcome. The advance was then pushed on in the oppressive heat of autumn until it began to approach Cherson.

During the fighting of 19 August 1941 Meyer led his unit with such decisiveness and panache that he was recommended for the Oak Leaves to the Knight's Cross. He was awarded that distinction during February 1943, and the recommendation reads:

> During the fighting that took place on 19 August 1941 Meyer carried out a wide, outflanking attack from the east of the heavily defended town of Cherson. As a consequence of that operation the enemy's defence of the town collapsed and Cherson was taken with its port and factories almost intact. A number of armed river vessels were destroyed. Traffic across the Dnieper was halted by the road being blocked, and this led to the retreat of the enemy's forces being seriously obstructed.

Soon the LSSAH were on the banks of the Dnieper river ready to continue the advance. During the fighting Meyer went over to a pair of 88mm guns in order to direct their fire. Not long after he had left that position a hail of Russian artillery fire smothered the area with high-explosive shells, killing or wounding the gun crews. During 15 and 16 September the LSSAH won more ground to the east and then began a march southwards towards the Crimean peninsula. The isthmus at Genitschchek was reached and promptly captured, thereby cutting the road and rail links of the Soviet forces in the Crimea. The Red Army's counter-attacks were many and comprised infantry assaults strongly supported by armour and artillery. Beating down the Russian assaults, Meyer smashed his way forward and set up a bridgehead in Terpento, out of which the LSSAH burst to take up an active pursuit of the fleeing enemy.

After taking Berdjansk on 7 October, Meyer went on to capture Mariupol and with such speed that most of its installations and factories were seized intact and undamaged. The Soviet troops pulled back in confusion, offering diminishing resistance to the German drive. Meyer described in graphic detail the pursuit battle that then ensued. From his vivid description it is clear that his No 1 Company had to fight its way through a confusion of retreating Red Army artillery batteries, and he recorded how his men leaned out of their vehicles to shoot down the Russians who were blocking the road to an unblown bridge which they had been ordered to capture intact. It did not remain long undamaged but was destroyed as the SS reconnaissance unit approached it.

It was during this storming advance to the Don, during October 1941, that Meyer fell ill, and he did not return to his battalion until the beginning of January 1942, during which time his promotion to the rank of Obersturmbannführer (Lieutenant-Colonel) had been authorised. Shortly after his return to duty the young commander was also awarded the German Cross in Gold.

On 9 January 1943 the SS Panzer Corps, to which the Leibstandarte belonged, was refitting in France when it was ordered to return to Russia at top speed. Corps was given the highest priority on the railways and roads and was taken to the area of Kharkov. The sector it held there was over 80km wide, and through the divisional front flooded a confusion of units retreating from the Stalingrad débâcle. Immediately behind those broken formations stormed the Russians. Under the Red Army's massive assaults the Leibstandarte divisional outpost line was driven in. On either side of the LSSAH, units of lesser determination than the SS gave way and soon a potentially dangerous gap had opened up one of the division's flanks. Corps ordered it to be closed and for contact to be restored between the open flank and that of the right-hand neighbour, the 320th Division. The Leibstandarte was ordered to capture Merefa, a small town on the Red Army's main road forward, and by that action to close the gap and to re-establish a continuous front line.

A strong battle group of the LSSAH was created. One of its three attacking prongs was Meyer's reconnaissance battalion, reinforced by a Panzer battalion. Merefa fell to that advance but Meyer carried on southwards, past that town and through Alexeyevka-Bereka, and, in conjunction with other battle group columns which had come forward, drove for nearly 50km across the spearhead of the Soviet advance, cutting it off completely. An entire Red Army cavalry corps was attacked and destroyed, chiefly as the result of the actions by Meyer's battalion.

That was not the end of the battle. The towns and villages so recently recaptured by the SS were taken from them by the Red Army and then lost by the Russians by being captured again by the SS. The objective of the Soviet effort was to capture Kharkov, and among the command staff in that city there was indecision. Hitler had ordered the SS Panzer Corps to hold Kharkov, although military sense demanded that the Germans retreat. The army group commander, von Manstein, ordered his forces to pull out of the city so that to the west of it he could launch a massive attack against the units of the Red Army, flagging now after many months of strenuous active service in winter conditions. The operation that von Manstein intended to launch would deal a devastating blow to the Red Army and neutralise it for months to come.

On 22 February 1943 the SS opened von Manstein's counter-offensive. Despite the thick and clinging mud, Meyer's reconnaissance battalion brought the advance forward to Valki. Kharkov itself lay ahead, and during the second week of March Meyer's unit succeeded in fighting its way through to the eastern edge of the city and cut the main road along which the Red Army would have to withdraw. Kharkov finally fell on 15 March, and there then followed a period of relative calm. For Meyer one product of the winter battles, and particularly that of the fighting for Merefa and Bereka, was the award, on 23 February 1943, of the Oak Leaves to the Knight's Cross. The future for Meyer was to include a change of unit and the chance to lead a regiment of Panzergrenadiers in a formation yet to be created.

The Hitler Jugend (Hitler Youth) Panzer Division was raised in the summer of 1943. The 1st Panzergrenadier Regiment of the division, later to be renumbered the 25th Panzergrenadier Regiment, was Meyer's new command. The division was moved first to Belgium and then into Normandy. A High Command report had stated that, except for the mortar and anti-tank battalions, the HJ was in all respects operational.

The War Diary of the 1st Battalion of Meyer's regiment recorded that the unit stood-to at 0300 hours on 6 June 1944 and was ready to march only three hours later. Acting upon the alarm signal that had been given, Meyer went out on a provisional reconnaissance in the Caen area, where his formation was to be deployed. Upon his return to the regimental area he found an order directing him to take his regiment to that part of the coast where the 716th Infantry Division was holding position, and in a battlefield conference with the commander of that formation, as well as with Feuchtinger of the 21st Panzer Division, he learned that the 716th had been broken, that the road to Caen was open and that the gap in the battle line was likely to be exploited by the Allies.

In response to Feuchtinger's gloomy forecast that the Carpiquet airfield was probably already in Allied hands, Meyer sent out reconnaissance patrols which reported back that both the airfield and the villages around it were still held by the Germans. Brigadeführer Witt, the General Officer Commanding the Hitler Youth Division, ordered that an attack by the HJ and the 21st Panzer Divisions was to go in on the following day, 7 June, and that the advance was to be made on either side of the railway line which runs from Caen to Luc sur Mer. The intention was to drive the Allied invaders back into the sea. In the event only Meyer's 25th Panzergrenadier Regiment and a single SS tank battalion were available to take part in the operation. The other units of the HJ lay dispersed all round Caen, while the 21st Panzer Division was in an even more serious situation, being involved in a defensive battle. Thus, instead of two Panzer divisions sweeping to the sea, the German counter-attack was to be made by a single Grenadier regiment and a handful of tanks.

This was the situation at the start of the invasion, and it remained so for much of the campaign in Normandy—too few units that were too widely dispersed to support each other, being committed piecemeal to action instead of a concerted mass drive by entire Panzer divisions. But if at High Command level there was confusion and indecision, at regimental level there was firm resolve. How well Meyer had trained his young soldiers for battle was shown when his 25th Panzergrenadier Regiment carried out an attack to cover the northern and western approaches to Caen. This small force, backed by a couple of the division's Panzer detachments and the regimental artillery, stood to arms to contest the advance of the 9th Canadian Infantry Brigade which was driving on towards Franqueville.

When 'green' troops are committed to battle there is always the danger that they will open fire prematurely. The fire control of the HJ was exemplary. The Grenadiers allowed the Canadian Stuart tanks to roll past them. Then a vedette of Panzer IVs moved out from cover behind a reverse slope, crossed the crest of the ridge and opened fire. The anti-tank guns of the 25th then joined in, and in the confusion of battle the Grenadiers of the 3rd Battalion of Meyer's regiment raced forward to cut off the Nova Scotia Highlanders from the armour they had been supporting. While the Grenadiers of the 3rd Battalion were locked in battle, the sister battalion had been closing up and then charged in an assault that bit deep into the flank of the 9th Brigade.

Under the fury of this assault the Canadian formations began to give ground, and they lost the villages and hamlets that they had so recently captured. It seemed as if the SS's intention to drive the Allies back into the sea might be realised by the Grenadier battalions of Meyer's regiment of the HJ Division. That attack had to be halted for a brief spell short of the objective. The regiment's right wing, which should have been covered by the 21st Panzer Division, was unprotected. It was wide open, and into that gap in the German battle line British armour had already begun to infiltrate, covered by a storm of artillery fire. Struck by that barrage of British tank guns as well as by the fury of field artillery fire, the attack by the 1st Battalion of the HJ began to waver. It was the time for personal example, and the officers of the battalion led their men into action. Quickly an anti-tank line was set up, opening up on the Allied armour, and then support arrived—a squadron of Panzer IVs which restored the situation. The German advance moved on.

When the forward movement by the 25th Regiment was finally brought to a halt the HJ had flung back the Canadian penetration more than four kilometres and the line that the SS then held was to remain intact for nearly a month against strong Allied attacks. In the words of a Canadian historian, 'The 12th SS, which defended this sector of Normandy, fought with a toughness and a determination which was never to be met with at any time again during the campaign in North-West Europe.'

As early as the evening of 7 June, Meyer's regiment had been forced on to the defensive as the Allied forces attacked, determined to capture Caen. To support the defence of his hard-pressed Grenadiers, Meyer relied upon the HJ Division's 3rd Artillery Battalion and the 2nd Bat-

talion of the Panzer regiment. The Allied assaults came in again on 8
June, when two infantry companies, with the armoured support of twelve
tanks, struck at the junction of Meyer's 1st and 2nd Battalions. Two of
the armoured fighting vehicles were destroyed by a tactic used in the
Russian campaign of 'killing' the first and last vehicles of the column,
thereby halting the advance of the rest, which could then be destroyed
at leisure.

June 9 passed with an attack by the Royal Ulster Rifles supported by
a barrage fired by the 3rd Division's artillery and the guns of a Royal
Navy cruiser as the Allies struggled to capture Caen. The Allied counter-
attacks came in again when an infantry assault struck at the junction of
Meyer's 1st and 2nd Battalions. The counter-fire of the German guns
was laid down by the 2nd Artillery Battalion supported by the fire of
massed machine guns—and to such effect that, according to British
sources, 'The intensity of the German fire in the woods to the north of
Cambes, between 1600 hours and last light, was of a nature which was
never to be experienced again throughout the whole campaign.'

The storm of British artillery fire which had endured for days eventually died down, and the days and nights that followed were filled with
patrols and with strengthening the Grenadiers' slit-trench line. On 10
June, according to the War Diary of Meyer's 1st Battalion, he visited
the trenches and brought with him Iron Crosses 2nd Class, which the
battalion commander then distributed to his men. One factor that had
obstructed the 1st Battalion's field of fire was the standing corn, and so
one night parts of this were cut down.

The HJ Division was heavily committed to defending Caen, a town
that had been a primary objective of D-Day. The first attempts to take
the town had failed in the staunch defence, principally by Meyer's
Grenadiers, and the Allies made other efforts to bypass it and by turning the German flank to force the defenders to give it up. The British
and the Canadians, in whose area Caen was situated, repeatedly changed
the point and direction of their attacks from one sector to another,
hoping to find some spot weak enough to be exploited.

In the first days of the Allied invasion it took the German forces
some time to come to grips with the situation in which they found
themselves, facing an enemy who would soon have a massive superior-

ity on the ground and who already dominated the air and the sea. It was the Royal Navy's command of the sea that was responsible for Meyer's receiving unexpected and dramatic promotion. On 14 June 1944 heavy units of the Royal Navy opened a barrage on the divisional headquarters of the HJ Division, in Venoix. One of the shells of that barrage exploded in a tree near the house and killed Fritz Witt, the general commanding the HJ Division. Meyer succeeded him and took over as the new divisional commander—the youngest in the German forces to that date. He learned that although the division had suffered severe losses in manpower, no replacements had come forward nor had the Panzers and guns that had been destroyed in battle been replaced. The supply situation, particularly of shells and fuel, was in complete chaos.

The most difficult situation he had to master in his first days as divisional commander was the three-day long attack by the British 8th Corps in Operation 'Epsom'. Meyer described in his book *Grenadiere* how that great battle developed as the Allies tried again to capture Caen and how he ordered Max Wüsche, the Panzer regiment's commander, to hold the vitally important village of Rauray. The text of the Wehrmacht communiqué dated 29 June 1944 shows how well that defence succeeded. It reads in part: '. . . The fighting was particularly hard to the south/west of Caen where the enemy was able to make a small penetration in the bush-covered terrain. A counter-attack in the evening hours forced the enemy back . . . In this area the 12th SS Panzer Division "HJ" under the leadership of SS Standartenführer Meyer . . . distinguished itself . . .'

However, despite the best efforts of Meyer's division and those of the other German formations, a crisis was developing. The swift advance by Patton's armour had outflanked the German forces in the heart of Normandy and had begun to trap part of the German Army in the West. The area of the encirclement was around Falaise, and it was important to hold the town so that the mass of the 7th Army could escape. The task of holding the town of Falaise fell to the young men of Meyer's division.

In the weeks before his military career came to an abrupt end—he was taken prisoner by Belgian partisans—Meyer was recommended for the award of Swords to the Oak Leaves of the Knight's Cross. The recommendation was signed by Dietrich, the General Commanding 1st SS Panzer Corps, and was authorised on 27 August 1944. Meyer was the 91st soldier of the Wehrmacht to receive this high decoration. Dietrich's citation is reproduced here, in full, because it gives in abridged form Meyer's military career from the day of the Allied invasion to the retreat of the German Army to the area east of the Orne river:

After being awarded the Oak Leaves, Standartenführer Meyer carried out fresh acts of outstanding bravery, in that on 10 and 11 March 1943, and on his own initiative, he cut the road between Kharkov and Belgorod and thereby the roads, which the enemy would use to retreat, between the Tractor Works and the edge of town. This success of Standartenführer Meyer and his reconnaissance battalion played a great part in ensuring that Kharkov was captured within three days.

When the invasion began SS Standartenführer Meyer was commanding the 25th SS Panzergrenadier Regiment, and on his own initiative carried out an attack on 7 June 1944 to the west and the north-west of Caen, a move which was later to be influential in the subsequent fighting. He was able to advance to the airfield at Carpiquet with armoured support and in a speedy, aggressive attack to drive the enemy back to the line Epron–Buron–Rots. It was due to his decisive handling of the situation that the main front line to the north of Caen could be brought forward.

After he took over the division the enemy attacked the left flank of the (HJ) Division, using his 11th Armoured Division, the 49th Infantry and the 15th Scottish Divisions. The enemy intention was to gain a bridgehead across the Orne near St André. In a bitterly fought, two-day long battle Meyer was successful in preventing an enemy breakthrough and to halt him in the Odon sector. In this fighting 117 enemy tanks were destroyed.

On 8 July the enemy attacked Caen using the 3rd Infantry Division and the 3rd Canadian Infantry Division. In the bitter fighting of those days the enemy suffered heavy casualties. Although the enemy succeeded during 8 July in penetrating the sector held by the right-hand neighbour, the (HJ) Division held most of its positions and prevented the enemy armour from breaking through. As a result a new front line south of Caen could be set up. The enemy lost 103 tanks in the fighting.

On 8 August the enemy attacked the sector held by the 89th Infantry Division using the 1st Polish Armoured Division and with the intention of seizing Point 140, 4km north-east of Potigny. While a battle group of the HJ Division was engaged in fighting against the enemy who had broken through with tanks and infantry, another battle group was locked in battle to the east of Wire and a third one was battling against the enemy who had broken through near St Aignan–Bretteville sur Laize. In these battles the 1st Polish Armoured Division was struck severely and 90 tanks were destroyed.

Despite our own losses in the fighting of 7 and 8 August, the [HJ] Division carried out an attack on 9 August against the 4th Canadian Armoured Division along the line St Sylvain–Seignolles–Point 111, to the north-west of Rouvres–Quesnay–Bray en Cinglais, and halted its advance. The enemy lost 103 tanks. This enabled a new front line to be established north-west of the River Liaison.

It was the single-handed effort of SS Standartenführer Meyer, who worked day and night with his regiments and battalions, that Caen was held for another day, despite the destruction of the 16th Luftwaffe Field Division. Braving all dangers, Standartenführer Meyer was always to be found where the situation demanded it. Together with his subordinates he was the life and soul of the fanatical resistance that stopped the enemy from capturing Caen.

It was the unequalled brave actions of Standartenführer Meyer that brought his soldiers forward in the most hopeless situations and prevented a breakthrough by the enemy into the better tank country east of the Orne river. When the enemy tried, using massive material superiority, to break through our front to the east of the Orne, it was Standartenführer Meyer whose division, despite the crippling loss of 6,000 men, remained the backbone of the defence. The successes and performance of the division speak for the exemplary bravery and decisive leadership of its commander.

I consider SS Standartenführer Meyer to be worthy to be awarded the Oak Leaves with Swords to the Knight's Cross of the Iron Cross for his outstanding services.

By the beginning of September Meyer's division was retreating through Belgium and was nearing the Maas river. On the evening of 5 September he sent a motorised recce battle group to establish how many German units in the Namur area were capable of carrying on the fight and also to check whether the Maas bridges had been blown. A second battle group was sent out by him to reach the division's right flank and there to wipe out the US bridgehead at Moux. Towards midday a despatch rider brought news that an enemy armoured column was approaching. Meyer, who had been forward with one of the division's battalions, returned to his HQ and upon learning of the approach of the tank units gave orders for the battle group along the Maas to disengage and to conduct a fighting retreat to the higher ground around Emptinne. The personnel of his headquarters then took up their weapons and left the building in Volkswagen staff cars, intending to engage the tanks. Soon they were confronted with the need to make a decision—whether to turn right and join the battle groups pulling back from the river or to turn left to avoid being cut off. Meyer turned left, as did three or four of the Volkswagen staff cars. They did not get far. In a nearby village the divisional commander's group was fired on by a pair of American tanks. The crews of the VWs abandoned their vehicles and took refuge in nearby ditches.

Meyer and three others did not answer when their names were called: it seemed clear to the remainder of the group that they had left the village and had crossed the high ground which surrounded it. In fact Meyer and a battle group were still in the village and were endeavouring to escape. Meyer hid, first of all, in a chicken coop and decided to wait until nightfall, when, under the cover of darkness, he would rejoin his comrades. After a number of little adventures, including some time spent in a churchyard cemetery and then in a cow stall, he gave himself up to a group of partisans who handed him over to an American unit. Meyer was then moved to a Catholic hospital and treated for his slight wounds.

Thereafter for Meyer it was a prisoner-of-war camp, and at the end of the war his trial as a war criminal. This took place in Aurich in Ostfriesland, and Meyer was accused of ordering the execution of seven Canadian soldiers who had been captured in the first days of the invasion. The prosecution was able to find only two witnesses. One was a deserter from the German Army who had dictated his accusation to a Belgian resistance group. The second was a Pole who promptly withdrew his accusation. Despite the defence testimony of leading German generals together with that of former Canadian prisoners of war, Meyer was sentenced to death. Protests by Canadian officers reduced that sentence to imprisonment for life, and this was later reduced to fourteen years' imprisonment.

Meyer was then transferred to Werl civilian prison from which he was released on 6 September 1954 after ten years' imprisonment. Accused of having been a member of a criminal organisation—the SS—Meyer was tried again as having been responsible for everything that happened in his area of command. Shortly before his birthday Meyer was taken from his cell to a Canadian officers' mess and in the course of the evening was told that if he had been found guilty, then on the following day the Canadian Army would have had no general officers. They would all have resigned in protest.

In post-war years Meyer wrote his book *Grenadiere* as a tribute to the men he had commanded. He lived in retirement in Hagen, in Westphalia, with his wife and the children of the marriage, remaining active in working for the rights of his former comrades. On 23 December 1961 he suffered a severe heart attack, which killed him.

Oberfeldwebel
Heinrich Schaefer

The defender of Cactus Farm in Tunisia

Oberfeldwebel Heinrich Schaefer is renowned and honoured by two countries—by the Germans for his action as a paratroop soldier in three campaigns, Crete, Russia and Tunisia, and by the British 1st Army, which fought in the North African campaign, for his staunch defence of Cactus Farm near Medjez el Bab in Tunisia. At the early age of 30 he was decorated with the Knight's Cross of the Iron Cross in a ceremony held in the American prisoner-of-war establishment Camp Harne.

Heinrich Schaefer was born on 27 April 1914 in Eberbach on the Neckar river, the son of a soldier who had been killed in the battles of the Great War. He grew up in post-war Germany and his widowed mother lacked the money to provide the young Heinrich with the means for an education other than that of a working-class boy. When he left school Schaefer found employment as a sailor in a transport on the River Rhine.

In 1936 he was conscripted into the Army and at the end of his two-year period of service had risen to the rank of Corporal before being discharged. Schaefer was later recalled to the colours but decided that the paratroop arm of service offered better opportunities for advancement than the infantry. His transfer from an Army infantry regiment to the Luftwaffe paratroops was authorized early in 1940, and he trained as a recruit in the Stendal para training school. Once he had completed recruit training his soldierly conduct and keenness brought him to the attention of his superiors, who marked him out for promotion. On the several courses to which he was posted Schaefer quickly demonstrated his aptitude for leadership and he was posted to the Sturmregiment (Assault Regiment) that General Meindl had raised. The task of the

Sturmregiment was to undertake the most difficult missions and to spearhead the airborne assaults that would gain the objectives it had been given.

The military operation in which Schaefer underwent his baptism of fire was that which the Germans launched to capture the island of Crete. This mountainous island lies in the eastern Mediterranean approximately 100km from the southernmost point of the Greek mainland. Earlier German operations in the Balkans had quickly overrun both Jugoslavia and Greece and had driven the British from the European mainland. The capture of Crete would be a stepping-stone to German control of the Mediterranean and would also cut the British link between Gibraltar in the western Mediterranean and the Suez Canal in the east. But the Royal Navy dominated the Mediterranean, and the task of seizing Crete seemed to be an impossible one.

To negate British control of the sea, the commander-in-chief of the German paratroop arm of service, Kurt Student, laid before Hitler a revolutionary plan—the capture of Crete from the air using paratroops and glider-landed detachments. The concept excited Hitler, who gave his consent and support for Operation 'Mercury'. It would go in on 20 May 1941 and was to be completed within ten days. The battle plan for 'Mercury' foresaw the first assaults being made by Kampfgruppe West, around the capital Canea. General Meindl, the commander of that battle group, had under his command the Sturmregiment with which Schaefer was serving. Because of a shortage of suitable aircraft, the paradrop part of the operation would have to be made in two separate sorties.

The major part of the 1st Battalion of Meindl's regiment was to take out the anti-aircraft guns on either bank of the Tavronitis river. One assault group was to capture the bridge across the small river while No 4 Company was to attack Point 107, a hill that dominated the small airstrip at Maleme. The capture of that hill was not only the most difficult of the tasks that were to be attempted, but also the most important, for it was upon the Maleme airfield that the follow-up troops—airborne soldiers as well as Gebirgsjäger (mountain troops)—would land to relieve the paras of the first two assault waves. But positioned on Point 107 were the artillery observers of the New Zealand units which were defending Crete. It was one of the first tasks of the Sturmregiment, therefore, to neutralise the New Zealand artillery units, otherwise their fire would slaughter the incoming aircraft and soldiers.

On D-Day, 20 May 1941, the opening assaults went in with Schaefer's group in the first wave, but it was soon clear that the group on Point 107 was isolated and under immense pressure. The New Zealanders mounted attack after attack to take out the scrape holes and sangars that the para groups had set up. If the attackers could destroy enough para positions they would be able to infiltrate the German defence line and force back the 1st Para Battalion's No 4 Company.

Each New Zealand attack against Schaefer's group ran into the fire of two MG 34s. Their rate of fire, varying between 150 and 300 rounds a minute, smashed the Allied assaults. Not content with merely destroying these attacks, Schaefer led his few men into counter-attacks and in one of these captured a 3in mortar and ammunition. Now the group had what was known in the German service as the 'poor man's artillery', and this meant that any New Zealand attack could be broken as a result of fire from the heavy, iron mortar bombs. Schaefer sent out patrols to bring in more ammunition for the mortars as the captured supplies were running low. Shortage of ammunition was only one problem facing the German paras. Another was that on the bare and rocky slopes of Point 107 there was no water source, and thirst plagued the paras most of all.

The airborne force that had invaded Crete was fighting in three main groups, an eastern battle group around Heraklion, a central one around Suda and Rethymon and the western battle group fighting to gain the Maleme airstrip. Despite fierce fighting which lasted for several days, Point 107 had still not been taken, and in an effort to halt the barrages that the New Zealand artillery was firing Schaefer planned a night operation. He sent out runners to co-ordinate and to collaborate with the other groups that would take part in this mission. The attack opened and, moving from rock to rock, the paras worked their way higher up the slope towards the New Zealanders until they had reached their assault positions. Then Schaefer fired his signal pistol. As the red flare curved across the sky the paras rose to their feet and charged into the New Zealand positions. They drove back the defenders and reached the object of the raid—a pair of field guns that had been firing on the airfield. Satchel charges smashed the breech mechanisms and rendered the artillery pieces inoperable. Searching through the abandoned positions, Schaefer's group found a second 3in mortar, more ammunition and boxes of rations. These last made a change from the hard tack that had been the paras' fare from the first day.

Days passed in a succession of Allied thrusts and German counterthrusts. Although Point 107 remained uncaptured and New Zealand gunfire was still directed on to the airstrip, a number of German pilots had managed to land their Ju 52 transport machines laden with soldiers. These men were Gebirgsjäger from Ringl's 5th Gebirgs Division, and they erupted out of the aircraft and went to ground. Officers detailed them to reinforce the para detachments; in such circumstances there was no time for a formal arrangement of companies. By these primitive means a row of positions was set up, at first a thin line but one which was solid and which at least held firm. But, despite the Gebirgsjäger reinforcement, it was still too early for the paras to be relieved from their positions on Point 107. The trickle of mountain troops reaching Crete had to be put in to strengthen other weak sectors of the line in both the eastern and the central sectors of the battle area.

For seven long days and nights Schaefer's para group in the western sector of the island held their positions on Point 107, short of everything except courage and the will to succeed. On the afternoon of the eighth day the Gebirgsjäger of Colonel Utz's 100th Regiment reached the area in sufficient numbers to take over the defence from the exhausted paras.

The battle for Crete ended victoriously for the Germans. Then came the time for awards and rewards. Schaefer was promoted to the rank of Oberfeldwebel and was decorated with both the 2nd and 1st Classes of the Iron Cross for bravery in the field. More pleasing to him was the special distinction of the Paratroop Badge in Gold. The paras stayed on occupation duties throughout that hot summer while back in Europe a new war had begun—that against the Soviet Union.

Three vast German army groups struck into Russia and at first made spectacular progress. Then the pace began to slow and Army Group North, which had been given Leningrad as its objective, was halted at the south-eastern approaches to the city. In the early autumn days Hitler issued a series of bewildering and conflicting orders, one of which sent the Panzer divisions of Army Group North heading south towards Army Group Centre, there to bolster the offensive that he had ordered to take out Moscow. The German units around Leningrad, now bereft of armour, were attacked in overwhelming strength by Red Army tank units. The army group's battle line began to give way and to bolster that wavering front against the massed assaults of the Soviets the 7th Flieger Division was rushed post-haste to the Leningrad sector.

Schaefer's unit, the 1st Battalion of the Sturmregiment, went into the line late in September. An indication of how serious the military situation had become at that time can be seen from the fact that as the Ju 52 transport planes carrying the battalion touched down, the paras were taken from the airstrip and rushed to Petroschinko, where the Red Army had established bridgeheads across the Neva river. Into those perimeters Soviet engineers had succeeded in ferrying a number of armoured fighting vehicles. There was little time for the Germans to plan their counterstroke, even less for co-ordination with neighbouring units and none at all for reconnaissance. The need was immediate. Machine-gunners of the divisional anti-aircraft battalion laid down a barrage of fire, and, covered by that hail of bullets, the assault battalion went into the attack with such élan that the Russians were thrown out of the bridgeheads and driven back to the river bank. It had been no easy victory, and the battalion's losses, already severe, continued to mount as the Red Army flung in one counter-attack after another. Then, on 7 October, the assault battalion was pulled out of the Petroschinko position and put in on the Viborgskaya sector to firm up the line at that place.

In rapid succession came the battles in the Volkhov sector in the woods of Ssinyavino. The bitterness of the fighting there cannot be completely understood by anyone who did not take part. The 55th Red Army had been ordered to sweep the formations of Army Group North from the southern shore of Lake Ladoga. On that sector it was then to combine with the 54th Red Army, which was driving from the east. The point at which the two Soviet forces were to meet was Ssinyavino. It was to prevent the conjunction of those two Red armies that the assault battalion fought the hardest battle of its life.

135

By this time winter had set in and a day consisted of a few hours of murky light and long hours of freezing darkness. On another part of the Volkhov front, Schaefer added to the reputation he had gained in Crete. The 1st Battalion of the Assault Regiment was put in to defend the airfield at Anissovo-Gorodischtshe against the attack by crack Siberian troops who had been brought in to capture this vital transport point. In his battalion's fighting to hold the airfield Schaefer played a prominent part. Night after night he led para patrols out into the darkness to dominate no man's land, and such was the confidence that his comrades had in him that they volunteered to serve on the missions that he led. By day he was like a rock, holding and flinging back the assaults of the Siberian crack troops. And when one of these attacks prevailed and a position was lost, then it was Schaefer who led the counter-attack that regained it. He seemed to be tireless; he seemed to be everywhere; and he was completely without fear. On many occasions the assault battalion faced an enemy who had a tenfold superiority in numbers, who was acclimatised to the bitter winter weather and whose attacks seemed to have cut off the battalion. But still the battalion held.

In May 1942 Para High Command issued orders that a 3rd Airborne Division was to be raised. One of its constituent formations was to be the 5th Regiment. The regimental commander, Koch, chose men for his new regiment whom he knew to be first-class soldiers, and among those he selected was Oberfeldwebel Schaefer. The training was rigorous, for the operation that had been planned was 'Hercules', the capture of Malta from the air. The intention was to gain for Rommel's army in Africa a safe port from which the Axis forces could be supplied. The plan was straightforward. German and Italian airborne troops would drop over the island and the Royal Navy would be prevented from interfering with the operation by the intervention of the battle fleet of the Italian Navy. Then Hitler abandoned the plan, giving as one of his reasons that, once the Italian Navy knew the British Fleet was en route, the Fascist admirals would turn tail and head for the safety of the Italian harbours. A more compelling reason was the fact that the capture of Tobruk in June 1942 made an attack upon Malta redundant.

In the deserts of North Africa the following summer and early autumn were a period of stalemate with neither the Axis forces nor the

British 8th Army able to win a decisive victory. That situation changed in October 1942 when Montgomery attacked the German-Italian forces at El Alamein. By the first week of November the Axis army was in retreat, and to make that serious situation more alarming an Anglo-American invasion force had disembarked in strategic harbours in Algeria and Tunisia and was racing eastwards to capture not only Tunis, the capital, but also the French naval base at Bizerta. By that move the Allies hoped to place a military force behind the Axis armies, and if they succeeded the German-Italian Panzer Army in the desert would be crushed between the British 8th Army and the Anglo-US formations in Tunisia.

Hitler demanded action to prevent this potential crisis degenerating into a catastrophe. He demanded that a force land in Tunisia and frustrate the Anglo-US intentions. But the only complete and ready formation to undertake that task was Koch's 5th Para Regiment. A hastily assembled armada of Ju 52 transport aircraft was concentrated at Trapani in Sicily, and it was in one of these machines that Schaefer flew across the Mediterranean and disembarked on the airfield at Tunis. The first and main task of the German para groups was to seize the airport and hold it so that follow-up troops could land safely. As soon as standard Army units began to land and disembark from the transports Schaefer knew that his unit's first mission had been completed. He reported for further orders and was told to prepare his group for an advance westwards.

Orders from Kesselring, the Supreme Commander South-East, in Rome were that the German troops in Tunisia—Koch's 5th Regiment and little else—were to advance as far as possible westwards into Algeria and were to block the Allied advance. With only a few lorries and motorcycles to make them mobile, the groups moved out on their new mission. Schaefer led his group into the fighting in and around Medjez el Bab, but by 20 November the Sturmregiment, which had advanced too far, was forced to pull back from that hotly contested area—and it had been a hard and costly battle. The name Medjez el Bab means the 'Key to the Gate', and the capture of that town would give an enemy advancing from the west (i.e. out of Algeria, as the Anglo-Americans were) a free run to the capital, Tunis.

The fighting then moved from Medjez el Bab to the Tebourba sector, where the German and Italian troops were hoping to encircle the Allied formations. The fighting lasted for three days and the Axis forces were victorious. When the battle ended a German-Italian perimeter had been flung around Tunis and was holding fast against Allied pressure. Fighting flared up again along the western side of the perimeter, and it was usually the 5th Regiment that was at the centre of events— and wherever the 5th Regiment was embattled there were Schaefer and his men.

Hitler was unable to reinforce the units in Tunisia to the point where they could gain a decisive, strategic victory, but much had been achieved. By their actions the paras had stopped the Allies from thrusting down through Tunisia and into the back of Rommel's desert army. The garrison in Tunisia did not have sufficient strength to do more that hold the perimeter, although its units often attacked and launched limited-objective offensives aimed at expanding the bridgehead or disrupting the Allied plans.

Throughout the winter of 1942/43 the Axis forces fought hard, and, as always, leading the attacks were the companies and battalions of Fallschirmjäger. One group of Koch's regiment held a ridge of low hills near Medjez el Bab, the central feature of which was a small, white-washed collection of buildings that have passed into British military history by the name 'Cactus Farm'. If the British 1st Army could clear that low ridge then the advance towards Tunis could begin. Longstop Hill had been captured from the Germans during April 1943, and Cactus Farm had now become the focal point of operations in central Tunisia. Throughout the spring of 1943 the British had attacked to take the ground, and each attack had been repulsed by Schaefer and his handful of men. The British 1st Army, this time strongly reinforced, was able to launch incessant assaults upon the small group of defenders holding Cactus Farm.

On 28 April the British 4th Division put in its 12th Brigade with orders to overrun the Germans and to gain the ridge. On the German side Schaefer knew well the strategic value of the ground he and his men were holding. For as long as the ridge and the dominant Cactus Farm were held, then so long could the Germans dominate the main road to Tunis and thereby halt the Allied drive upon the capital city. After a series of British attacks had been driven back, the 1st Battalion of the Queen's Own Royal West Kent Regiment put in a two-company attack to bypass and outflank the Cactus Farm position. 'C' Company (with which the author was serving) gained its objectives but the left flank company failed in its assault, allowing the paras of Major Schirmer's battalion to infiltrate and to counter-attack 'C' Company.

In the light of early morning on 29 April, what was left of 'C' Company were prisoners of war and were being rounded up before being marched away. The sound of firing reached them. On their right stood Cactus Farm, enveloped in the smoke of shell explosions and with a thin line of British infantry marching into the attack. Through the smoke the author remembers seeing the flashes of fire from the muzzles of the German machine guns in action. Only later did he learn that Schaefer, alert to the danger, had ordered the mortar teams to fire so that their bombs fell only fifty metres from his group's positions. It was a calculated risk undertaken to overwhelm the approaching British infantry with a storm of fire and to break the coherence of their attack. As the British infantry closed in, Schaefer gave his mortar teams the order to fire and he added to that hurricane of fire with all the automatic weapons of the defenders. Teller mines flung through the air detonated among the leading ranks of the British infantry and tanks. The fighting at close quarters lasted for more than an hour, but slowly the British platoons began to pull back.

A few hours later British armour tried to gain the objective that the infantry had failed to achieve. Two squadrons of tanks rolled up the grassy slope towards the farm, halting and then firing their main armament. The para defenders did not have even a single anti-tank gun with which to offer long-range assistance, but Schaefer hurried to the wireless set and ordered the artillery to fire on to his positions. The guns opened up and were supported by the fire of the para mortars and machine guns. That fire separated the infantry from the tanks. As the British AFVs penetrated the German line Schaefer gave orders that they were to be attacked with satchel charges. He himself set an example by rising to his feet and placing a hollow charge grenade on the outside of one of the vehicles. A few seconds later the massive charge blew the machine up. His men followed the example that Schaefer had set them, and within minutes ten enemy vehicles had been destroyed. The remaining five turned away and sought to escape, only to be caught by two para groups who attacked and destroyed them all with Molotov cocktails.

Schaefer ordered the German guns to cease firing and led his men into a counter-attack to take out the British infantry who were seeking cover behind the burning tanks. A few hours later the Allies sought to gain what neither their infantry nor their armour could achieve when thirty Mitchell bombers unloaded their freight of bombs upon Cactus Farm. During the attack the last vehicles remaining with Schaefer's battle group went up in flames, but only two paras had been killed. Again the British tanks and infantry went into the assault, but again they were driven off.

On 30 April they attacked once more and were again repulsed. Then the bombers and fighter-bombers came back. The Allied infantry and tanks that had been flung back in the morning hours of 30 April came in again during the afternoon. All day the fighting went on and by last light fourteen more armoured fighting vehicles lay destroyed or burning on the Cactus Farm ridge.

The exhausted paras slept only fitfully and then Schaefer was awakened. A para lieutenant had brought orders: Schaefer and his group were to hold out for one more day. Then a wireless message was received. The British 1st Army offered Schaefer's group the chance to surrender with honour. His reply spurned the offer. The British retaliated with a four-hour long artillery barrage. This was followed by yet another British attack, chiefly an infantry assault but supported by a few tanks.

That early morning assault was beaten off, as were the others that succeeded it. Then at 1800 hours Schirmer's para battalion headquarters issued the order for Schaefer's group to pull out of Cactus Farm. Anything that could not be carried away was destroyed, and then, towards midnight, Schaefer at last led his men back towards the new German defensive line that had been set up at Mohamalata. From that place Schaefer took his group towards the sea, hoping that he would find there the ships to take his men back to Europe. But there were no ships, and the group, together with the rest of Panzer Group Africa, passed into captivity.

A footnote to the activities of Schaefer's group was the report by the officer who had come forward to tell the group to hold. He stayed with the Cactus Farm garrison throughout the final day and counted 37 enemy tanks destroyed and over 400 British dead. He recommended that Schaefer be awarded the Ritterkreuz. On 8 August 1944 Schaefer was called to the office of the commander of the American prison camp. There he was advised that for his heroic defence of Cactus Farm he had been awarded the high decoration for which he had been proposed.

Schaefer returned to Germany from POW camp but did not long enjoy his freedom, for on 7 December 1963 he died from the effects of his war service compounded by an infection which he had picked up during his time as a prisoner of war.

Generalmajor
Theodor Scherer

The Hero of Cholm

Generalleutnant Theodor Scherer, who passed, as a Generalmajor, into German military history as 'The Hero of Cholm', was born on 17 September 1889 in Hochstadt, Bavaria. After completing his education he enlisted into the Bavarian Army as a cadet officer during July 1908 and was commissioned as a Leutnant (2nd Lieutenant) in the 12th Bavarian Infantry Regiment in 1910.

He served throughout the First World War, and at the end of hostilities was not one of those officers who were retained in the 'One Hundred Thousand' Army of the Weimar Republic. He joined the Bavarian State Police Force and served with the Landespolizei until the expansion of the German Army came about in 1935. He applied to rejoin the Army, was accepted and was commissioned in the rank of Oberstleutnant (Lieutenant-Colonel).

By the time the Second World War broke out, in 1939, Scherer had risen to the rank of Oberst (Colonel). He took over command of the 56th Infantry Regiment, but his tour of duty with that formation was brief. In 1940 he was appointed to command the 507th Infantry Regiment, towards the end of that year was promoted to the rank of Generalmajor (Brigadier-General) and in 1941 was appointed to the post of Commandant of OKH Headquarters. Following that staff appointment he was given field duty again, namely command of the 281st Security Division, a post he took up on 1 October 1941.

By this time the war in Russia had already run for four months and much else had happened. The German Army's summer and autumn offensives had conquered great areas of the western part of the Soviet Union. In the north of that country, one German army group was investing Leningrad, in the centre another was moving on Moscow, while Army Group South had overrun much of the Ukraine. But the strategic intention of Hitler and the High Command Staff had not been met: the Red Army had not been defeated west of the Dnieper. It is true that millions of Russian soldiers had been killed or captured, but in other parts of the country vast reserves of men were being mustered and trained for battle. Out of the Soviet Far East a mass of Siberian troops had been transported westwards and were forming up in preparation for the great winter offensive that Stalin and the Red Army High Command—the Stavka—had planned.

The principal elements in the Stavka plan were to relieve the pressure on Leningrad and Moscow, but of interest to us are those winter battles that came in against Cholm. This small town is situated some 100km from the isthmus which separates Lake Ilmen and Lake Seliger and lies, therefore, within the area of the Pripet Marshes. The whole area of central Russia is covered by that vast swamp and almost primaeval forest. The Pripet is a feature extending for 600km on a north–south line and 300km from east to west. This expanse of almost impassable terrain was, in 1941, a barrier to any enemy advancing from the west, as were the Germans. Cholm is one of the few areas that rise above the surface, and because it is an area of dry ground the land bridge there was an important communications centre upon which seven roads converged, and it was also crossed by a main highway and a railway line. The peacetime population of the town had been about 10,000, but conscription and forced labour had reduced that number. The land bridge of Cholm is cut by the River Kunya, a tributary of the wider and deeper Lovat, and both flow through the town on its western side. Being both a land bridge and a communications centre Cholm was strategically important—and fought for by both armies.

The Red Army's winter offensive opened at 0300 hours on Friday 5 December, a bitterly cold morning with temperatures which dropped to minus 30 degrees and with more than a foot of snow on the ground. The first move in that Russian offensive was made by units of the Kalinin Front, and this was followed on the next day by an extension of the operation to include Zhukov's armies. The long-term strategic intention has already been explained, but of more immediate concern to the

Stavka was to entrap and to destroy the Panzer armies operating with Army Groups North and Centre. That intention succeeded in part, and Guderian's Panzer group was severely mauled. To add to his difficulties, the only rearward road that his forces could use was soon cut, compelling the German motorised units to move off the roads and march across country through blizzards and snowdrifts, obliging them to consume greater amounts of petrol.

At the beginning of January 1942 the Stavka produced plans for a continuation of the successful December offensive that had gained most of its strategic and tactical objectives. The second stage of the Red Army winter offensive was to open on 9 January 1942 and it was aimed at nothing less than the destruction of Army Group Centre. In the Stavka plan, and concurrently, the German units of Army Group North that were investing Leningrad were also to be destroyed, while Army Group South was also to be attacked in strength.

The operation began on 9 January, as planned, when five Soviet armies struck and shook the German 16th Army of Army Group North. The 16th was one of the two German armies positioned to the south of Leningrad. The Red Army's main thrust struck at the junction of the 16th and 18th Armies and was spearheaded by no fewer than three shock armies. A further four Red armies struck at the right wing of the German 16th Army, the 11th Red Army striking towards Staraya Russa, the 34th seeking to gain Demyansk and the 3rd and 4th Shock Armies seeking to split Army Group North from Army Group Centre.

What happened on the left wing of the 16th Army during those dark and desperate winter days lie outside the parameters of this story. We are concerned only with the town of Cholm and the German garrison that had been flung together to defend it. The assault by the 3rd Shock Army, despite making massive gains, soon came up against stiffening resistance on the part of German formations that were fighting for their lives and knew it. They fought with desperate courage but could not altogether withstand the weight of the Russian assault.

Ten Soviet divisions, together with other assault troops, advanced across the frozen ice of Lake Seliger on that first day of the new offensive, as the commander of the 4th Russian Shock Army, Yeremenko, drove his forces forward into the junction between the 16th Army (Army

Group North) and the 9th Army (Army Group Centre.) The advance
of the soldiers of Yeremenko's Shock Army was made through chest-
high snow but was supported by the fire of a strong artillery barrage.
The Red Army troops forcing their way through the snow were struck
by the fire of massed German machine guns, but their advance seemed
almost irresistible until on Yeremenko's flank the 3rd Shock Army, aim-
ing for Cholm, was held by strong resistance put up by the 123rd Infantry Division. The General Commanding the 3rd Shock Army had
to call upon Yeremenko's 4th Shock Army for help. This was given,
and a week later both formations had resumed their interrupted advance, though this time on diverging lines.

While the 4th Shock Army was striking for Nelidoye, the 3rd continued its advance towards Cholm and on 17 January, under its pressure, the regiments of the German 123rd Division were driven back.
Two days later Generalmajor Scherer arrived and took over command
of the garrison at Cholm. He found that the force he now led was not a
homogeneous one but was composed of men from all three branches
of the Services—Army, Navy and Air Force—as well as from various
arms of service within the Army. In addition there were fragments of
other major units, including some from the 123rd Division and part of
the 280th Division. There was also a Luftwaffe contingent in battalion
strength and a police reserve battalion. The naval group was made up
of drivers who had carried troops from the Leningrad front and had
not been able to return to their parent units. To complete this miscellaneous collection of sub-units, there were also Latvians and other non-
Germanic units.

The first impressions that Scherer must have gained from his new
command could only have been depressing. The little town of Cholm
stood in the middle of a snow-covered plain with most of its wooden
buildings gutted by fire and with its more solid brick-built houses marked
by shell explosions. His troops came from half a dozen sources and
numbered less than 5,000. That collection of fragments did not pos-
sess between them a single piece of artillery nor even, at that time, an
anti-tank gun. The garrison did not have armoured fighting vehicles of
any mark, there were no mines, barbed wire or other defensive materi-
als, ammunition was scarce and food was in such short supply that half

rations were the order of the day. All in all Scherer's task seemed to be hopeless, but he had been ordered to hold Cholm and hold it he would. He knew Hitler's order that if the Russian winter offensive forced back the Germans from their positions, those troops holding strategic places were to form 'hedgehogs' and were to maintain them, because when campaigning weather returned those winter defensive outposts would be summer-time springboards for the next German offensive.

Cholm and its garrison were isolated in a sea of Red Army formations. Militarily, the town and its units came under the aegis of von Arnim's 39th Corps, and both the corps commander and the garrison commander of Cholm were aware of the importance of the town and of the Führer's order to hold it. Von Arnim was also aware that Scherer's troops were totally isolated, and he was determined to end that isolation as quickly as possible. It was an almost automatic reaction on his part to the situation that made the corps commander raise and put into action the first of his rescue attempts. This was to 'run' a lorried convoy carrying winter clothing, rations and, most importantly, fodder for the horses, together with ammunition. The first convoy of heavily loaded lorries reached Cholm but on the return journey was fired on by Siberian ski-troops who had cut the road. Now 'Hedgehog Cholm' was truly cut off from the larger '39th Corps hedgehog' and nothing could get through the Red Army which was manning jump-off positions, ready to undertake, once again, the advance westwards.

With the realisation that Cholm was cut off by road not only from the main German battle line but, more importantly, from its parent unit, the 39th Corps, Scherer welcomed any increase in strength, and during the first day a detachment of Gebirgsjäger numbering some 200 men fought its way through the Red encirclement and was taken on to the Cholm defence establishment. The arrival of these mountain troops not only represented an increase in the garrison numbers but was also a morale boost, for it showed that men and units were willing to fight their way into the encirclement to support the 'hedgehog' defence. In addition, the weapons that they brought added to the defenders' firepower. The MG units were put into action on the second day of the siege when they were used in a counter-attack that drove back the Red Army from the north-western part of the town, which they had captured only the previous day.

The problems facing Generalmajor Scherer have already been mentioned, but we must also consider the hardships that his men were suffering. Most were still wearing the uniforms they had on when they marched into the Soviet Union in June and now, in the depths of a bitter winter, were without any sort of warm clothing. They were always cold and underfed, and such sleep as they could gain was only in brief snatches of not more than an hour or so. Sentry duty came round too frequently for them to enjoy long periods of uninterrupted sleep. The garrison outpost line was set out in the snowfields surrounding the town. The ground was too hard for trenches to be dug and so sangars (walls of tightly packed snow) were built, behind which they sheltered and froze. Primitive machine-gun posts were made by using explosive charges taken from the garrison's small supply to blow holes in the frozen earth. That earth was then used to build walls to surround the machine-gun positions.

The area that Scherer commanded was small, and when he weighed the few troops of his garrison against the task he had been given he knew that his men could hold the Cholm 'hedgehog' if this were no more than 2km square. With the road blocked, the only certain method of receiving supplies was for these to be brought in by air. From the Luftwaffe officers on his *ad hoc* staff Scherer learned that a Ju 52 transport aircraft needed a runway only 70m long by 25m wide. The construction of such a runway was certainly feasible, and the Soviets were not yet able to shell the area so seriously as to stop the flights. That would come in time, but initially landings could be made under only Russian rifle or machine-gun fire. Airdrops, the other option, were necessarily inaccurate. A parachute container dropping from as low as 1,000m could be blown off target and would land in the Russian lines. Such accidents could not be avoided, and if landings on the primitive airstrip by Ju 52 machines failed, then airdrops would have to replace them. Contact between the garrison in Cholm and Arnim's corps had to rely upon wireless contact, and that link never failed.

Although the town was cut off from the 39th Corps 'hedgehog' on 21 January 1942, it was not until two days later that the first major attack was made. It is a fact that from the first hours of the encircle-ment Russian patrols and probes had come in around the whole pe-rimeter. These light thrusts were made to test the fighting resolve of the garrison as well as its strength. Scherer himself recalled that the first serious attacks to come in during 23 January produced a number of crises because they were made by tank units against which the Ger-mans had no anti-tank defence. The first assault came in from the west, and then a fresh one was made from the east. A third assault followed from the south and, finally, there was one from the north. The guns of the Russian tanks shot everything to pieces for the Soviets were deter-mined to deny the Germans the cover of those houses. One of the few defences against the Soviet armoured vehicles was the Teller mine, which had to be thrown under the tank tracks. An alternative method was to construct a 'Geballte Ladung', a cluster of hand grenades around a central grenade that had a nine-second fuse. But if there were no artil-lery pieces upon which the men of Cholm could depend, they were adept in utilising other methods of close-quarter defence. One such was to erect a pair of barricades across a street. An explosive charge was laid on top of the barricade and as the tanks approached an infantryman lit a fuse that ran along a cable and detonated the charge, thus destroying the lead tank.

Scherer based his defence upon four key positions in the town. These were the KGB prison (the KGB was known at that time as the GPU); a deep ravine known as the Police Ravine; the Hairpin Bend, so called because of the sharp bend which linked the Kunya and Lovat rivers; and the church cemetery, the sector upon which the airdrops were to be made. The KGB prison was located on the eastern side of the town, the Hairpin Bend was on the town's western side and the cemetery was on the north-eastern edge of the defensive perimeter.

In the early days of the siege an airstrip was built, and it was upon this runway that the Ju 52s landed and unloaded their freight of sup-plies, ammunition and medical stores. For the pilots, landing in such a confined area was always a risk, and once a landing had been made they and the rest of the crews had to wait inside the machine with engines running while the plane was quickly offloaded and the wounded taken on board. When that small airstrip came under direct fire from artillery pieces and, eventually, from mortars a new area was selected, but this turned out to be too dangerous to use and the garrison relied more and more upon airdrops. This method of supply was also fraught with difficulties, not least of which was the cramped area of the Hairpin Bend on to which the supplies were expected to be dropped. To aid the Ju 52s to identify the drop area the garrison fired prearranged sets of signal flares. When, in time, the drops proved too costly in terms of lost supplies, the Luftwaffe used gliders to bring them in.

It does not need to be emphasised that a glider landing was a single-enterprise mission. The wood from a crashed glider quickly became a source of fuel. Many of those who were besieged in Cholm wrote of the airdrops and of the measures that were taken when a towed glider was seen approaching the drop zone. Two sorts of patrol were either on standby or else were quickly formed. A fighting patrol was assigned to collect the supplies that the glider carried and a MG group fired their weapons to keep the Reds at bay. On those occasions when a glider overshot its mark and landed in Russian territory there were pitched battles to rescue the precious supplies. During the siege of Cholm over eighty supply gliders landed in the fortress area, but against that modest success it had to be admitted that the Luftwaffe lost twenty-seven of its Ju 52 transport planes.

It was mentioned above that the Cholm garrison did not have a single artillery piece inside the perimeter. However, this was not as serious a problem as it might have first seemed. Although the German main front was nearly 60km distant, von Arnim had opened a salient which was being manned by a battle group of von Uckermann's 122nd Infantry Division and into which he had brought forward the bulk of his corps' heavy guns. From positions in that salient the heavy guns of the 122nd Division fired upon targets indicated to them by a pair of officer artillery observers inside Cholm. These officers and their subordinates worked out and operated the fire plans that were brought into play. In time the skills of the gunners outside Cholm and the observation abilities of the spotters inside the perimeter were such that together they could and did pick off individual Soviet tanks with complete accuracy.

The one hundred and five days and nights of the siege passed with a deadly similarity that was no less frightening for all its familiarity. Every day witnessed barrages by Soviet artillery that seemed never to suffer an ammunition shortage. These bombardments would follow failed attacks, usually by infantry but often accompanied by tanks. The attacks would come in following a predictable pattern. An attack on one side of the perimeter would be driven back and the shellfire would die down. Punctual to the schedule, a second attack would come in on another sector of the perimeter. Once this had been driven off there would be a period of calm before another assault came in on the third side, followed at the correct interval by an attack on the fourth side. The very predictability of the assaults aided the organisation of the defence. Once an attack had been beaten off on one sector it was safe to assume that there would not be another on the same sector for many hours. Scherer knew that he could then withdraw the bulk of his infantry from that sector and deploy it against the next attack.

Over the course of days, aircraft, gliders and airdrops by Heinkel 111s from Kampfgruppe 6 brought in the ammunition and the mines which the defence needed to protect itself. But there were never so many mines that the defenders could relax. Searches carried out in the ruins of the town found several Teller mines, which were gratefully incorporated into the anti-tank defence line. There was also rejoicing when an 81mm mortar was found, together with a supply of ammunition. But greatest of all was the rejoicing when in the cellar of one shattered house a 3.7cm anti-tank gun was found buried in the rubble. Hastily excavated and cleaned, it was then found to have no sights. This meant that all sighting had to be made along the length of the barrel, and this led on one occasion to an unusual result. The gun, wheeled into position to meet a Russian tank attack, opened fire on the leading vehicle and seemed to have achieved no result. But the third tank in line halted abruptly, swung to one side and began to burn. The aim had been inaccurate. It was fortunate for the gunners that the Russian machines which had been put into that attack had been the lightweight T-26 tanks: against the T-34 the gun would not have had the power to penetrate its armour, and even against the T-26 the gun crew had to wait until point blank range in order to achieve a 'kill'.

The Soviet High Command—the Stavka—had put in artillery and armour against the Cholm infantry. Their attacks had all been unsuccessful. Then, as the weather began to improve, the Red Air Force was brought into action, bombing and machine-gunning suspected German positions. In one of the first air raids the Russian planes dropped leaflets urging the civilian population still living in Cholm to leave the town because a fresh Red Army offensive was imminent. It is bizarre to consider that many Russian civilians deliberately chose to stay in the ruins of their town, short of fuel and of food, rather than pass through the encircling Red Army units in order to re-enter Soviet society. Among the many Russian civilians who did choose to stay with the German garrison there must obviously have been some who were spies and agents, but most were not. The Soviets knew every move that the Germans made or were intending to make, whereas the only intelligence sources available to the garrison came from Ic reports from Corps or from the interrogation of deserters from the Red Army—and there was a steady stream of such men. From Corps intelligence sources, Scherer then learned that his attackers were General Purkaev's 3rd Shock Army and that the immediate vicinity of the town was under attack by three Red Army divisions.

One of the principal sources of worry for Scherer was the care of the wounded. For as long as the Ju 52s could land and take off they took with them the most serious cases. Then the landings were stopped and because it was not possible to evacuate the wounded these were taken to any one of the less damaged buildings and housed there. It was a matter of honour among the wounded that if one could carry a firearm then one was fit to fight, and the growing numbers of wounded formed the garrison's only reserve of troops.

The deserters from the Red Army, as well as those Russian soldiers who had been taken prisoner during attacks or patrols, received the same rations as the soldiers of the garrison. Little enough it was, to be sure, but the fact that it was fairly distributed paid dividends for the Germans. Through the usual sources the soldiers of the Red Army who were investing Cholm learned that their former comrades were being well treated and soon they too came over to the Germans in a small but constant stream, bringing with them details of Soviet attack plans, news of the positions of machine guns and other snippets of information that could be used immediately or reserved for future use. Some of the deserters even volunteered to collect the warm winter clothing from the fallen Soviet soldiers. When those clothes were brought back into the perimeter they were cleaned of blood and mud and were repaired by the Russian peasant women still living in the town. Only then were they passed to the fighting units where they were most urgently needed.

During that first winter of the Russo-German war temperatures of between 30 and 40 degrees of frost were recorded. The Russians may have been acclimatised to such abnormally low temperatures, but to the Germans they were another example of the frightening nature of Russia. The German soldier could only be stationed on guard for an hour at a time—any longer than that and his concentration faded as the numbing cold spread through his body. Sentries were always posted in pairs because there were many instances of single sentinels being knifed in the back or of having their throats cut. Because the period of guard came round so frequently, there was never any chance of a long rest in a warm room. An hour on guard and two off guard was the reality. Usually guard duty was followed by a lie-down in a rubble-strewn cellar where a brazier might give off a little warmth and a cup of hot tea or coffee and a smoke provided a brief respite.

Wireless messages from Corps advised Scherer that from the forces in its own 'hedgehog' it had selected one that would make attacks to reach the garrison. The unit named was that of General von Uckermann. Over the air Scherer and von Uckermann then entered into discussions on plans that would be put into operation when the latter gave the word. Within the perimeter Scherer organised assault companies and had these armed and ready to fight their way westwards as von Uckermann's men drove eastwards. Von Arnim, the corps commander, had neither forgotten nor abandoned the Cholm garrison. Knowledge of its plight had been with him from the first day. In those early days he had launched a number of Panzer thrusts to gain touch but these had been totally unsuccessful. Then German infantry were committed but their efforts made no progress: either deep snow or Russian opposition had caused them to fail.

Between 9 and 20 February von Uckermann launched fresh drives to raise the siege, but the efforts of his division achieved nothing. In order to link up with these relief efforts Scherer created battle groups from the Cholm garrison and committed the first of these. But the deteriorating weather and determined resistance by the Red Army halted the battle group's advance after only 3km and there the position remained for the next few days. During that period two Ju 52s from the Luftwaffe managed to land on the airstrip, but the fury of the Russian artillery forced them to take off without being able to evacuate any wounded. On 13 February the Luftwaffe made a fresh attempt to land and deliver supplies, and one of the machines was able to take out some wounded, but they were only a few. There were more than 500 seriously wounded men in the ruined houses and hovels that substituted for hospitals inside Cholm.

When 15 February dawned it seemed like another ordinary day but events soon rose in a crescendo. To begin with there was a heavier than usual bombardment which covered the thrust by a wave of tanks. This armoured assault was rebuffed, but the Reds came in again and again until after the ninth attack they had gained ground in both the eastern and southern sectors of the perimeter. Using Luftwaffe support, Scherer's men drove back all the incursions except for two minor ones on the south-eastern edge of the perimeter. Over the following days there was a certain amount of confusion in the matter of air supply. The airdrops that were carried out on 15 February failed because nearly a quarter of the canisters either burst on impact or landed in the Russian lines. A fresh attempt at landing on the airstrip on the 15th succeeded and some anti-tank guns and supplies were delivered. The Soviets retaliated promptly and the fire of heavy artillery destroyed one of the transport machines that was waiting to take off. The wrecked aircraft blocked the airstrip, and Russian artillery fire finally managed to close the strip altogether on 20 February. The garrison then had to depend not only upon the usual airdrops but also upon gliders.

A new airdrop zone was set up in the Hairpin Bend at the confluence of the Kunya and Lovat rivers. It was at this time, between 13 and 20 February, that repeated and heavy attacks came in, causing Scherer to radio for help from the Luftwaffe. The first German air force raid made in response to Scherer's request came in on the 21st. The use of Luftwaffe aircraft intervening in ground operations took the pressure off the ground troops and brought them some relief.

Towards the end of April 1942 it became very clear to Scherer that the Soviets intended to launch a major offensive against Cholm in order to capture the town as a present for Stalin on May Day. Scherer's defensive task was made more difficult by the thaw which had set in during April and which caused the ice of the Lovat and Kunya rivers to break up. The result was flooding of the low-lying parts of the town, which caused the perimeter defences to be split into several areas. In those flooded areas no trenches could be dug and the soldiers huddled on small patches of dry ground ready to move into action against Soviet attacks.

At 0500 hours in the morning of May Day a heavy and prolonged bombardment opened which was followed by mass infantry attacks supported by armour. The local Red commanders had learned the lesson that unco-ordinated attacks against single sectors of the defence brought heavy casualties. They had begun to organise their assaults and on May Day flung in one attack after another from the south, east and north of the perimeter. Scherer put into action his counter-attack companies and these soon recaptured the ground lost on the northern and eastern sectors. But the Red Army's penetration in the south threatened to break through the German defence line, forcing Scherer to commit his final reserves. They held the line intact and foiled the Soviet attempt at a breakthrough. Cholm did not fall to the Russians on May Day, and the cost of their operations was to be seen in the piles of bodies of their fallen soldiers.

Thwarted only temporarily, the Reds came back in again during the 2nd and 3rd of the month, causing the defence such an expenditure in ammunition that Scherer asked for extra supplies to be glider-landed or airdropped as a matter of the utmost urgency. He also asked for (but did not expect to receive) replacements for the soldiers he had lost as a result of the Red Army's most recent operations. He was fortunate in both respects, however: more supplies were rushed in, and replacements were landed in gliders and put immediately into action.

Throughout January and February heavy and prolonged Soviet attacks had gained small footholds in the perimeter that were quickly driven out by the determined garrison. With the onset of warmer weather, Army Group North determined to carry out operations to 'tidy up' the battle line, and among these operations were renewed efforts to break the Russian ring. On 4 May the 49th Corps opened a new effort to raise the siege and one battle group advanced against fanatical resistance to within 1½km of Cholm. The battle group resumed its advance at dawn on the following day in pouring rain and sleet and by 0620 hours had broken through using the main Lokvitsa road as its line of advance and with the garrison's airfield to the north-east of the town as its chief objective. Behind the battle group came SP guns and infantry groups from the 122nd Division that pushed forward so that, by 6 May, mopping-up in the town had been completed.

The Reds holding out in the north-eastern and south-eastern parts of the town continued to offer such determined resistance that dive-bombers had to be employed to destroy them. Even under these aerial assaults the Russians held out. The Red Army units in the south-east were finally overcome by 18 May, but the determined resistance of those in the north-eastern part of the town was not broken until the second week of June. To the west of Cholm Soviet strongpoints continued to prevent a firm link-up, and AFVs from the 8th Panzer Division had to attack these groups in order to clear the route so that supply columns could reach Cholm.

The evacuation of the wounded was Scherer's immediate priority after the first troops of von Arnim's corps had broken through, and there was by this time the added worry of typhus. Then the garrison marched out as the relief troops marched in. There was a short period of rest and home leave, and for Scherer promotion to the rank of Generalleutnant and command of the 34th Infantry Division before he went on to command the 83rd Division.

Scherer served with Generalleutnant rank and in the appointment as General Commanding the 83rd Division up to the beginning of April 1944. There then followed a staff post as Inspector of Coastal Defences on the Eastern Front until the end of the war, when he returned home. On 15 May 1951 General Scherer was killed in an accident.

For his part in the defence of Cholm, Scherer was decorated on 23 February 1944 with the Knight's Cross of the Iron Cross, and when Cholm was liberated on 5 May he received the Oak Leaves to the Knight's Cross. A few months later, on 1 July, Hitler approved the design of the Cholm Shield which was awarded to the men of all services who had fought and held out in the town or else had dropped supplies. The shield shows on its obverse an eagle with extended claws, which hold an Iron Cross. Below that are the single-word legend 'Cholm' and the year, '1942'. Dress regulations stipulated that the shield was to be worn on the upper left sleeve of the tunic.

Ferdinand Schörner

The last commander of Army Group Centre

erdinand Schörner was born, the son of a police officer, in Munich on 12 June 1892. His first intended vocation was to be a teacher, and in his studies he showed an aptitude for modern languages that was to stand him in good stead in later years. After matriculation he went on to read languages at three universities, Munich, Lausanne and Grenoble, and his future career seemed to be assured.

In common with most German academics, Schörner signed on as an 'Einjährig Freiwilliger' for the year 1911–12, a course of action open to university students and graduates, for this bestowed certain privileges, notably the reduction of conscripted service in the armed forces, the freedom to choose one's branch of service and the advantages of being treated almost as an officer. By the outbreak of the Great War he had already risen to the rank of Vizefeldwebel of the Reserve, an NCO rank. When war was declared Schörner enlisted in an élite unit, the Bavarian Leib Infantry Regiment, part of the Royal Bavarian Household Troops, and went into the field with that regiment on the Western Front.

In action he quickly demonstrated his bravery and he rose from an NCO platoon commander to become an officer cadet, from which he advanced to a commission as a Leutnant of the Reserve. At about this time the mountain troops of the German states were being amalgamated into the Alpine Corps and it was as an officer in the Deutscher Alpenkorps that Schörner was posted first to the Tyrol and then to the Italian Front in May 1915. In the autumn of that year Schörner's regiment was posted to Serbia and in the bitter fighting in that country he was wounded. He recovered quickly and returned to his No 12 Company after only a few weeks. There then followed a return to the Western Front, and after a period spent in a quiet sector the Leib Regiment was posted to Verdun. It was around the village of Fleury that Schörner's regiment fought and endured during June of 1915, and it was on the 22nd of that month that he was hit and badly wounded by shell fragments.

From the Western Front the Leib Regiment moved east again and into the mountains of Romania. In the battle for Hermannstadt, Schörner and his company seized an important feature near Riul Vadului, in the Red Tower Pass, and by holding a position in the rear of the Romanian 1st Army blocked its retreat as he and his men defended the position against strong and repeated attacks. On 6 January 1917 he and his company stormed the heights of the Magura Odobest before the Alpenkorps returned to the Western Front for a brief period, but they were quickly rushed back again to Romania to take part in the fighting for Pusha and Supita, where the corps broke through the Romanian lines. In that fighting Schörner repeatedly demonstrated his courage and decisiveness. On 12 August 1917 he led his company some distance ahead of the main body of the regiment and established a bridgehead on the northern bank of the Sufita river. He held that perimeter against the enemy's mass attacks, which came in not only frontally but also against the flanks and the rear. In the fighting between 29 August and 3 September 1917 he beat back massed Russian attacks with heavy losses to the enemy. Throughout the two offensives Schörner fought so well and was so consistently brave that he was recommended for Prussia's highest military award, the Pour le Mérite.

The military emphasis then swung again to Italy, and it was in this theatre that Schörner led his No 12 Company to fresh triumphs. To set the background, it was in Italy that the Central Powers, Germany and Austria-Hungary, were planning to launch a pre-emptive strike against Cadorna and the Italian armies he commanded. This new operation by the Central Powers was the twelfth in the series to be fought along the line of the Isonzo river and its aim was to smash the Italian Army in the field and to produce a final victory on the southern front.

The Central Powers had gathered together two powerful armies for the twelfth offensive. The main thrust was to be made in the Flitsch–Tolmein–Karfreit sector where the Italians held the upper peaks and which they had not only fortified but had also strongly garrisoned. It was, therefore, vital to the progress of the offensive that the peaks in that area be seized without delay. They were to be attacked and taken in quick succession. It was stressed that any delay in the first five days of battle would have a disastrous effect on its outcome.

Schörner's regiment of the German Alpenkorps began to arrive in the Tyrol on 16 September 1917, and all preparations for the offensive had been completed by the 24th. The appalling weather of that autumn caused the opening day for the offensive to be postponed until 24 October, with H-Hour set for 0200. The attack on that rainy morning opened with a barrage of gas shells, succeeded by the conventional fire of high explosive. Behind that barrage came Austro-Hungarian and German divisions that rolled over the Italian front-line defenders. In the advance through the Julischen Alps Schörner won fresh glory at Monte Kolovrat, the most important strongpoint and cornerstone of the entire Kolovrat position. He led his No 12 Company through a trackless mountain waste, his soldiers labouring under the weight of the heavy machine guns that they would need to defend themselves once they had gained their objective.

Schörner went forward with his men, encouraging those who needed encouragement and inspiring them all. One man died from the exertion of the climb and others sank to the ground, too exhausted to continue. Towards last light the leading files of Schörner's company reached a point just below the northern crest of Point 1114 and he grouped his men to lead them in a charge that would throw the enemy troops from their positions. His soldiers found a gap in the Italian barbed wire defences and then the Bavarians charged. There was a short but intense period of hand-to-hand fighting before Schörner's men won the day and the enemy began to surrender. More than 300 Italians, including the commandant of the defensive position, were taken prisoner, and included in the booty taken were machine guns and a vast amount of ammunition, as well as other weapons and a quantity of rations.

It was the first day of the offensive, and thanks to Schörner's aggressive attitude Point 1114, the most important defensive position in the Kolovrat complex, was in German hands. The regiment forwarded

Schörner's name to Supreme Headquarters for the Pour le Mérite. The citation read, in part:

> He is an exceptionally confident and courageous leader in action who has commanded his company extremely well. In the attack upon the Italian positions to the west of Tolmein . . . he and his company succeeded, late in the evening, in seizing Point 1114, the dominating, strongly fortified key point of the Italian main positions. The capture of that position led directly to further successes on 25 October. It is very unlikely that this strongpoint would have been taken on the following day . . . I consider this officer, who has once again demonstrated his bravery through this decisive act, to be worthy of a very special decoration . . .

The commander of the Alpenkorps also wrote about the importance of the operation carried out by Schörner and his endorsement to the recommendation included these words: 'The capture of Point 1114 was of enormous importance for the future victories along the whole front. It is with the greatest possible pleasure that I recommend Lieutenant Schörner for the award of the Pour le Mérite . . .' The recommendation was authorised by Kaiser Wilhelm II on 5 December 1917 and the award was bestowed upon Schörner by the commander of the Leib Regiment, Ritter von Epp. Schörner was the only Bavarian company commander to have won Prussia's highest gallantry award.

The regiment then moved back to the Western Front and Schörner was promoted to the rank of Oberleutnant (1st Lieutenant) on 22 March 1918. During the following month he took part in the struggle for Mount Kemmel in the Ypres salient. In August 1918 he was badly wounded again, and it was not until shortly before the Armistice of November 1918 that he returned to active service with his company, which had, by that time, been posted again to the Balkans. The soldiers of the Leib Regiment were the last German troops to leave Serbia.

The armistice of November 1918 and the end of hostilities on the Western and Southern Fronts did not mean the end of the war for Schörner. His old commander of the Leib Regiment, Ritter von Epp, had raised a Freikorps, a band of volunteers who fought against anti-government uprisings inside Germany as well as against those external enemies who sought to occupy Reich territory which they claimed as their own—notably the Poles in Upper Silesia. With Freikorps Epp, Schörner again distinguished himself when he returned to his home town of Munich and helped to crush the communist regime that had usurped power. From Munich he led his men to the Ruhr, where they took an active part in putting down the revolution brewing there. In the course of time both the external and the internal threats to the nation's security faded and Schörner was free to take up again his profession of soldiering.

With the Armistice and the signing of the Versailles Treaty the German Army was reduced in size to just 100,000 men. Schörner, who had been raised to the status of a regular service officer, was invited to stay on in the Army of the Weimar Republic. His first employment was as a regimental officer in the 19th Bavarian Infantry Regiment, and after he had been reduced to the substantive rank of Captain he took over the 10th Company of a Gebirgsjäger (mountain) unit. In accordance with the usual German military practice he spent a period away from his regiment, to take up the post of adjutant in the Dresden Infantry School, where he was promoted, once again, to the rank of Major. The choice then lay before him: to remain a regimental officer or to try to gain admission to the covert General Staff. He chose the latter option and improved his knowledge of languages. He was then appointed to be an aide de camp or 'command assistant' in the Munich military district and served in that capacity for three years, from 1923 to 1926. His period on the staff was then succeeded by one of regimental duty. Five years later his linguistic abilities caused him to be posted to serve with the Italian Army in the role of interpreter before being moved again, this time to the military college in Dresden where he lectured on tactics.

In 1935 Schörner was given another staff appointment, in the Foreign Armies Branch of the General Staff, and two years later he was promoted and again returned to regimental employment when he was given command of the 98th Gebirgsjäger Regiment with the rank of Lieutenant-Colonel. He was again promoted two years later, to the rank of Colonel, and in that rank he led his regiment into the campaign in Poland in 1939.

Schörner's 98th Regiment was part of the 1st Gebirgsjäger Division, which, for the Polish campaign, served with the 18th (Gebirgs) Corps, which had been given the city of Lemberg as its principal objective. The story of the corps' approach to the city is one of incredibly

long marches from southern Slovakia and into Poland. These were repeated day after day, and were interspersed with battles against brave
and determined Polish defenders. The 1st Gebirgs Division's operations plan was to capture that important objective by a *coup de main*,
and for this a battle group from Schörner's regiment was set up consisting of four Jäger companies as well as detachments of anti-tank gunners, pioneers and batteries of 15cm artillery and of Flak.

'The Race to Lemberg' opened with the capture of Sambor during
the evening of 12 September. Schörner then received an order from
the divisional commander which read: 'Today's task is to conduct an
all-out advance upon Lemberg . . .' Schörner interpreted that in his
own way: 'Drive as fast as if on a motorway and create as much dust as
possible.' He knew that clouds of dust arising from the advance guard
column would deceive the Poles into believing that the troops advancing under that dust cloud towards them were in greater strength than
was actually the case. The advance guard set off at high speed and
raced toward Malovanka. It was anticipated that there would be determined resistance at that place because the area through which Schörner's
formation was advancing narrowed as it passed between two lakes.
The battle group moved swiftly to force the narrows, but a storm of
Polish fire halted the advance. Disdaining to take cover, Schörner stood
in the open and reorganised his battalions, creating a new battle group
made up of just motorised units. The newly formed advance guard
spearheaded the attack and was followed by regimental headquarters,
a pioneer company and a Jäger battalion mounted in lorries.

At top speed the battle group crashed into and then through the
enemy's roadblocks and, once through the narrows between the two
lakes, reached open country. The advance continued without halt until
the first houses of West Lemberg were reached. Then determined opposition was met. Schörner's advance had created a salient that pro-
jected into the main body of the Poles' Eastern Army, and that salient
was under constant attack by Polish units that had been bypassed by
the advance guard in its careering progress. Those Polish detachments
had regrouped and had taken up the fight again to smash the walls of the
German salient. Polish resistance was everywhere determined but grew
to such an intensity in West Lemberg that the advance had to be halted.

The area was strongly garrisoned by an enemy determined to resist the advance of Schörner's Gebirgsjäger. All along the line of the regiment's advance, machine gun groups and snipers fired upon the German regimental column. In the words of an officer who took part in the 'The Race to Lemberg' with the advance guard,

> Our few troops were grouped together with regimental headquarters in a few houses in West Lemberg. They were determined to hold the ground they had won until the main body arrived. From reports which came in, the German advance was being contested as Polish groups which had been bypassed regrouped and took up the fight again.

The divisional commander, General Kübler, together with his Ia, fought their way into West Lemberg during the afternoon of 12 September and having taken stock of the situation ordered the sister regiment, the 99th Gebirgsjäger, to drive for the city using all available motorised detachments. To carry out this order the Gebirgsjäger of the 99th carried out a foot march that lasted most of the day. Sambor was reached and the motorised advance upon Lemberg was to begin on the following day.

The 99th's battle to break through and reach the 98th lasted for eight long days. While Schörner's battle group defended the high ground at Zboiska Holoska and the surrounding hills, the Poles struck first of all on one front, then on a second, and on a third, and then the fighting developed on a fourth front. Schörner's men were completely surrounded and cut off not merely from the division but also from supplies and reinforcements. The Poles were superior in numbers to Schörner's group and put in repeated attacks to drive the Germans out of the city. The TAC headquarters of Schörner's regiment was set up in the latter's defensive perimeter and was constantly threatened with being overrun and destroyed. There was so little German artillery support that fire had to be rationed and the advance guard group was limited to the support of just one or two batteries of guns. The Poles suffered no such shortages and continued to bombard the Jäger positions with fire from every calibre of weapon up to and including 12cm.

On 21 September Schörner's determination to hold out was rewarded when Lemberg surrendered, and as a result of the invasion of eastern Poland by the Red Army the Poles capitulated. But the time that the

Jäger spent in the city was brief. On the day following the surrender the Jäger had to evacuate it and hand it over to the Red Army, into whose zone of occupation it fell. The 18th (Gebirgs) Corps had been the formation that had penetrated deepest into Polish territory.

With the campaign in Poland at an end the 1st and 2nd Gebirgs Divisions moved to the Western Front. While the war in the West was still being fought, Schörner was given command of the 6th Gebirgs Division, which had been raised on the military training ground of Heuberg. The cadre around which the 141st Gebirgs Regiment was raised was made up of men who had formerly served with the 139th Gebirgs Regiment but had been left out of battle when that formation went to fight in Norway. The second Jäger regiment, the 143rd, had been raised originally for the 4th Gebirgs Division.

Schörner was determined to have his division ready for action in the shortest possible time, and such was his drive and enthusiasm that it appeared on the strength of the 7th Army as early as 13 June 1940. Two months later, on 1 August, Schörner was raised in rank from Oberst (Colonel) to Generalmajor (Brigadier-General), and in the New Year he received orders to move his division to the Balkans. Hitler had ordered a military operation against Greece and Unternehmen 'Marita' was the result. The Führer had decided upon that campaign because, as he saw it, the British occupation of Crete would allow RAF bombers to attack the Ploesti oilfields in Romania, so vital to Germany's economy. A deterioration in the political situation soon brought orders for an extension of Operation 'Marita' to include a war against Jugoslavia.

Two German armies went into the field in the Balkans, and included on the strength of those armies were four divisions of Gebirgsjäger. The 1st and 4th fought against Jugoslavia while the 5th and 6th were employed in Greece. Those two latter divisions, combined into the 18th (Gebirgs) Corps, had the task of smashing the Metaxas Line. With this defensive position neutralised the 5th Division would open the Rupel Pass and would then spearhead the advance southwards.

The Metaxas Line was a series of field fortifications and bunkers on the peaks and crests of the mountains that formed the frontier between Greece and Bulgaria. Many of those peaks reached to over 2,000m in height, but they declined as they ran westwards towards the valley of the Struma river. Once the Gebirgsjäger had scaled the mountains and had opened the Rupel Pass, the way would be open for an advance towards Salonika.

Schörner's 6th Division fought on the right flank of the 5th Division and was positioned in the Belshanitsa mountain range between Bulgaria and Jugoslavia. The 6th Division had as its main task that of thrusting southwards through the mountains and then advancing to the valley of the Kumli river. On the lowest slopes of the mountains in which the division was to operate there was only scrub vegetation, and this died out at higher levels until on the upper peaks there was nothing but bare rock. The valleys that scored the mountain slopes were deep and narrow and there were no roads in the area—often not even tracks. Movement in that mountain wilderness was restricted, and every mouthful of food, as well as every round of ammunition, had to be portered up from the valleys thousands of feet below. Mules could only bring the rations up to a certain height and then it depended upon the Jäger to carry the great burdens of food and ammunition to the fighting companies. So difficult was the terrain that it was estimated that a man carrying a message from battalion TAC headquarters would expect to climb for six hours to reach the front-line platoons provided that runner was not burdened with the heavy weight of a ration or ammunition pack.

Schörner's battle plan for his division's operation foresaw six columns in battalion strength, advancing side by side. The column on the extreme right flank was made up of the 2nd Battalion/143rd Gebirgs Regiment, from which one company had been detached and sent marching westwards almost as far as the Jugoslav border. Once in position it would form the protection for the right flank of the 6th Division. The 3rd Battalion of the 143rd Regiment held the center, and on the regiment's left flank the advance was to be made by two columns. As these advanced they were to link up and were then to descend from the high ground and combine to attack, and then go on to capture the regiment's final objective, the village of Makriatitsa. With that village in German hands the road between Jugoslavia and the Rupel Pass would be cut—and cut so effectively that the Greeks would be able neither to receive reinforcements nor to retreat. A company of pioneers and a battalion of mountain artillery augmented the attack by the 143rd Regiment of Schörner's 6th Gebirgs Division.

Schörner placed the 141st Regiment on the left flank. It was deployed with the 2nd Battalion on the right and the 3rd in the centre. The 1st Battalion, holding the left flank, touched the right-hand battalion of Ringl's 85th Regiment. Once again, the attack was to be supported by a company of pioneers and two battalions of artillery, one of which had been detached for the operation from Ringl's division. In order to achieve the rapid penetration of the mountain barrier, the artillery fire plan was for both batteries to open a close-range bombardment of the enemy's positions. Once the double line of Greek defences had been taken the guns would then be brought forward to give the closest possible support to the Jäger in the final stages of the attack.

It was a tribute to Schörner's drive and tactical skill as well as the courage of his men that the 6th Division passed through the mountain barrier and gained the valley of the Kumli river within a day. During the second day of battle those enemy strongpoints which had been bypassed and which still continued to resist were attacked and destroyed. Schörner regrouped his division and moved it to aid Ringl's 5th Division, which was still embroiled in the Metaxas Line defences. Then, according to a special OKW communiqué, 'the Greek Army . . . realised its hopeless position . . . and laid down its arms . . .' This was not, however, the end of the campaign in Greece, and both divisions fought against the British and Colonial forces as these conducted a fighting retreat down to Corinth. During the campaign it was a unit of Schörner's division that raised the Reichs war flag over the Acropolis in Athens.

The war in the Balkans ended, but only a few months later a new theatre of operations opened on the Eastern Front and it was in the area of northern Finland, commonly called Lapland, that Schörner's division was posted. He was to spend the next two years in that isolated and desolate region. Northern Finland was so far removed from the main battle areas of the Eastern Front that the High Command did not send to units in northern Finland the supplies and reinforcements which were needed. Lapland was seen as a minor front and one that was to be given a very low priority. Yet it was from the mines of Petsamo in northern Finland that the Reich obtained the supplies of nickel that it needed for the German armaments industry. That fact alone should have afforded the Lapland front a very high priority. Indeed, in April 1940—long before the opening of the war against Russia—Hitler had drawn specific attention to the importance of the Petsamo area. Its supplies were vitally important and the German High Command predicted that in the event of Finland entering the war as Germany's ally the first Russian reaction would be an advance westwards from Murmansk to seize the nickel mines there. Hitler had declared that military economics had been the imperative that caused a German force to be sent to protect the Petsamo deposits, but the formations he sent there were denied almost everything they needed.

The Führer made it clear that the German troops were not to be confined defensively to that small but important area but were to attack eastwards. The 100km between Petsamo in Finland and Murmansk in Russia were considered by Hitler to be a derisory distance. But then he had never been to that region, whereas Dietl, the Gebirgskorps commander, had visited it and knew it well. It was a region so inhospitable that the Finnish General Staff considered it to be one in which it was impossible to conduct military operations. Before the onset of winter weather they withdrew their forces in northern Finland to areas well below the 65th parallel.

It was to this bleak and frozen desert that Hitler had ordered the Gebirgskorps to be sent. In time and as the result of reorganisation the forces there were renamed the Lapland Army and formed three corps, each of which was given a separate objective. Dietl's 'Norway Corps' had Murmansk as its objective. Two hundred kilometres to the south of Dietl lay the 36th Corps, which was given the task of cutting the railway line at Kandaleshka. Some 340km farther south again, the 3rd Corps of the Lapland Army was to cut the railway line at a place called Louhi. The railway line was of strategic importance for it linked the ice-free port of Murmansk with Leningrad. When it was cut it would interfere with the movement of supplies and reinforcements between the second largest city of the Soviet Union and the far north.

However, the blindness of Hitler and the General Staff to the strategic possibilities of the war in Lapland meant that the German campaign in northern Finland was one of lost opportunities, starting from Hitler's bizarre military order for the widely separated corps to march separately and unsupported. Moreover, the failure by OKW to accept the economic factor as being of prime importance as well as the failure to reinforce that front were to lead, in time, to the retreat of the Lapland Army—by that time known as the 20th Gebirgs Army—out of Finland and into Norway.

On 15 January 1942 Schörner was given command of the 19th Corps and led it in its operations on the Lapland Front. Although much of the military activity in that theatre was restricted to patrols, there were many offensive operations, chiefly from the Russians who were trying to drive the Gebirgsjäger back on land while Soviet marine detachments made assault landings from the sea. Schörner was very conscious of the sensitive sector on the left wing of his corps, a spot which became known as the 'Fisherman's Peninsula'. Despite the many and furious attacks launched by the Red Army and Navy, the 19th Corps did not lose a metre of territory while Schörner was in command, but did give ground under other commanders and during subsequent Soviet offensives.

Schörner tended to minimise the difficulties of life in Lapland with the expression 'The Arctic is nothing'—a saying that gained currency in his corps and passed from that unit into the Lapland Army in general. His command of the 19th Corps lasted until October 1943, when he was suddenly moved to take over the 40th Panzer Corps, later to be known as Army Group Nikopol. He had barely settled into his new post when the Soviet winter offensive broke against and shattered the neighbouring 30th Corps. Soviet troops smashed through and began to encircle the German forces. To prevent the corps from being cut off Schörner decided to retreat and held open a narrow, 3km wide corridor, through which he led his men out of the Red encirclement and into safety.

The German front in the East was, by the last years of the war, no longer firm and cohesive but had begun to crumble. Schörner, whose troops were holding a bridgehead on the east bank of the Dnieper river, went to see for himself the situation on the ground. His tour of inspection soon showed him that the Führer Order to hold the bridgehead was a ridiculous one. On his own initiative Schörner gave the order to withdraw and his units carried out a complicated retirement operation in good order. He lost only a minimal number of men in that retirement; had he obeyed Hitler's order his whole command might well have been lost. Already promoted to General of Mountain Troops, Schörner received another promotion at the end of March 1944 and became a Generaloberst (Colonel-General) when he was appointed to command Army Group Ukraine. Only two weeks earlier he had been awarded the Oak Leaves to the Knight's Cross.

The Army Group that he now commanded held an important position for it protected the approaches to Romania. The prevailing political situation was precarious. With the Red Army's advance into eastern Europe it was feared that the government of Romania might make peace overtures to the Soviets and would then cease to be Germany's ally. Were this to happen, then the oil supplies from the Ploesti fields would be cut off. From a military viewpoint it was important to hold the Romanian Army formations in the line, and Schörner resolved that problem in his command area by mixing German and Romanian units so closely that the Romanian formations could not withdraw.

Drastic situations require drastic solutions, and Schörner extended his control over all his soldiers in a direct way. He was already known to them as a staunch member of the Nazi Party and also as a strong disciplinarian. He had been an infantryman and knew full well that rear-echelon troops frequently stole the rations intended for front-line units. In his opinion those who risked their lives in combat deserved the best rations and supplies. He was also aware that the same rear-echelon troops were capable of building little empires to hold the men they had under command and sought for ways to increase their power. He also knew that any man who deserted his post left a heavier burden for his comrades to bear. Schörner was relentless in his pursuit of those who were slackers, those who stole their comrades' food and those who tried to stay away from front-line dangers by remaining in rear-echelon posts when they could have been better employed in a fighting unit. His visits to rear-echelon units were feared by the idle and the cowardly, but were welcomed by the front-line soldiers who knew that their commander was of the same mind as they.

Schörner was ruthless to his subordinates but did not lack the courage to defy his superiors. As commander of the Odessa area he found the military situation fraught with dangers. He appealed to Hitler, as the Supreme Commander, asking for authority to withdraw his forces from the city. Hitler refused to accept Schörner's appreciation of the situation. However, despite the Führer's order Schörner withdrew the 6th Army to positions behind the Dnieper, where he was able to set up a new, shorter and therefore stronger front.

He was next appointed to be Commander-in-Chief of Army Group Kurland, but before he reached his new headquarters the Red Army had attacked and had crushed the German front. Masses of Russian troops were pouring through the gaps that had been created. Schörner made the decision to abandon ground and thereby save his soldiers from a hopeless battle. He gave orders for the outnumbered 16th and 'Narva' Armies to pull out of their positions in the northern Baltic States and to join the main body of the German Army in Kurland. His decision, carried out in defiance of Hitler's orders, saved both the 16th and the 'Narva' Armies. Paradoxically, despite this act of disobedience, on 28 August 1944 he had bestowed upon him the Swords to the Oak Leaves of the Knight's Cross. Meanwhile a personal reconnaissance of the Baltic island of Oesel persuaded him to order the evacuation of the garrison.

On 1 January 1945 Schörner was awarded the Diamonds to the Oak Leaves and Swords of the Knight's Cross, and later that month he took over command of the newly renamed Army Group Centre, created out of the former Army Group A. The Red Army was attacking and was fortunate in the weather conditions it encountered. Severe frost had hardened the ground, allowing the Russian tanks to operate, and had also frozen the rivers so hard so that these were able to bear the weight of AFVs. The Red fronts made good progress in their advance from the Oder towards Berlin and the roads behind the German lines were crammed with masses of refugees, all fleeing from the Russian forces.

Schörner was now confronted with a new dilemma. If he held on to territory his men would be sacrificed, but their sacrifice would not have been in vain: behind their firm and unyielding front hundreds of thousands of German civilians would be able to escape the fury of the Red

Army. The final test of Schörner's military leadership came with his refusal to obey Hitler's order to hold the industrial region of Upper Silesia. The Führer had ordered the area to be held at all costs.

For his part, Schörner was determined to prevent the Red Army from sweeping through eastern Czechoslovakia and into Moravia and decided to use the troops that would have been employed in the short-term defence of Silesia in protecting Moravia. On 23 January 1945 he telephoned Hitler and announced his intention to withdraw and to set up the next defence line along the Oder river. Hitler reluctantly agreed that he had made the correct decision. Schörner's army group then carried out a three-week fighting retreat. He and his men fought with such skill that the Soviet troops were forced to halt their attacks on 3 April. For all their crushing superiority in men and *matériel*, the Soviets had been held, and as a reward for his efforts Schörner was promoted to the rank of Generalfeldmarschall. Three weeks later, in a local German offensive, the towns of Bautzen and Weissenberg were recaptured from the Russians, raising hopes in the Führerbunker of a massive counter-offensive. But it was clear that the Third Reich was dying, and in those last days Hitler entrusted Schörner with the post of Commander-in-Chief of the Army.

Deeply conscious of the critical need to hold every town and village in order to thwart the Allied advance, Schörner used his considerable gifts of organisation and the full force of his authority to ensure that his orders in that respect were fully and totally obeyed. As a result of his action and his uncompromising orders, one and a half million people from the eastern provinces of Germany were able to escape the Red Army and were saved.

It was the end of the war and Schörner had one last and controversial task to carry out before he surrendered himself to the Americans in the Tyrol. There had been confusion about the Field Marshal's activities when he was accused of having deserted his men. His explanation was that he had been ordered by Hitler to take charge of the Alpine Redoubt, and because Czech and Austrian insurgents held the area over which he would have to fly from his headquarters in Czechoslovakia he had changed out of uniform and into a dark suit. During the early hours of 9 May Schörner flew in a Fieseler Storch light aircraft and landed near a small town in the Tyrol, where be changed into leder-hosen. Discovering that the German officers he had expected to meet had all been taken prisoner, Schörner formally surrendered himself

Then began a life of degradation as a prisoner in the Soviet Union. One part of the torture he underwent was to be kept standing for hours knee-deep in icy water, and in another camp he was locked up with criminals. Although invited to join the communist-run 'National Committee for a Free Germany', Schörner refused, and his strength of character is shown by his response to a demonstration against him in the officers' prison camp at Krasnogorsk. He opened the door of his hut on hearing their shouts and told them: 'If you had only shown the same energy in battle as you do now, then neither you nor I would be here today.' At the end of his captivity he found himself the victim of a left-wing hate campaign. He had served in the Freikorps after the First World War and had helped civilians to escape the Red Army during the Second World War. The anti-Schörner campaign had a more sinister reason according to some German authors. At that time, in 1955, the question of a new German Army was being mooted and those who rejected it used Schörner, the 'Hitler General' as the tool with which to condemn the raising of such a force.

During Schörner's time as a prisoner of war his wife and son had both died, but release from a Soviet prison was followed by four and a half years in a German jail accused of crimes against German soldiers. Ferdinand Schörner died on 2 July 1973 in Munich.

Leutnant
Erich Johannes Schuster

The paratrooper par excellence

In the opinion of many of his superiors and his subordinates, one of the most celebrated paratroopers of the Second World War was Erich Johannes Schuster. He was born in the Rhine/Pfalz village of Morbach on 6 November 1919 and was killed in action on 12 December 1942 on an isolated Tunisian hillside.

As a child Schuster witnessed at first hand the humiliation of his native land, for Germany had lost the First World War and was occupied by the Allied armies. His schooling was conventional, and at its end he decided to enlist into one of the armed forces. He chose the paratroop arm of service that had been set up in the newly formed Luftwaffe.

That arm of service was a new one, and little was known of it outside German military circles. Hitler's party comrade Hermann Göring had been one of the first men to appreciate the shock effect produced upon an enemy by a parachute landing literally at his back. A detachment of paratroops in Göring's regiment of Prussian police had gained a series of successes against communist cells in that province: parachute-landed assaults by the Prussian police had routed them, and those results, gained against the Nazi Party's political enemies, led directly to the setting up of a Luftwaffe airborne company which was expanded and became in time the 1st Fallschirmjäger Regiment. It was that formation which Schuster intended to join, and in the autumn of 1938 he was ordered to report to the Para School in Stendal. There he completed his course as a paratroop soldier, having made the necessary qualifying jumps. He was then posted to No 1 Company of the 1st Regiment, which was at that time stationed in Stendal.

In addition to Göring, other military men had been active in promoting a paratroop force, and with Hitler's active encouragement two major Luftwaffe airborne formations were soon in the process of being raised—the 7th Para Division and the 22nd Air Landing Division. The German paratroops made their first appearance in public on 20 April 1939, the occasion of Hitler's birthday and only months before the outbreak of the Second World War.

Neither of the two airborne formations was employed in the first campaign of that war, against Poland in September 1939, but both expected that they would have a role at some stage of the conflict. This came with the attack in the West, which opened in 1940. The task which lay before the airborne soldiers, but which was in those early days as yet unstated, would be to attack and to overcome the defences of Belgium and Holland.

For this first assignment a special assault detachment was raised and placed under the command of Captain Walter Koch. Schuster had volunteered for the assault detachment and in November 1939, while serving as an NCO in the 17th Company of the 1st Para regiment, he was transferred to Koch's battalion. Early in the spring of 1940 the OKW, the Combined Services High Command, changed its battle plan for the attack upon France and the Low Countries. Details of that change of plan are described more fully in the chapter of this book that deals with Walter Koch, but an outline here will refresh the memory.

Koch's assault battalion was split into four groups, 'Concrete', 'Steel', 'Iron' and 'Granite'. These were to be glider-landed shortly before dawn on 10 May, and each was to attack and to take out an objective—the fortress of Eben Emaël (Granite), the bridge at Veldwezelt (Steel), the bridge at Vroenthoeven (Concrete) and the Canne bridge (Iron). The capture of the fortress and of the three bridges intact would allow the German 6th Army to 'bounce' the Albert Canal and go on to cross the River Maas, the first major water barrier against an invading army coming from the east.

To assist the 6th Army to advance into the heart of Belgium swiftly and with little hindrance, the battle plan for the four storm detachments was that each of them would touch down on its stated objective at 0535 hours, before dawn. Approaching silently in gliders, they would swoop out of the darkness to surprise and overwhelm the Belgian defenders, and each group was ordered to hold the objective it had captured until relieved. So vital were these four operations considered to be that the advance of the 6th Army across the Belgian frontier was held back until five minutes after the gliders had landed.

Erich Schuster was an NCO in the 'Steel' detachment, which had the task of capturing the Veldwezelt bridge. Late in the evening of 9 May, Koch's battalion assembled on the airfields at Cologne-Ostheim and Cologne-Butwzeilerhof and during the night each pair of aircraft—a Ju 52 to act as the tug for the DFS 230 glider—was made ready and prepared for take off. At 0420 hours on 10 May, the eleven officers and 427 NCOs and men, including the glider pilots, began to board the forty-two wooden gliders and only minutes later the air armada took off and circled to gain height before heading westwards into the dark night sky.

Nearly an hour later Lieutenant Altmann, the commander of 'Steel' detachment and Schuster's superior officer, looked through the window of his glider and identified, from its shape and size, the town below—Maastricht. It was now only a matter of seconds to touchdown and already the Belgian anti-aircraft guns were in action. Altmann told the pilot to descend and ordered his men to brace themselves for the impact of landing.

The glider touched down, raced over the uneven ground, rocking, shuddering and shaking the soldiers inside it. Then it skidded to a halt and the occupants carried out the oft-rehearsed drill of deplaning and of setting up machine-gun groups to cover the flanks. By the time these tasks had been completed the other gliders of the group had also landed, not always without incident. One machine dropped almost vertically and landed so hard that that two paras were killed and the others were knocked unconscious. But the Veldwezelt bridge, 'Steel' detachment's objective, was close; the glider pilots had done their work well. More importantly, that bridge was still intact.

Groups of paras raced towards it and from pillboxes at its eastern approach the Belgian garrisons put down curtains of machine-gun fire. The paras reached the entrance to one bunker, flung in hand grenades and then followed those with an explosive charge that detonated with a loud roar. The pair of Belgian machine guns fell silent; the small garrison was dead or wounded. It was now a matter of getting on to the roadway of the bridge and carrying out the double task of beating down the opposition and of locating the explosive charges. Individual paras, trained in pioneer work, swung themselves along girders below the bridge roadway, found and removed every visible charge and then went on to search for any skilfully concealed packets of explosive. Soon the para pioneers could report that all the charges had been removed. The Belgians would no longer be able to blow up the bridge. But it was still not in German hands. Opposition was coming from bunkers on the bridge's western side and the German airborne troops fought their way through bursts of machine-gun fire until they were close enough to destroy the pillboxes with more explosive charges.

The opposition had been overcome and the objective had been taken. Now it was a matter of holding it until the advance guard of the 6th Army came up to relieve 'Steel' group. The time was a little after 0615 hours. The battle for the bridge had lasted less than an hour, and, in addition to the success of 'Steel' group, 'Concrete' detachment could also report that it had completed its task. But 'Iron' group, which had attacked the Canne bridge, had the frustration of seeing the target destroyed by a series of mighty explosions. A signal that went back to Koch reported that although the bridge had been blown up it had not been totally destroyed and that engineers could soon make it usable again.

Throughout the day there were frequent and heavy Belgian infantry counter-attacks to retake the lost bridges. The first para-dropped reinforcements for 'Steel' detachment came in during the late afternoon, although it as not until 2130 hours that the group could be withdrawn and taken to Maastricht. The enterprise had been a costly one, and 'Steel' lost eight dead and thirty wounded, half of them seriously. As a junior NCO in that operation, Schuster had played a prominent role, and this was commented upon by his commander, Lieutenant Altmann, in a post-battle report.

In the months after the campaign promotions were made and awards were issued. Under German Field Service Regulations it was not possible to gain the highest award for gallantry without having first won the lesser awards. Thus a single act of bravery was insufficient to gain, for example, the Iron Cross 1st Class unless the 2nd Class had already been awarded. The German service overcame this problem by awarding the 2nd and 1st Class Crosses simultaneously, and on 13 May 1940 Schuster was awarded both.

A year passed with Schuster sharpening his skills and passing on his tactical knowledge to the volunteers who flooded into the para schools. Then in May 1941 came the greatest test of the airborne arm: it was to capture the island of Crete from the air using a limited number of troops and within a matter of days. Schuster was at that time in Leutnant von Plessen's No 3 Company of the Assault Regiment, and on 20 May 1941 his group's glider landed near the airport of Maleme in the western end of the island. The glider touched down in the boulder-strewn bed of the Tavronitis river with the landing so severe that the commander of No 2 Platoon was knocked unconscious. Schuster grasped the situation immediately and took command of the platoon.

Among the tasks of the Assault Regiment was the neutralisation of the anti-aircraft guns which were positioned at the approaches to the bridge, and Schuster led the men of his platoon in an assault which took out the whole anti-aircraft battery. Going on from that small success, he led his men towards a new target, the western edge of the small but tactically important airfield. The NCO who had been knocked out in the landing took over command of No 2 Platoon once again and continued to lead it, but Schuster had done enough to be recommended for the Knight's Cross of the Iron Cross. He had been an inspiration to the men of his company and had held it together after the company commander had been killed in action and the No 2 wounded.

The campaign ended and the paras spent some time on occupation duties in Crete while far away the great mass of the German Army had invaded and was fighting in the vastness of the Soviet Union. By the time the airborne men were posted to the Eastern Front the German campaign in Russia had slowed down and the three army groups, particularly Army Group North, had been forced on to the defensive and were soon to be driven back in the first retreat suffered by the German Army in the course of the Second World War.

The first area to which the para units were posted was around Leningrad. There the Red Army had suffered a crushing defeat during the course of the German *Blitzkrieg* of autumn 1941 and had since that time been making strenuous efforts to break the ring that the Germans had thrown around the city. The Assault Regiment and other para units were rushed to the Eastern Front and put into the line in small groups in an effort to close gaps, to spearhead assaults, to strengthen a wavering defence or to act as 'fire brigades'. Against the thin line of German soldiers the Russians put in divisions of highly skilled Siberian infantry who struck for the airfield of Anissovo-Gorodischtshe near Chaikova.

In December of that year and on a new area of the Eastern Front, the central sector, the Red Army's winter offensive was so overwhelming in strength that reinforcements to man the line had to be brought from as far away as Smolensk. During mid-January the headquarters of Meindl's regiment together with Koch's reinforced 1st Battalion were taken partly by air and finally by train to the area around Vyasma. There Meindl took command of a hastily assembled group of fragments of units named 'Battle Group Meindl'. This was moved to positions to the north of Yuknov and given the task of stopping a threatened Red Army penetration through the front of the 4th Army. Having successfully beaten back the Russian attacks, the 1st Battalion of the Assault Regiment, together with the 7th Airborne Artillery Battalion and a company from the 7th Para Machine Gun Battalion, took post to the south-west of Yuknov on the right wing of Meindl's battle group. It was given the task of defending the airfield, which was located to the east of the Yuknow–Roslavl highway.

The fighting to defend that place lasted for months. During those many weeks of physical and mental strain the battalion was often surrounded and cut off from the main body of the battle group but still managed to hold the area against the furious and repeated attacks by the Siberian divisions. It was also during this time that Schuster was wounded and Leutnant Arpke killed while leading his 3rd Company in a counter-attack.

The fighting in Russia was hard, bitter and costly in manpower, and 'fire brigade' units were rushed from one threatened place to another. At the beginning of March 1942 Meindl handed over the Yuknov sector to the 12th Corps and his unit foot-marched to new positions around Cholm and Starya Russa, leaving the 1st Battalion to defend the Shalkova area. It was not until April that the Assault Battalion was relieved by an infantry regiment and was taken back to Germany.

In May 1942 OKL ordered Koch to form a 5th Para Regiment, which was to be incorporated into a planned 3rd Airborne Division. When he had completed the task and the regiment had been created, the 'old' Assault Regiment ceased to exist, but the name lived on when the traditions of that regiment were taken over by the 12th Para Regiment of the 4th Division after the remnants of the 5th Regiment were taken prisoner in Tunisia. Throughout the summer of 1942 Koch's new unit carried out occupation duties in France while its constituent formations were brought up to strength and trained for a new operation.

At the end of 1942 the invasion of French North Africa by the Western Allies demanded that the Axis respond to this challenge, and Hitler ordered that all available troops be sent to the Tunisian theatre of conflict. Schuster had been promoted to the rank of Leutnant on 1 July 1942 and was a company commander in the 5th Para Regiment. On 21 November he landed in Tunisia and moved up the line to the combat zone.

The struggle to expand the Axis perimeter was intense and hard, with the German force, predominantly paratroops at first, fighting against an Anglo-American advance guard which, although initially in no great strength, was to grow in time to become a major force. The western side of the perimeter, which the German-Italian troops were holding, and the area that the paras were defending saw the heaviest fighting. The area of that struggle was in the central western sector around the key town of Medjez el Bab, from which place ran a good road straight to Tunis.

In the middle weeks of December Schuster's No 1 Company left its positions and took up new ones some 15km north-west of Pont du Fahs, where the platoons were quartered in a French farm. Schuster sent out reconnaissance and fighting patrols in order that his men became quickly familiar with the area and with the type of mission that they would be fighting.

On 10 January 1943 the company moved once again towards the combat zone along the Bou Arada–Goubellat road and reached a point where it gained touch with the 3rd Battalion. Captain Jungwirth, the battalion commanding officer, held an 'O' group and gave orders to Schuster that his company was to occupy the high ground of Point 311. Schuster then relayed those orders and directed his 3rd Platoon to carry out the operation on the following day.

During the morning of the 11th Schuster, still uncertain of the situation in his sector, decided to undertake a reconnaissance. Taking a motorcycle combination and a truck, he prepared to set out to establish the situation on the Bou Arada road. If his reconnaissance showed that the road was clear, then the 3rd Platoon was to move forward an hour later and was to occupy the objective, Point 311. Schuster, together with a group of NCOs and another officer, stood waiting to begin the reconnaissance. All around them small groups of their men were taking up position. Two para groups had occupied the left and right slopes of the hill and had begun to dig-in. A support group of a pair of Italian 3.7cm Pak came forward and took post at the foot of Point 311. Schuster set up his TAC headquarters some distance up the slope of the hill and had a small reserve consisting of a heavy machine-gun detachment. Behind TAC headquarters, and some distance up the slope of the hill, there was a small detachment of para riflemen and then another group armed with two 81mm mortars.

The reconnaissance began well and a defensive position was laid out on Point 305, before the group went on to the nearby Point 306. There the advance was halted because it was noticed that on Point 316 British infantry had occupied the high ground on the far side of the road. From the British-occupied area machine-gun fire opened up on the German group, but without effect. Schuster ordered the driver of the truck to move further along the road to reach Point 315 and the vehicle bounded and jerked its way up the reverse slope of the hill. It halted, and Schuster's group jumped out of the lorry and then began to make their way uphill on foot.

When they reached the crest they found that the ground was already occupied by British soldiers. There was also the sound of heavy motor engines, and when Schuster looked through his binoculars he saw a troop of Valentine tanks advancing towards him. He gave orders for an NCO to check on the number of tanks, now rapidly closing in, and followed that order with another for the NCO and his detachment to fall back and to report to Leutnant Flemming's follow-up platoon. The NCO took his group downhill and contacted the platoon commander. As he was making his report more British tanks rolled forward and opened fire. The paras were not equipped for close action against armoured fighting vehicles and withdrew to Point 311. Almost immediately it was realised that Schuster was missing, and it was at first believed that he had been taken prisoner. Accordingly Lieutenant-Colonel Koch had leaflets printed and dropped over the British positions. These demanded that Schuster be returned and in exchange a British officer prisoner would be released. If this demand were not complied with by 1900 hours then a Stuka squadron would attack and destroy the British positions.

During the rain-filled night of 11/12 January Schuster's 1st Company, of which Flemming had taken command, moved forward and consolidated its hold on Points 305, 306 and 311. The advance was fired on by British artillery in a barrage that lasted the whole night. Then, towards dawn, the storm of high explosive stopped and was replaced by smoke shells. It was clear that under that cover the British infantry would attack and attempt to sweep the paras from the hill. Out of the thick clouds of smoke there then appeared the figures of British soldiers. Flemming had little time to organise a defence before the British closed in, supported by tanks. Two of the tanks ran over mines that had been laid in the grass and one after the other the Valentines blew up.

A firefight then developed on the blue mountains—blue because of the colour of the vegetation that covered them. From positions immediately behind the para line mortar crews went into action and were then joined by the paras' heavy machine guns. Flemming ordered his men to drive back the British infantry, and as he led them into a counter-attack he was severely wounded. Two of his men also fell, killed in action, and a further three were wounded, but the British attack had been broken and the enemy infantry were pursued down the slope of the hill. The artillery of the newly arrived 10th Panzer Division then entered the battle and fired a curtain barrage to protect the para positions. This was not the end of the fighting. Two Valentines that had approached along a wadi emerged from it and as they rolled towards the German positions were knocked out.

In the period of relative calm that followed that episode German stretcher-bearers went out to bring in the wounded of both sides. In the area between the British and German positions one of the paras saw a figure lying on the ground some way ahead of him. As he made his way towards it he realised with a shock that it was Schuster. He called his three comrades and together they made a quick examination. It was indeed the company commander, and he was dead. A bullet had struck the artery in his thigh and he had bled to death. Schuster died not knowing that an order had come through which promoted him from 2nd Lieutenant to 1st Lieutenant.

On 13 January Erich Schuster, together with twelve of his company, was laid to rest in the cemetery of La Mornaghia. In the words of his comrades and of his superiors, he had been one of the finest soldiers in the Para arm of service. He had died a soldier's death.

SS Obergruppenführer
and General der Waffen SS
Felix Steiner

The innovator who rose to command
the 'Wiking' Division and then the 11th Army

S oldiers in today's armies who wear coloured, camouflage-patterned jackets and trousers, even on non-combat duty, perhaps are unaware of the debt they owe to the SS commander Felix Steiner. He was the first officer to put soldiers—specifically, the men of his 'Deutschland' Regiment—into that type of clothing. Steiner was also the commander responsible for the introduction of the battle drills first employed by his regiment and which were to be used to good effect on the battlefields of the Second World War, firstly by the SS and then by the German Army. Both those innovations, as well as others that he introduced, were born of his front-line experience in the Great War, where he first learned that hard training off the battlefield reduced casualties on it—or, in his own words, 'Sweat saves blood.'

Felix Steiner was born in Stallupönem in East Prussia on 23 May 1896. His forefathers were originally Austrians who, in 1732, had left the Salzburg area to live in Prussia's eastern province. Otto was baptised, raised and confirmed in the Protestant faith, for his father was a devout man, like his ancestors before him.

The young Steiner had the standard education of a German boy and between the ages of 12 and 18 was at school in Königsberg, where he finished his education and gained the certificate of matriculation on 9 March 1914. A week later Felix enlisted into the 41st (5th East Prussian) Regiment of Infantry in the appointment of a Fahnenjunker (Ensign). On 1 June he was promoted to the rank of Lance-Corporal in the Fahnenjunker class and only a few months later, on 1 August, was again raised in rank, to Corporal Fahnenjunker.

Upon the declaration of war the 41st Regiment moved into action in East Prussia, and early in 1915 Fahnenjunker Corporal Steiner was gazetted in the rank of 2nd Lieutenant. Between 3 and 20 August 1914 his regiment was in action along the German frontier in the East and took part in the Battle of Tannenberg as well as in the fighting in the Masurian lake district, followed by battles during October at Goeritten, at Suwalki and then around Kutno. On 14 November, during the fighting for Kutno, Steiner was badly wounded in the right arm and the left leg. After convalescence he returned to the Front and found that the war had changed from one of movement to one of positional (i.e. trench) warfare. He was next involved in the campaign at Jakobstadt and in the fighting along the Duna river.

In the years that followed, Steiner served in a machine-gun battalion and for his war services was awarded both the 2nd and the 1st Class Iron Crosses. He continued to fight on the Eastern Front until the spring of 1918, when his regiment was posted westwards. He served in Flanders as well as at Cambrai and was fighting on the Western Front when the German government asked for an armistice. Returning to Germany, Steiner helped to raise Freikorps detachments that took part in battles around Königsberg and in Memel, defending German territory against revolutionaries and incursions by Polish regular forces.

As a born soldier, Steiner considered the military life a vocation rather than an occupation, and this attitude caused him to be retained in the Army of the Weimar Republic. Promotion in such a small force did not come swiftly, and although he had been a 1st Lieutenant at the war's end in 1918 it was not until 1927 that he was promoted to the rank of Captain. When Steiner retired from the Army in December 1933 he had risen only to the rank of Major, but he promptly joined the police force in the Rhineland, intending to train the men under his command along military lines. This he did in order that they would be ready to be incorporated into the new and expanded German Army when the order for expansion was given.

Steiner was then invited to become Head of Training in one of the branches that had been set up by the Weimar Republic's Ministry of War. It was his task to develop new methods of training and in particular to determine how quickly a soldier could become proficient. His

service with that department did not last long. When the Nazi government reintroduced general conscription, as it did in 1935, the Training
Department was abolished and Steiner had to decide with which branch
of the Army he wished to serve. He chose the Verfügungs formation of
the SS, for it was clear to him that these units would be amalgamated
one day to form a division. When that happened this new type of keen
and dedicated soldier would be the ideal material on which he could try
out the kinds of training that he had been formulating in his mind. As a
former Major of the Army, schooled in war and decorated for bravery,
he was quickly appointed to the position of a battalion commander in
an SS Verfügungs regiment and within a year had been promoted to
command the whole regiment, which had by that time been given the
name 'Deutschland'.

He had chosen his new arm of service well. His men were young,
keen, dedicated and eager to learn the new methods of warfare. Steiner
appreciated that it was a question of how an individual or a group
reacted when under fire. What would hold a man or unit in the line was
dependent upon morale, upon each soldier knowing that he was superior to the enemy. That feeling was the vital element and it was one that
Steiner inculcated into the men of his regiment. Each of his volunteer
soldiers knew that he was superior to the ordinary conscripted recruit
of the Army and that being better trained, having sharper instincts and
having quicker reflex actions placed him above the others. In short,
each knew that he was an all-round warrior.

The influence that Steiner exerted upon the training of the SS units
under his command cannot be too strongly emphasised. It was as commander of the 3rd Battalion of the 'Deutschland' Regiment that he had
first begun to develop his theories on the employment of infantry on
the battlefield, and he had gone on to introduce these at regimental
level. The successes that were produced in peacetime manoeuvres and
which were later to be repeated under active service conditions en-
sured that these revolutionary concepts—revolutionary at that time—
were taken up by the whole Waffen SS organisation. The subalterns
and field officers who learned Steiner's battle tactics took that knowledge with them when they were posted to new units. Thus, it can be
claimed that these drills played an important part in producing the

spirit of moral superiority that enabled the divisions of the Waffen SS to achieve their outstanding victories on both the Eastern and the Western Fronts.

Steiner refused to drill his men in the conventional methods of training and turned his attention and his considerable energies to instructing them along his own lines. He discarded parade-ground drills that produced, as he saw it, the type of soldier who functioned best within a military formation and instead taught his men to act as individuals who combined physical fitness with hunting skills. Equipped with these two abilities, his soldiers should be able to operate in any type of terrain or climatic condition.

Steiner's intention was to have his soldiers so physically fit that at the end of a long and gruelling approach march to battle they would still have sufficient energy to carry out an infantry attack. His men were trained not just to meet physical demands but also to overcome the psychological stress of taking command decisions. To enable them to do this each was taught to take over the duties of his immediate superior so that if that man became a casualty the given mission could be successfully concluded. His groups were taught assault tactics so that they would be worthy successors to the German Sturm (assault) battalions of the First World War. To what degree of physical fitness Steiner's men were trained can be gauged from the fact that when, at the conclusion of a long-distance marching competition, his unit, which had entered a 450-man-strong team, not only completed the 25km course at an average speed of 7kph carrying full packs and equipment but then passed the saluting base carrying out the 'goose-step', the strenuous parade march.

During May 1939 Hitler, who had learned of Steiner's methods, expressed a wish to see a battle drill in which infantry and artillery were to collaborate. Steiner's regiment was to begin an attack without artillery support and was to overrun the 'enemy' outpost line before going on to drive the defenders back to their main-line positions. The artillery would then fire a barrage upon the 'enemy' positions. Under that fire, infantry storm detachments would blow up the barbed-wire defences with Bangalore torpedoes and would finish with a charge upon the 'enemy' positions. It was explained to Hitler that two battalions of

Steiner's regiment would carry out the assault while the third battalion was held in reserve.

The Führer waited for the demonstration to begin and eventually asked with some asperity how much longer he was to be kept waiting. He was told that the attack had been under way for over twenty minutes and then he noticed individual soldiers, visible for only a second or two, moving swiftly across the ground towards the objective. Hitler watched the attack unfold all the way from the covering artillery barrage and saw the storm troops take the objective using hand grenades, machine pistols and flame-throwers. It was a splendid demonstration of Steiner's training and tactics.

The years 1936 and 1937 had seen the introduction of a number of new developments. Acting upon the suggestion by of one of his officers, Steiner introduced the wearing of camouflage-patterned helmet covers and followed that by outfitting the soldiers of his regiment in similar-patterned jackets. Among the new pieces of equipment that he brought in were the simplified form of battle pack, new-pattern pouches for machine-pistol magazines and a waist belt with supports for hand grenades.

In 1938 two political crises threatened the peace of Europe. The first of these, in March of that year, was the annexation of Austria and the second, in the autumn, was the occupation of the Sudetenland. The outcome of the latter led to the invasion, in the spring of 1939, of the rest of Czechoslovakia. Steiner led his regiment into the newly annexed territory—a regiment that had changed in status from being infantry to becoming a fully motorised formation. It carried out its move into Czechoslovakia in blinding snowstorms and along ice-bound roads, difficulties that Steiner considered as opportunities for the vehicle drivers to learn to cope with such problems.

The year 1939, which had already seen the occupation of the rump of Czechoslovakia, saw a worsening of the political situation as the Third Reich began to threaten Poland. The 'Deutschland' Regiment was moved by sea to East Prussia to take part in the ceremonies commemorating the 25th anniversary of the Battle of Tannenberg. As the political crisis worsened there was an organisational change for Steiner's regiment with the creation of Panzer Division Kempf, in which

'Deutschland' formed the motorised infantry component. Kempf's division was unusual at that time because it had on its order of battle both Army and SS units and leaders.

Upon the outbreak of war on 1 September 1939, Steiner's regiment, supported by the 7th Panzer Regiment, crossed the East Prussian frontier and entered Poland, thrusting towards the heavily defended Mlava positions. That first drive into the Polish complex of defences was unsuccessful, whereupon Steiner swiftly reorganised his regiment and formed three battle groups, each named after its commander. He led one, the second was 'Battle Group Kleinheisterkamp' and the third was 'Battle Group Landgraf', a unit of the 7th Panzer Division. The composition of each group was identical—a battalion each of infantry, tanks and artillery.

It was the task of Steiner's battle group to outflank the defences of Mlava by an advance to Ciechanov and to cut the roads leading north and south of that place. The attack, carried out in conjunction with the Kleinheisterkamp battle group, forced the Poles to evacuate the Mlava positions. Then followed the battle for the Roshan position, another system of prepared defences. The fighting for that objective was later to be described as the hardest of the whole campaign. At one point in the conflict, on the eastern bank of the Vistula river, the fog of battle was such that the regimental battle groups found themselves facing both eastwards and westwards as they fought against Polish formations seeking to break through and to reach Warsaw.

Plucked from that bitter fighting along the Vistula, 'Deutschland' was then road-marched 350km to go into action in the Modlin area. The objective in that sector was the modern fortress that guarded the north-westerly approach to Warsaw and the battle to subdue the fortress lasted from 19 to 28 September. One episode during this two-week battle was the conveying out of Warsaw of the families of diplomats who were accredited to the Polish government. This took place on 21 September and was so unusual that it was mentioned in the Armed Forces Communiqué of the following day.

On 25 September the corps commander issued orders for the storming of the Modlin fortress. 'Deutschland', supported by the 7th Panzer Regiment, was given the task of breaking through between two of the main forts of the complex. During the fighting it was reported to Steiner that enemy resistance along the regiment's front seemed to be slackening and that a surprise attack might be successful. Immediately the commander decided to carry out a reconnaissance of his own and worked his way forward until he was only 300m from the Polish positions. Concluding from that reconnaissance that resistance to 'Deutschland''s advance had indeed weakened, Steiner reported his intention to launch an attack upon Zacrozym and the north-western corner of the defensive positions at 0530 hours the following morning. This was agreed by Division, who subsequently ordered the opening of the assault to be delayed by an hour. At 0615 hours the artillery barrage opened up and a quarter of an hour later Steiner's infantry went into the attack. Shortly after 0900 hours the objectives had been taken, and with these victories the participation of the 'Deutschland' Regiment in the Polish campaign came to an end. Recognition of Steiner's part in the campaign came with a bar to the Iron Crosses 1st and 2nd Class that he had won during the Great War.

In the spring of 1940 training began for the new campaign that lay ahead. On 10 May 1940 this opened, and for Operation 'Yellow', as the first part of the new offensive was code-named, Steiner's regiment formed part of the SS Verfügungs Division. He lined up his regiment in columns along the road between Hamminkeln and Raesfeld where, as the regiment had ordered, all vehicles had been camouflaged against air attack. Operation 'Yellow' opened and 'Deutschland' advanced from the Wesel area to S'Hertogenbusch and thence to Breda, thrusting along the Dutch-Belgian frontier. The town of S'Hertogenbusch was taken and the advance carried forward, across the Beveland Canal, where the first really serious resistance was met. Within three days 'Deutschland' was approaching Vlissingen.

The pace from the start of the campaign had been fast and hard. Thanks to Steiner's insistence upon physical fitness, his soldiers, although tired, had met all the demands that he had made of them. As always, he was well forward and up with the leading elements, repeatedly risking his life and demonstrating coolness under fire. One worrying fact for the whole Army was that enemy armour could not be penetrated by shells fired from the German 3.7cm anti-tank gun.

'Deutschland''s line of advance then took it across the Lys via Haze-brouk, Cassel and Poperinghe, for Steiner's regiment was one of those which had begun to cast a Panzer ring around the Allied forces in Dun-kirk. It was clear that the Allies had been hit hard, and the OKW Order of the Day for 16 June stated that 'the enemy front has broken and the retreating troops are likely to cross the Loire. It is the High Command's intention to hold the enemy frontally so as to cut off his other troops in the eastern fortress areas [the Maginot Line] and there to destroy him . . .'

While the Verfügungs Division had been fighting in Holland in von Bocke's Army Group B, the mass of the German Army in the West had cut through Belgium and into northern France. That main force, now approaching the Channel ports, had driven so fast that a salient had been created between the German forces in the north, in Flanders, and those in the south, which were preparing to battle along the Somme river line. The walls of the salient were weak and needed more units to strengthen them. The Dutch surrender on 14 May allowed part of the German forces in Holland to be redeployed for the purpose. The Verfügungs Division, with Steiner's regiment on its strength, was one of these and accordingly wheeled southwards into Flanders. It was dur-ing its advance across the battlefields of the Great War that 'Deutschland' first encountered British troops. The 3rd Battalion War Diary for 28 May records that the unit had taken 107 British soldiers prisoner.

The La Bassée Canal had been crossed and bridgeheads forced against the bitter resistance of British 2nd Infantry Division. While that fighting was in progress the Verfügungs Division was ordered to clear the British out of the forest of Nieppe. When that difficult task had been accomplished the SS troops were totally exhausted and the contraction of the perimeter around Dunkirk allowed the division to be taken out of the line and rested. It was as well that the soldiers were able to relax, for ahead lay Operation 'Red', the battle to defeat the French Army, which had positioned itself to the south of the Somme river. The army groups in the eastern parts of France were collapsing, and that, coupled with the fall of Paris, broke the fighting spirit of the French.

Once the Somme had been crossed a battle of pursuit opened—exhilarating but exhausting. One feature of that advance was the 60km penetration of the French front by Steiner's regiment. He was, as always, up with the leading elements of his 'Deutschland' Regiment and halted outside the town of Angoulême. He ordered a group of his men to arrange the surrender of the town and they, having captured a group of officers at a conference, were then ordered by Steiner to take prisoner the remainder of the garrison. A small detachment of SS men acting in the spirit of their commanders' training behaved so confidently that the officers of the garrison, who had been surprised while at lunch, promptly surrendered. Still not satisfied with the day's haul, Steiner then ordered that the French armoured regiment that was stationed in the town should also be told to surrender. More than 116 of its officers were captured by a handful of SS men.

The campaign in France and the war in the West were brought to a successful conclusion. After a short period in southern France along the Spanish frontier, Steiner led his regiment northwards again to take up occupation duties in Holland. For his part in the war in the West, Steiner was awarded the Knight's Cross on 15 August 1940.

During the time that 'Deutschland' was in Holland, some of its units were posted away as cadres around which other SS divisions could be created, for these new formations needed veteran soldiers around which their units could be built. These unit postings were followed on 1 December 1940 by the transfer of Brigadeführer Steiner to take over command of the 'Wiking' Division, a formation that was still not fully raised. In order to increase its strength Steiner added units and sub-units from his former regiment, for he was determined to instil into the soldiers of 'Wiking' Division the same spirit that he had created in 'Deutschland',

The new division was to be manned by soldiers from 'countries with the same racial composition as the Germans', and the first contingents came from Norway, Denmark and Holland. The raising of this new division was begun in Munich and it was there that the disparate divisional formations were eventually to be concentrated. To begin with, the designation for 'Wiking' was 5th SS Infantry Division (Motorised) 'Germania', but that title was changed and it was soon given the name by which it has passed into military history.

Steiner was well aware of the difficulties that he faced. He was later to write that the initial training given to a new unit determines its success on the battlefield: 'Mistakes made during the formative stages of a unit's history are difficult to correct . . .' Part of Steiner's difficulties in respect of this training was that the components of his division were in various parts of Germany and thus could not train together as a homogeneous whole. They did not achieve this unity until April 1941, when 'Wiking' concentrated in the Neuberg training ground. On 1 April that year Steiner's 'Wiking' Division was accepted as being ready for war and was taken on to the strength of the Field Army. He knew that within months his new command would face its baptism of fire, and it would be then that judgements could be made about how well his training methods had succeeded.

At the beginning of June 1941 Steiner's division was moved eastwards through Germany, and near Breslau a halt was made to bring all units up to full war establishment in men and weapons as well as to liaise with senior formations. The division was then road-marched through Poland, and during the night of 20/21 June it concentrated around Lublin. The war against the Soviet Union began on 22 June, and for the opening moves of Operation 'Barbarossa', as the offensive was code-named, the artillery regiments of 'Wiking' and the 9th Panzer Division were moved forward in order that their fire could support the armoured thrusts by the 3rd Panzer Corps. The operations on the Eastern Front were indeed the baptism of fire for Steiner's volunteer formations, and the fact that they acquitted themselves so well was a tribute to the level of training insisted upon by the divisional commander.

The Panzer Corps advanced rapidly towards Kiev, but in the third week of July 'Wiking' met fierce Soviet opposition. The Nordland Regiment was attacked by an entire Soviet corps that tried to work round the northern flank of the German corps. The regiment stood fast and in a savage battle not only held the enemy force but also struck it such blows that the outflanking attempt was thwarted. This was the first of many major battles that were to be fought out over the next four years.

Towards the end of July 1941 'Wiking' was taken on the strength of the 3rd Corps. That formation was attacking towards Korsun and the Dnieper river. The division's principal task was to protect the left flank of the 1st Panzer Group. Then a change of plan by the High Command altered the divisional thrust line from eastward to southward so as to follow the line of the Dnieper river. As divisional headquarters was about to begin its move, Steiner noticed movements on a nearby hill that turned out to be a mass of Russian soldiers, who then crossed the main road and effectively cut it. To evade capture by the Red Army Steiner gave orders for all vehicles to make a U-turn and as most of them swung round to obey a pair of 88mm guns went swiftly into action, opening a destructive fire upon the swarming Russians and scattering them.

With that incident cleared up, the divisional commander ordered the advance to continue even though it was clear that large numbers of enemy stragglers were firing at German vehicle columns as these headed towards the Dnieper. Some time earlier a vast Russian force had been encircled around Uman, and it was these remnants in Steiner's area that were fighting desperately to avoid being trapped. A report written by an officer of the motorcycle company contains these illuminating words: 'Every front-line soldier knows from his own experience just how dangerous these seemingly harmless situations can be.'

To pursue and to bring these evading units to battle, Steiner formed his division into battle groups and sent them into action. The situation rose to a crisis as the Red Army fought with determination as its divisions strove to defend the Dnieper river line. Wave after wave of Russian infantry attacked 'Wiking''s bridgeheads on the river's eastern bank, and those assaults grew to a suicidal fanaticism when Steiner led his division across the Dnieper during the night of 7/8 September with the intention of expanding the bridgeheads and then to go on and break out of them. A strong German barrage was mounted, to which the Red Army responded with a hurricane of fire so fierce that the corps commander left Steiner's headquarters having decided not to order the attack to begin, qualifying his decision with the words 'I would rather forgo it [the enlargement of the Kamenka bridgehead] than sacrifice a division to achieve it.'

A little later the Russian artillery fire slackened, and Steiner seized the opportunity and ordered the attack to open. From the swift successes that were then achieved it was likely that the Russian artillery defence had been a rearguard fighting hard to allow other Russian units to make good their escape. Steiner's Order of the Day praising his men for their efforts announced that 'Wiking' had not only destroyed eight enemy divisions in the bridgehead perimeter but had also tied down a number of other Soviet forces. One interesting fact given in that Order of the Day was that on no fewer than three separate occasions Soviet propagandists had reported the destruction of the 'Wiking' Division.

The fighting in the Dnieperpetrovsk bridgehead that followed that in the Kamenkov bridgehead endured for four bitter weeks and was followed by battles for other rivers, leading to the capture of Rostov. But it was clear that campaigning weather for the year 1941 was coming to an end. There was, however, one last encirclement battle to fight—one which was intended to destroy two whole Red armies numbering twelve infantry divisions. When it was concluded the Soviets had lost 65,000 men as prisoners as well as 500 guns. It was a splendid success, in which 'Wiking' had played no small part, but within days of the offensive closing down winter had set in.

Among the principal features of the battles in that first winter of 1941/42 was the fighting in the Mius positions, a struggle which did not end until July 1942. The German summer campaign of 1942, code-named Operation 'Blue', saw one part of Army Group South striking eastwards towards Stalingrad while a second arm drove into the Caucasus. The advance was carried across the Sambek river and captured Rostov and Bataisdsk as the German Army raced to gain the Caucasian oilfields. Then Russian resistance hardened, resulting in bloody and prolonged fighting for the anti-tank ditch of Malgobek.

In the bitter struggles of those days Steiner was an example to his men. Once when a mortar bomb exploded near him and wounded him afresh he remained unperturbed and refused to allow the medical staff to bind his injuries. He would not waste time in that fashion: it was more important for him to bring the advance forward and he was right to refuse treatment. Tuapse lay ahead, and that place was a key point in the battle for the oil of the Caucasus. In December the 'Wiking' Division was mentioned in the Wehrmacht communiqué, and on a personal level Steiner, now a Gruppenführer and Lieutenant-General of the SS, was decorated with the Oak Leaves to the Knight's Cross in December 1942. He was not at that time with his division. On 14 November 1942, while fighting still raged in the Caucasus, there was a change of command in 'Wiking' Division. The General Officer Commanding the 3rd Panzer Corps was posted away to take over command of the 1st Panzer Army, and the vacancy in the command structure of the 3rd Panzer Corps was resolved by appointing Steiner to the post.

The first and most immediate task for him to master was to stop a breakthrough by Soviet Guards infantry. These had attacked and broken into the positions in the Chikola valley that were held by the 2nd Romanian Mountain Division. Steiner ordered an immediate counterattack by all available units. These were weak in number—just an SP battery and a company of policemen—but they were sufficient to break the Red Army ring surrounding the Romanian division. Steiner's corps was too weak to hold the front for any length of time and under Russian pressure it was forced to retreat to Chikola. The Russian advance threatened the only road along which supplies could be brought forward and Steiner needed to find a more powerful group if he was to ensure that the single strategic route was not cut. Knowing the capabilities of his former division, he ordered 'Wiking' forward, but that formation was locked in battle and could only spare, to begin with, a single battalion. This was later reinforced by a battle group made up of armour, guns and infantry. The potency of that battle group, weak but determined, flung back the Soviet thrust.

The purpose of OKH in promoting Steiner to command the 3rd Panzer Corps, an Army and not an SS formation, was that at that stage of the war there was to be an expansion of the Waffen SS organisation and Steiner had been selected to gain experience in handling a major unit. The experience that he did gain was to prove invaluable later in his career, but when he first took over the corps his task in December 1942 was to lead it in a fighting retreat out of the Caucasus. The whole of the German southern front was pulling back from the areas of southern Russia that it had won in the summer offensive of 1942.

In January 1943 Steiner reverted from his corps post and resumed command of 'Wiking' Division, which he then led into battle against the 1st Russian Army. On 30 March 1943 the order to raise the 3rd (Germanic) Panzer Corps was issued, and just over two weeks later its detachments had begun to concentrate in Upper Franconia. Its order of battle included the 'Wiking' and 'Nordland' Divisions. Steiner, who was its first commander, strongly opposed the proposal to transfer his new corps to Western Europe, fearing that a conflict of loyalty might arise when the anticipated Allied invasion took place. He proposed, instead, that his units be 'blooded' in an operational theatre of war other than the Russian theatre, and High Command, agreeing to this concern for his corps, deployed the unit on anti-partisan operations in Jugoslavia during August 1943.

The employment of his grenadiers on anti-guerrilla missions quickly turned them into skilled soldiers and soon Steiner's corps could be posted to the Eastern Front—specifically, to the Oranienbaum sector of Army Group North. That area of the Eastern Front had been dormant for several months, but there were signs that the Red Army intended to launch an offensive to raise the siege of Leningrad. Intelligence sources reported a great build-up of forces in the area and stated that this was particularly strong in the 75km long Orianenbaum salient. This lay to the south-west of Leningrad, and the German 18th Army, of whose establishment 3rd SS Panzer Corps now formed part, was placed on the western side of the Soviet salient with a Luftwaffe force on the eastern side.

Neither German group had been long in position before the first major Russian offensive was mounted on 14 January 1944. This arrived in such overwhelming strength that it was estimated that the Reds had a 4 to 1 superiority in men. Subjected to that pressure, the 18th Army's left wing began to give way, and under orders from the army commander the forces south of the line of the River Luga began to withdraw. This act uncovered the flank of Steiner's corps, and the Red Army broke through despite counter-attacks launched by his SS regiments to close the breaches in the corps' front. Army then ordered Steiner's 3rd SS Panzer Corps to hold bridgeheads over the Luga and to build a new front along the line of the river and across the swamp that surrounded it. Steiner argued that the Luga line was indefensible and that a withdrawal should be made to a defensive line around Lake Peipus. The High Command rejected his advice and its decision embroiled him and the 3rd (Germanic) Corps in month-long struggles as the Soviet forces sought to destroy this bastion on the Narva while Steiner and his men fought equally hard to maintain it.

The Russian offensive rumbled on throughout January and February, and by mid-July Steiner's corps had been bled white. There was such a shortage of men and equipment that the only solution was for him to form mixed-arms battle groups and to put these into action against the most menacing Red Army thrusts. The stand which the 3rd Corps had made was recognised by a mention in the Wehrmacht communiqué of 1 August, which stated that 'under the leadership of Waffen SS General Steiner [it] had played a prominent role in stopping the enemy in this [the Tannenberg] sector'. The recommendation by General Grasser of the Narva Army reads:

> To the Reichsführer SS. I recommend that the General Officer commanding 3rd SS Panzer Corps, SS Obergruppenführer Steiner, be awarded the Swords to the Oak Leaves of the Knight's Cross.
>
> SS Obergruppenführer Steiner, who was awarded the Oak Leaves on 24 December 1942, has set a splendid personal example by always leading from the front and has repeatedly distinguished himself. His leadership has led to the Army's present successes
>
> In detail:
>
> (1) In particularly difficult circumstances he raised the Nordland Division as well as the Nederland Brigade. In partisan-infested Croatia he not only trained the formations that he had raised but also took an active part in the fighting.
>
> (2) Thanks to his initiative and zeal the young and inexperienced troops of his command threw back all the enemy attacks in the Orianenbaum pocket.
>
> (3) The Russian breakthrough on the Leningrad and Orianenbaum fronts during January 1944 once again placed a severe burden on the leaders of his almost immobile formation. Thanks to his determination the units of his corps were kept under such a firm hand that they were able to fight their way through to the Narva.
>
> (4) When the Russian 2nd Assault Army opened its offensive in July 1944 he immediately led his subordinates in the defence of the Tannenberg positions. From 23 July the enemy attacked the 3rd (Germanic) Corps repeatedly each day in overwhelming force but did not succeed in breaking through. This defensive success is due to the special efforts of Obergruppenführer Steiner.

General Grasser's recommendation was warmly supported by the commander of Army Group North. The award was bestowed on 10 August 1944 and Steiner received the decoration as the 86th soldier of the German Army.

Throughout the late summer and early autumn of 1944 the German forces maintained their defence of the Narva, but at the end of July

Army Group North began to pull out and Steiner's corps was given the task of forming the rearguard and holding the land bridge between the Narva and the Joevi. Three separate battles were fought to hold that ground, but at the end of September Steiner led his corps, which had been surrounded and cut off, out of Estonia and broke out to the south. He then divided his corps and sent 'Nordland' southwards towards Riga while 'Nederland' went eastwards into action near Wolmar.

There then followed the three battles of Kurland in which the corps took a prominent, if not a decisive, part. On one occasion near Prekuln it was cut off and isolated but still fought off the enemy's attacks. It was not until February 1945 that the corps was evacuated and taken by sea to Pomerania. In the area of Kekkau, the 'Nordland' and the 14th Panzer Division struck and dispersed the 3rd Red Army Guards Mechanised Corps, sending it fleeing towards Mitau. The intention of that pre-emptive attack was to protect the mass of Army Group as it withdrew westwards. In Pomerania Steiner was busy organising the evacuation by sea of his military units from Tallinn in Estonia. As a result of his efforts and organisational skills more than 80,000 soldiers and civilians were shipped to Germany.

This was one of the last acts that Steiner could render his corps, for he was then promoted to lead the 11th Panzer Army in Pomerania. There, confronted by the overwhelming Soviet pressure, he decided to pull his army back so as to prevent its total destruction. Operating on a reversal of the fire-and-movement tactic of the earlier attacking years, he brought back his formations during the night of 21 February 1945. Within a month the German forces in the East were manning the line of the Oder river and were preparing themselves for the battle that they all knew would shortly open. That offensive had Berlin as its final objective. Soon the German capital was under attack by Red armies driving in from two directions. Hitler, in what he thought was a brilliant strategic counter-stroke, had formed the 11th Panzer Army, had appointed Steiner to lead it and had given him authority not only over his own military formations but also over all the other military, naval and Luftwaffe formations in Mecklenburg. Hitler's directive was that the 11th Army was to strike from the north-west of Orianenburg and into the flank of the Russian masses thrusting westwards towards Nauen.

That attack by the 11th Army was to be co-ordinated with a drive by Busse's 9th Army.

At 1050 hours on 21 April Hitler gave the order for Steiner to open the offensive, the message relaying those instructions containing the threat that Steiner would pay with his head if he failed. Hitler's final words read: 'Upon the successful conclusion of your mission depends the fate of the German capital.' Had either the 9th or 11th Armies been up to strength or made up of fresh troops, then Hitler's strategy might have had some chance of success, but these were worn-out fragments of major formations. They had no hope of success.

By 27 April one of the divisions of the 11th Army had been taken away and, as Steiner was to testify years later,

> I had nothing with which to attack. The three divisions in reserve at Schorfheide had already been swallowed up attempting to stop the Russian juggernaut rolling westwards. Two new divisions that Army Group Vistula had promised never arrived. I refused to put the inexperienced units into action in an operation that was doomed from the start. The plan of attack was based on facts that had no basis in reality, but only in the fantasies of the Chancellery.

It is perhaps true that Hitler had withdrawn a division from Steiner's army because he did not believe that the 11th Army was making a strong enough effort to reach Berlin. The problems facing Steiner were many and almost insoluble. In addition to the lack of strong forces, mentioned above, his front stretched from Orianenburg to Eberswalde.

Steiner opened his attack on 24 April, and the Soviets, surprised by this aggressive action, pulled back in panic. Then Stavka regrouped its forces and counter-attacked, forcing back the 11th Army. It is, perhaps, the fact that Steiner's army had made so little ground that caused Hitler's breakdown, which ended with the words 'It's all finished, everything, everything . . .' That Steiner had no army worthy of the name was irrelevant to the Führer. He had, once again, been betrayed.

Seen from another perspective, Steiner must have long realised that the Third Reich was going down in defeat. As he doubtless saw it, his greatest loyalty was to the men of his 11th Army and he was determined to save them. He gave orders for a paced withdrawal to the Elbe and then for his units to face westwards and to engage the Americans. Under the terms of the capitulation, all German units had to surrender to the nation against which they had been fighting, and Steiner's order meant that many of his soldiers were spared the degradation of a Soviet concentration camp.

In post-war years Steiner busied himself with work for his former SS comrades and was instrumental in setting up the organisation HIAG, which aided former members of that arm of service. He wrote several books dealing with the war, specifically on the role of the Waffen SS in the conflict. He died in May 1966.

General der Kavallerie
Siegfried Westphal

Chief of staff to three senior commanders

I n the ranks of the German Army that fought the Second World War there were many senior officers who reached high position but who were not masters of the battlefield. Such men did not win battles or command the operations in which major formations were engaged; instead they were the officers who produced the battle plans for the field commanders and who oversaw the development and execution of these plans. Such men, the chiefs of staff, reached their positions as a result of their intellectual power and their mental ability. Among the most outstanding of these military advisers was Siegfried Westphal, whose mental powers and organisational skills were such that he was chosen to serve as chief of staff to three field marshals—to Rommel in the desert, to Kesselring in Italy and to von Rundstedt, the Supreme Commander West, in France. In 1945 Westphal again served Kesselring when that officer took over as Supreme Commander West from the dismissed von Rundstedt.

Siegfried Westphal was an East German, born in Leipzig on 18 March 1902. His military career began when he entered a junior cadet academy in 1918, but his poor physical condition coloured the first months he spent in that establishment. Determined to meet the physical challenges demanded by his tutors, he trained hard and eventually passed from the Junior into the Senior Cadet Academy in Berlin-Lichterfelde. Westphal had succeeded in the challenge of becoming physically fit, hoping to go out on active service, but the Armistice of November 1918 denied him that ambition.

For the officers and NCOs of the former Imperial Services the Armistice was an unsettling period and one that lasted for many years.

Under the conditions of the Versailles Treaty the German Army was reduced in number to just 100,000 men and it was a force that was not allowed to have heavy artillery, armoured fighting vehicles or, indeed, a General Staff system. It was that limit upon the numbers of men who could serve in the Army that concerned the professionals in the service. Uppermost in the mind of each soldier was whether he would be retained in the Army or discharged into the ranks of the unemployed, whose numbers continued to rise in a defeated Germany. Westphal was one of the lucky few to be retained, and he passed from cadet status to the rank of Ensign, a probationary grade that had to be achieved before an officer's commission could be awarded.

In January 1921 Ensign Westphal was posted from the 6th Cavalry Regiment to the School of Infantry in Munich as one of a class of more than a hundred potential officers. The group to which he belonged was made up of men from all ranks of the Army, including former NCOs who, under the egalitarian regimen of the socialist republic, were to be given a chance to become officers. A great many of the candidates had been former officers who, fearful that they might not be allowed to stay in the service in their commissioned rank, had resigned and had promptly re-enlisted as private soldiers. The remainder of the candidates were those from cadet schools who had not yet been gazetted.

The whole of the intake to which Westphal belonged was divided into six groups, and each group was taken on to the strength of an infantry company of the School, where it was drilled and where it received infantry training. Westphal's physical condition deteriorated again and the physical training instructors frequently humiliated him. However, despite the adverse reports on his physical condition he made such progress in both his academic studies and his regimental duties that he eventually passed out fourth of all the candidates who sat the examination. He was then posted to the Cavalry School in Hanover, where the regime was, if anything, more severe than in the Infantry School. Reveille was at 0400 hours and riding instruction, the first parade of the day, began two hours later. Academic lessons started at 0900 hours.

Westphal graduated from the Cavalry School and returned to his parent regiment, the 6th Cavalry, where he was promoted to the grade of Senior Ensign, the final stage before a commission. Then followed a posting to the 11th Cavalry Regiment, and it was during his time with this unit that he was promoted to the rank of Leutnant (2nd Lieutenant). To further his military education he was sent to serve with the military district headquarters in Oppeln for three months before returning to regimental duties with the 6th Regiment. In October 1924 he was ordered to take up the post of adjutant to the regiment, and what followed was not a particularly happy time for the 22-year-old Westphal. There were many officers in the 6th who were senior to him in both years and in service and these men resented his rapid rise to such a responsible position.

In the post of regimental adjutant Westphal took part in military manoeuvres. It was not usual for officers of such junior rank to participate in such occasions, and in order for him to be present he was given the temporary post of aide-de-camp to the divisional commander. Westphal also spent much time acting as a 'galloper', carrying orders from his superior to units in another part of the manoeuvre area. Although still young he was already suffering from arthritic pains, which affected his back so badly that at times he had to be helped to mount or to dismount from his horse.

During 1926 he returned to the 6th Regiment, where he was often called upon to lecture on those occasions when senior officers visited his unit—which they usually did at the end of a field exercise. Westphal's brief was to comment upon the way in which the exercise had developed, its outcome and the lessons that were to be learned from it. In 1927 came promotion to the rank of Oberleutnant (1st Lieutenant) and then followed a succession of courses, of which those with the artillery and the signals branches of the service were of particular interest to him. It was well that he gained good marks in these disciplines because Army High Command had introduced qualifying examinations to test officers before they were promoted to the rank of Captain. It was from this rank upwards that an officer could apply, or be ordered, to sit the General Staff entrance examination. Westphal sat the qualifying examination and passed with such high grades that he was transferred swiftly from regimental duties into the General Staff structure.

It will be appreciated that, because the size of the Army was so severely limited, the service had been able to select only the finest brains
to serve on the General Staff. As mentioned above, a General Staff
system was forbidden to Germany under the terms of the Versailles
Treaty, but by deft changes of name and title, for example, to Troops
Department and to Army Department, the Versailles restriction was
overcome and the General Staff continued to function, albeit with a
much lower profile. It was a paradox that the difficult entrance examination to the Staff, which had, during the years of the Weimar Republic, rejected so many otherwise capable officers, was found to have had
an adverse effect when the service expanded as it did under Hitler. It
was discovered at that time that there were too few General Staff officers to fill the posts in the new, expanding Army. As a consequence,
there were some officers who had never had staff training but who
went on to reach senior posts, and when war came these men achieved
very senior command positions.

In September 1933 Westphal married, and a month later, on 1 October, he was sent to Berlin to undertake another General Staff officers'
course. It was at this time that Hitler began the first moves to expand
the German Army. Hitler and his government very soon learned the
truth of what the High Command had told them all along—that it is
not possible to produce a smooth-running military system over a period of months: to produce such a result has to be the work of years. In
the task of making an efficient machine—Hitler had demanded an army
numbering no fewer than thirty-six divisions—Westphal was soon hard
at work, although his superiors doubted whether the number of divisions that Hitler required could be met. The shortage of high-grade
officers in the Army worsened when a number of the most capable
men with the appropriate training were taken from the Army to serve
in the newly created Luftwaffe.

A more serious effect of Hitler's planned expansion of the armed
forces, particularly as it affected the Army, was that fighting efficiency
was reduced. The Army, hitherto restricted to just 100,000 soldiers, all
of whom were picked men trained to the highest pitch, was suddenly
enlarged, and that mass of first-class professionals was dispersed among
the newly raised formations, thus diluting it. To anticipate events, let it

here be stated that the strength of the German Army at the end of the Second World War was some 340 divisions. If the raising of just 36 divisions had caused concern among the High Command, what must their feelings have been when ten times that number were raised?

To add to the problems, there was soon discord at the highest level of command as to the strategy that the Nazi Party politicians proposed to dictate. Their intentions were aggressive and were certain to lead to war. The General Staff commanders realised that the service was unprepared for such a conflict. As early as 1935 they had been of the opinion that any future war in central Europe would of necessity be fought out on two fronts. In the West the massive army of France, one hundred divisions strong, was a constant threat, while in the East the military force of the republic of Czechoslovakia, some thirty divisions, would be put into the field so as to divide the strength of the German Army. The General Staff solution to this two-front threat was that a lightning war against the weaker partner, Czechoslovakia, should be initiated so that she would be defeated in a matter of weeks. Meanwhile in the homeland the Army's main strength would be held ready to be deployed and would stand on the defensive until the divisions which had been used in Czechoslovakia returned to the battle line. The whole German force would then be deployed to strike against France.

The threat posed by Czechoslovakia was removed as a result of the Munich Agreement of 1938, and at the outbreak of the Second World War, only a year later, Westphal was serving in the post of Ia to the 58th Infantry Division, a formation whose unpreparedness for active service and general incompetence came as such a shock to him that he then reported that the formation was not capable of being put into the field.

Several months later came Westphal's posting as Ia to the 26th Corps, part of the 18th Army, in Army Group B. For the forthcoming attack upon France and the Low Countries this army group had the task of invading Holland, and when war came in May 1940 the two divisions of the 26th Corps moved rapidly to relieve the paratroops who had been dropped over the west of Holland on 10 May, the first day of the new war. By 14 May the Dutch had been forced to surrender, and with that act the role of the 26th Corps in the war in the West came to an end. It was then sent eastwards to Königsberg in East Prussia. Westphal was not long in that place before being ordered to Koblenz to serve on the commission which had been set up to ensure that the French kept to the details of the armistice which had been signed. When General Mieth, the representative of both the Army and the OKW on the armistice commission, left that post it was Major Westphal who was called upon to replace him. He held the post until June 1941.

By this time the war in Africa had been running for several months, and the German Afrika Korps was in the process of being built up to the strength of a Panzer group when Westphal was ordered to report for a medical examination. This was to determine his fitness to serve in Africa. The examination disclosed a weak aorta and he was given the choice of going to Africa or serving in Europe. He followed his wife's advice and went to Africa, despite his own reservations about serving under a man like Rommel, who had a brusque manner and was disliked for the brutal treatment of his subordinates. Westphal was posted to Freising near Munich, where he took up the duty of forming the headquarters detachments of Panzer Group Africa. This was intended to become a force of four divisions and would replace the Afrika Korps, which had a strength of only two. Westphal's new task was a long and wearisome one, made more difficult by the Italians, partners in the Axis alliance, who placed obstacles in the way of a swift success.

It was, therefore, not until July that Westphal and his headquarters staff reached the African theatre of operations, and there he met Rommel for the first time. There was an immediate rapport between the two men and Westphal, still only a Lieutenant-Colonel in rank, was directed to work on a plan for the capture of the fortress port of Tobruk. On the other side of no man's land the British were making preparations for Operation 'Crusader', but Westphal was convinced that the enemy preparations would not be completed by the year's end and proposed that the Axis forces pre-empt this offensive with a German operation. There was a disappointment both to Rommel and to his Ia, Westphal, that the demands of the war in Russia did not allow the proposed expansion of Afrika Korps to a Panzer group to be realised at that time. Instead of German Panzer formations, a new Italian armoured corps and an additional three Italian infantry divisions were to be added to the Axis establishment. One German division was created, the 90th Light (Africa), and in addition the 5th Light Division, which had been one of the two original formations to serve in Africa, was upgraded to become the 21st Panzer Division.

As mentioned above, upon his arrival in the new theatre of operations Westphal had been directed to prepare an attack that would take out Tobruk. That planned operation had to be postponed because, once again, the supplies which the Axis forces needed to nourish the new attacks had failed to arrive. The offensive that the Axis forces had proposed then became a race against time—which the Germans lost. Both Rommel and Westphal received a shock when the enemy offensive opened on 18 November 1941. The British commander-in-chief, Archibald Wavell, had achieved total surprise. The climax of the British offensive was a massive tank battle fought out at Sidi Rezegh, but it was an operation which the British lost and Rommel was determined to pursue Wavell's army and to cut off its retreat.

He ordered the 21st Panzer Division to seize the strategically important Halfaya Pass. Westphal warned his superior that the divisions of the Afrika Korps were too weak for such an enterprise and that if he insisted upon removing the 21st then this would leave the Axis ring encircling Tobruk too weak to withstand a British attack. Westphal further warned that crises might develop both in the Halfaya Pass sector and around Tobruk and that the Axis forces would be unable to withstand both attacks.

Rommel left his TAC headquarters promising to return within two days, and before he left gave Westphal full authority to act upon his own initiative. Another minor crisis then developed when Bastico, the Italian commander-in-chief and nominally Rommel's superior officer, visited Corps headquarters expecting to find his subordinate there. By the end of the second day Rommel had still not returned and the Italian commander left the headquarters furious that the German leader was absent from his command post for so long. The weight of responsibility that had been put upon Westphal can be appreciated when it is realised that he was in effect directing the operations of the German 90th Light Division as well as those of a German artillery group and three Italian corps. All the officers of those units and formations were senior in rank to him, but each obeyed his orders and directives as if it had been Rommel who had issued them.

The situation around Tobruk began to reach crisis point. The intention of the British operation, 'Crusader,' had been to raise the siege of the encircled fortress from both outside and inside Tobruk. By the evening of 24/25 November Westphal needed a decision from Rommel in order to prevent the Axis ring around Tobruk from being split asunder. The attacks by British 8th Army forces outside Tobruk together with those of the garrison inside the perimeter were on a massive scale, and the Axis encircling ring was threatened with being broken.

The German and Italian troops fought with desperate courage to prevent a link-up of the 8th Army and the Tobruk garrison but failed. Considering the military situation to be hopeless, the senior Italian and German commanders recommended that the Afrika Korps should withdraw from the Tobruk area before the whole army was lost. Westphal refused to give the order to retreat, using the words 'Here we stand'. He realised that the Axis army would not be saved if it withdrew. It had no AFVs to put into action against the 8th Army's tank masses. Had it pulled back it would have been pursued, caught and destroyed.

In attempts to contact Rommel, Westphal sent off dozens of wireless messages and when those went unanswered ordered five Fieseler Storch aircraft to find the commander. All the machines were shot down. Rommel's absence can be explained by the fact that he had read battlefield reports that claimed that the 8th Army had been decisively smashed. This was not the case, and Rommel was unaware of the potentially perilous situation around Tobruk because he had not received news from Westphal of the situation in that sector. Six of the Afrika Korps' radio transmitters had been knocked out, and although the Ia's urgent messages had been received by the wireless operators the operations officers had not acted upon them and forwarded the messages to Rommel.

The commander's order, which was sent out on the evening of the 25th, was that the 21st Panzer Division was to advance upon Bardia. It was then that Westphal made what he later described as the most fateful decision of his military life. He could see from the battle maps that both parts of the Axis forces—the one around Tobruk and the other around the Halfaya Pass—were widely, indeed dangerously, separated and might be destroyed in detail unless immediate action were taken to concentrate them. He decided to act without his superior's permission and sent out the signal 'All previous orders are hereby cancelled. Afrika Korps will return at best possible speed to Tobruk.' The 21st Panzer, which had been under orders to strike towards Egypt, promptly turned round and hurried westwards, in the direction of Tobruk.

On that return march the division was intercepted by Rommel, who, when he learned the reason for that westward move away from Egypt, threatened to have Westphal court-martialled. Instead, having had the situation explained to him by his subordinate, he recommended him for the Knight's Cross. He finally realised what a burden Westphal had carried for five days—not the two days for which he himself had thought he would be absent from his headquarters. In the event Westphal did not receive the Knight's Cross for which he had been recommended, but was awarded instead the newly instituted German Cross in Gold.

Rommel had lost the battle of November 1941, and ordered a withdrawal back out of Egypt and into Tripolitania. It was Westphal who organised the retreat which the Axis forces now had to undertake, initially back to Benghazi and then, when the 8th Army pressed too hard, back to Mersa el Brega from where Rommel had opened his first offensive in the early spring of 1941. Following a reconnaissance flight in Corps' last remaining Fieseler Storch, Rommel and Westphal agreed that the Mersa el Brega positions could not be held if the British reopened their offensive. The few Panzer companies and artillery batteries that reached Tripoli restored the balance, and it was now the 8th Army which had to overcome the problem of a long supply line while convoys were arriving regularly to reinforce and resupply the Axis armies, which had the shorter supply lines. The improved supply situation meant, so far as Westphal was concerned, that the German-Italian forces could undertake a spoiling offensive to throw the British off balance. Rommel was not keen to undertake a new operation, but Westphal hammered home the point that the 8th Army was temporarily in an inferior position *vis-à-vis* the Axis forces.

Persuaded by Westphal's logic, Rommel gave orders for a new offensive to be prepared. To deceive British reconnaissance aircraft and ground patrols, Westphal ordered that during the hours of daylight all Axis vehicles that had to make journeys would undertake only those that took them in a westerly direction, i.e. towards Tripoli. At night the traffic could be in both directions. Thus in the British headquarters the belief grew that the Axis armies were planning a further retreat towards the capital city of Tripoli. Further to hoodwink the 8th Army, an old steamer and some barges were set alight, an act which was designed to confirm to the British High Command the story that the Axis forces were about to retreat.

The reverse was happening. On 19 January 1942 convoys arrived with sufficient armoured fighting vehicles to raise Rommel's force to over 100 Panzers, and, in addition, the Italians had ninety. It was time to strike, and only days later the offensive opened. Rommel and Westphal rode with the leading companies of the battle group that had broken through the British front. Benghazi was reached, and the two senior officers, now up with the attacking platoons of the 2nd Machine Gun Regiment, took part in the capture of that city. At about this time Rommel again recommended Westphal for the award of the Knight's Cross of the Iron Cross, but again the recommendation was turned down and his Ia was awarded instead the Panzer Combat Badge in Silver—an acknowledgement of the fact that, unusually for a staff officer, he was generally to be found in the front line. Rommel also offered Westphal a new post as Chief of Staff of Panzer Group Africa, but he turned this down as the holder of the post, General Gause, was not in Africa at that time and it might have seemed, had Westphal accepted the post, that he was exploiting Gause's absence.

The offensive in Cyrenaica lasted just over a fortnight and saw the 8th Army driven back. On 17 February 1942 Rommel and his Ia went to report to Hitler. After a further two days of discussions with Field Marshal Keitel, Westphal went home on leave. Upon his return to Africa he found Rommel in two minds whether he should open an offensive to take out Tobruk or attempt to capture the island of Malta and thereby ease the supply situation of the newly created Panzer Army. At Westphal's urging Rommel decided on a new operation to begin in Libya. The objective remained, as it had always been, to capture the fortress of Tobruk.

On 26 May Rommel opened the assault against the British line at Gazala. For the operation Westphal had gathered together an 'army detachment' consisting of the Rifle Brigade of the 90th Light Division, the 10th and 21st Italian Corps and the 104th German Artillery Group. That German formation was to open a barrage in the northern part of the Gazala line and behind it a mainly Italian force was to carry out a feint attack while the real and main attack by the rest of the German-Italian army was to go in. The main body was to make a 60km drive through the desert to reach the Bir Hachim position at the southern end of the Gazala Line. The 'box' at Bir Hachim was held by the Free French. At that point the Axis force that had marched through the desert was to swing northwards and drive up towards the Mediterranean, behind the British front, and during its advance to the sea it would take out the British armour.

Shortly before last light on the second day of the offensive, Rommel ordered Westphal to drive out and find Nehring, the new commander of the Afrika Korps, and give him orders to halt the northward advance until touch had been gained with the main body of the 90th Light Division, whose task it was to protect the eastern flank of the corps' thrust. When Westphal returned to Rommel's headquarters an hour or two later it was to learn that Rommel had departed and had taken a wireless group with him. Westphal was now, in the rank of Lieutenant-Colonel, the commander at Panzer Group Headquarters—senior, that is, because of his position as Rommel's Ia. He immediately commandeered eleven of the twelve Army signals formations that were at TAC HQ and returned to Nehring. Even there he did not have control of all the German units, for some of them were out of wireless range and all were widely separated. Forty-eight hours were to pass before they were all in touch again, by which time Rommel had returned to his headquarters and the tanks of the 4th British Armoured Brigade had impaled themselves on the 88mm guns of the Afrika Korps.

Rommel realised that his troops now had to fight on two fronts. He was told that they were effectively boxed in to the east and to the west, to which his only comment was that now the Afrika Korps would be able to show that it could fight as well in defence as in attack. He and Westphal then left TAC headquarters to visit the front-line units. The offensive/defensive fighting was hard, and Westphal, who was with Rommel in the front line, was wounded by a shell splinter. It could not be removed in the field hospitals and the Ia was loaded into a Ju 52. It was expected that the aircraft would fly to Europe, but it lost power in two of its engines and landed in Benghazi. The wounded had to wait until a second Junkers was brought in to carry them to Tripoli. From there Westphal was taken back to Germany, where he was operated on. As a result of the successes that had been gained in Libya Rommel was promoted to the rank of Field Marshal and Westphal received the rank of Colonel.

It was not until August 1942 that Westphal returned to Africa, where Rommel was planning a new operation. This was to be a re-run of the Gazala battle of May 1942. The Axis armies now held jump-off positions from which they could carry their attack towards the Suez Canal. As always in the war in Africa, the question of the Axis offensive and its follow-up pursuit to Cairo and Alexandria were dependent upon the supply of fuel for its vehicles. Rommel and Kesselring met, and during the discussion mention was made that two tankers were en route from Italy. Westphal, who was present at the conference, was far more aware of the situation than either of his superiors and advised Rommel not to open his planned August offensive until both vessels had landed and had discharged their cargoes. He pointed out that the minimum daily requirement of fuel for the Panzer Army was 600 tons, and that if the planned offensive rolled before the ships arrived, by the end of the second day the entire fuel reserves of the Panzer Army would have been used up. Upon Kesselring's statement that if the tankers did not arrive then he would guarantee a daily air lift of 600 tons of fuel, Westphal pointed out that the aircraft would themselves need 300 tons a day for the round trip. Kesselring, annoyed at Westphal's logic, asked him to leave the room so that he and Rommel could talk without interruption.

The logical advice was not heeded, and on 30 August 1942 the Panzer Army moved into the attack. This was soon halted in the 8th Army's forward defence zone, and with the Axis forces held in the British minefields the RAF struck in a series of swift and deadly raids. During one of those Nehring, commanding Afrika Korps, was wounded. The Panzer Army's slow and wasteful advance brought it, eventually, to the

Alam el Halfa ridge and there it was finally halted. As Westphal had predicted, the sinking of the tankers had brought about a crisis. Both had been attacked and sunk before they reached Tobruk, and meanwhile the Panzer Army's fuel reserves had been used up. Nothing came of Kesselring's promise to airlift supplies.

Westphal and Rommel visited the front-line areas, enduring the same privations as the men they commanded and enduring the shelling and air raids that were a constant feature of life for the Axis soldiers. Under the 8th Army's continuing pressure, the Panzer Army was forced to pull back from Alam el Halfa until its withdrawal reached positions laid out west of El Alamein.

With the German and Italian forces regrouped Westphal began to report on the 8th Army's build-up for its new offensive, but little notice was taken of his warnings. When the British began their offensive there was immediately a minor crisis on the German side. This was the death of the Panzer Army's chief signals officer and that of General Stumme, the commander of the Afrika Korps. More serious was the loss of the operations map that had been in Stumme's car, and to recover that document Westphal sent out a Panzer detachment to bring back both it and the General's body.

On Westphal's advice, Rommel, who was on sick leave in Austria, returned to Africa. While his superior had been absent Westphal had been carrying not only the burden of his own office as Ia but also the tasks of the Ib and the Ic. The first advice he offered when he and Rommel met was that the Axis forces should withdraw from the positions in which they were fighting against the 8th Army's El Alamein offensive. Rommel accepted the advice and ordered his forces to pull back. Then came a telegram from Führer HQ ordering the Army to stand and fight and either win or die.

Rommel was prepared to obey this ridiculous demand until he heard Westphal order the staff officers to draw machine pistols and hand grenades from the armourer and for them to prepare to fight a close-quarters battle. Even then Rommel still prevaricated until Kesselring flew to Africa on 4 November, looked at the situation map, heard the reports of the 8th Army's breakthrough and recommended a withdrawal to Fuka. That recommendation was accepted by Hitler. Panzer Army

Africa then withdrew, and during the weeks of its retreat the only positive action was the award of the Knight's Cross to Westphal; this was in addition to the German Cross in Gold, which he had received in 1941.

In the first weeks of December Westphal was given a field command and took over the 164th Light (Africa) Division. Rommel was at that time in Germany, where he discussed with Hitler the future of the Panzer Army. When Hitler asked for the name of Rommel's best officer the Field Marshal's immediate reply was 'Westphal'. That officer then received orders to create a defensive position at Buerat with such forces as were available. These were 30,000 veterans of the Afrika Korps, but their units had no Panzer support. There were also a few companies of Arabs. Shortly after organising the defence Westphal was recalled to Europe to take up a new post.

Upon arrival in Italy he reported to Kesselring. The two officers then went to see Mussolini, following that visit with one to the Chief of the General Staff of the Italian Army. Westphal then left for Germany to enjoy a period of leave, but during this he was ordered to report to Kesselring in Rome. Despite their earlier differences of opinion, Field Marshal Kesselring had asked for Westphal to be posted to his own staff. Westphal reached the Field Marshal's headquarters in Frascati and during the discussions with his new superior was informed that he had been promoted to the rank of Generalmajor. This happened in March 1943, and it shows concern for the men he had commanded in Africa that from the time he began to serve on Kesselring's staff almost to the end of the campaign in Africa Westphal flew often to Tunisia, where the German-Italian army was reaching the end of its life.

Westphal learned that a mass of soldiers was stationed in southern Italy expecting to be shipped to Africa, and with Kesselring's approval he grouped those men into units and sent them instead to Sicily, aware that the island would be the next objective of the Anglo-US armies. With the arrest of Mussolini in July 1943, Hitler put into operation his plan to disarm the Italian Army and to replace its units with German troops who would defend the peninsula. The Italians were indignant at this invasion of their territory and Westphal spent a great deal of time smoothing out the difficulties that arose between the officers of the former allies.

How seriously the situation had deteriorated was shown when US bombers attacked Kesselring's headquarters in Frascati, and during one raid Westphal was lucky to escape with his life. He asked to go to Monte Rotondo where General Roatta has his headquarters. Westphal set out but was halted by a patrol of the crack Italian Grenadier Division. He demanded to talk to Roatta, and it was in the Italian's office that he learned that an armistice between Italy and the Allies had been signed. Westphal returned to Frascati and called the General Staff of the divisions of General Carboni's corps to a conference. In his speech he expressed regret that they were no longer allies and gave them the option of laying down their arms or of being attacked by Stuka dive-bombers. On the following day an elderly senior officer arrived and signed the order for the capitulation of Carboni's corps.

The German Army then began to occupy Italy, and Westphal was busy organising and laying out defensive lines across the width of the Italian peninsula. The Allied landings at Anzio on 22 January 1944 were no surprise to him for he had anticipated landings on both sides of Italy and had expected one to be made up as far north as Venice. Hitler ordered a major counter-attack against the Allied beachhead at Nettuno near Anzio. The attack went in at the end of February but was broken off on 1 March without having gained its goals. The losses that the German Army had suffered were overwhelming.

Westphal was ordered to report to Hitler at Berchtesgaden to explain the reasons for the failure of the counter-attack and, unknown to him, a number of other officers had also been ordered to report on the failed mission. Westphal's report lasted for over three hours and the discussions that followed it were frequently interrupted by the Führer, who tried to catch out the commander on points of detail. Despite Westphal's report being accurate and complete, little changed on the Italian Front. There were no new troops; indeed, the opposite had happened, and there was a movement of formations out of the peninsula.

In April Westphal was promoted to the rank of Generalleutnant and two weeks later had to be rushed into hospital for an operation. He was evacuated to Merano in the southern Tyrol and was out of action until the end of August 1944. On the 31st of that month he reported to Hitler again and there met Field Marshal von Rundstedt, who had been reinstated as Supreme Commander West and who was given Westphal as his chief of staff.

The first task facing Westphal was to create order out of the chaos of the masses of soldiers who were retreating out of France. He succeeded so well that he was able to form a firm front to the west of the Rhine, a success that Hitler described as a miracle. On 24 October Westphal and Krebs, the chief of staff of Supreme Commander West and that of Army Group B, respectively, were ordered to report to Hitler, who gave them the astonishing news that he intended to undertake a new offensive in the West and that the objective was the port of Antwerp. This operation, which has become known as the Battle of the Bulge, was to be undertaken by thirty-six divisions. Both chiefs of staff agreed that the forces to undertake such an operation were insufficient in number and they proposed an alternative operation—a limited offensive around Aachen which would encircle and destroy perhaps as many as twenty US divisions. The proposal was rejected: the new offensive was to be carried out exactly as Hitler had laid it out, and no deviation from the Führer's plan was permitted.

It was Westphal's task to ensure that each of the three army groups that were to fight the imminent battle was equipped and disposed to meet the challenges it would encounter. He still had the gravest misgivings about Operation 'Watch on the Rhine' and expressed his doubts to Generaloberst Jodl: 'If our troops have not reached and crossed the Maas river by the second day of the operation then it must be seen as having failed and must be broken off.' The offensive opened on 16 December 1944 and, despite initial successes, failed to make the progress required. By 16 January the German army groups were in retreat. Westphal, who had by this time received promotion to the rank of General of Cavalry, had the task of creating new formations to be put into battle on two of the major fronts, West and East. One-third of the forces under the control of the Supreme Commander West were transferred to the Eastern Front, leaving western Germany dangerously weak.

Hitler and Westphal met on 6 March, and that meeting resulted in a bitter exchange of words on the effectiveness of the Siegfried Line defences. During the second week of March Field Marshal Kesselring took over from von Rundstedt as Supreme Commander West. With the Anglo-American forces now on the east bank of the Rhine, the end of the war was fast approaching.

Not long after hostilities ceased in Europe the war crimes trials began and Westphal acted as a witness for the defence in the trial of the German General Staff, and followed this by acting as defence witness in the prosecution of Field Marshal Kesselring in Italy. In all, Westphal spent more than 30 months as a prisoner, often under degrading conditions, and it was not until just before Christmas 1947 that he rejoined his family. He had no employment and used the disciplines he had learned to write his autobiography and a number of histories dealing with the war. Concerned about the fate of the soldiers who had served under him in Africa, he founded the Society of Afrika Korps veterans, as well as other ex-service organisations. The chief of these was the European Confederation of Ex-Servicemen. He then took up a career in the Ruhrstahl Company and rose to be a director of that organisation. He retired in 1972.

Westphal died in his 80th year, on 2 July 1982, and he was perhaps the only German general officer of the Second World War to have had bestowed upon him the rank of Commander of the French Legion of Honour.

Index